Judith Butler and Politica

Over the past 25 years the work of Judith Butler has had an extraordinary impact on numerous disciplines and interdisciplinary projects across the humanities and social sciences. She is self-described as wanting to trouble the most basic categories of human identity (such as gender, sex and sexuality) and to engage with the most troubling political issues of our time (such as the 'war on terror', hate speech and recourse to rights). This original study is the first to take a thematic approach to Butler as a political thinker. Starting with an explanation of her terms of analysis, *Judith Butler and Political Theory* develops Butler's theory of the political through an exploration of her politics of troubling given categories and approaches. By developing concepts such as normative violence and subversion and by elaborating her critique of heteronormativity, this book moves deftly between Butler's earliest and most famous writings on gender and her more recent interventions in post-9/11 politics. It explores her notorious deconstruction of the subject and supposed negation of political agency, and concludes that her work demonstrates a commitment to a radical vision of democracy troubled, but not constrained, by political theory itself.

This book, along with its companion volume, *Judith Butler's Precarious Politics*, marks an intellectual event for political theory, with major implications for feminism, women's studies, gender studies, cultural studies, lesbian and gay studies, queer theory and anyone with a critical interest in contemporary American 'great power' politics.

Samuel A. Chambers is Senior Lecturer in Politics at Swansea University, where he teaches political theory and cultural politics. He writes broadly in contemporary thought, including work on language, culture, and the politics of gender and sexuality.

Terrell Carver is Professor of Political Theory at the University of Bristol, UK. He has published extensively on issues relevant to sex, gender and sexuality in political theory and international relations.

Judith Butler and Political Theory

Troubling politics

Samuel A. Chambers and Terrell Carver

Routledge
Taylor & Francis Group

LONDON AND NEW YORK

First published 2008
by Routledge
2 Park Square, Milton Park, Abingdon, Oxon OX14 4RN

Simultaneously published in the USA and Canada
by Routledge
270 Madison Avenue, New York, NY 10016

Routledge is an imprint of the Taylor & Francis Group, an informa business

© 2008 Samuel A. Chambers and Terrell Carver

Reprinted 2009

Typeset in Times New Roman by
Taylor & Francis Books
Printed and bound in Great Britain by
MPG Books Group Ltd

British Library Cataloguing in Publication Data
A catalogue record for this book is available from the British Library

Library of Congress Cataloging in Publication Data
Chambers, Samuel Allen, 1972-
Judith Butler and political theory : troubling politics / Samuel A.
Chambers and Terrell Carver.
    p. cm.
    Includes bibliographical references and index.
[etc.]
    1. Butler, Judith, 1956- 2. Butler, Judith, 1956- Gender trouble. 3.
Feminist theory. 4. Feminism. 5. Lesbian feminism. 6. Power (Social
sciences) 7. Sex role. 8. Gender identity. I. Carver, Terrell. II. Title.
    HQ1190.C34 2008
    305.42092–dc22
                          2007022686

ISBN13: 978-0-415-76382-0 (hbk)
ISBN13: 978-0-415-38366-0 (pbk)
ISBN13: 978-0-203-93744-0 (ebk)

Contents

Acknowledgements

Samuel A. Chambers writes:

This book, or at least the idea of it, has been in the making for almost 10 years, and over that time I have incurred a lengthy and substantial list of debts. The errors are still all mine, including the failure to include everyone here. I start by thanking Lisa Disch not only for teaching me Butler in the first place but also for continuing to be a fabulous reader, a great friend and an invaluable colleague. The book owes its deepest, and for that reason least-articulable, appreciation to Jackie and Tim Chambers: despite their distance from the academy they possess a bountiful wisdom concerning academia, a wisdom from which I, and thus this book, have benefited enormously.

Although I have never taught a single class or module devoted specifically to Butler, much of the shape of the arguments and ideas in the book are inflected by experiences in the classroom. In particular, it is a great joy to acknowledge the outstanding undergraduate seminar students at St Mary's College of Maryland and the University of Redlands for their enthusiasm, commitment and genuine love of political theory, and especially the political theory graduate students at Penn State University for their keen insights, deep professionalism and unflagging support.

Portions and earlier versions of many of these chapters were presented to various audiences; comments, questions and discussions in those contexts proved profoundly helpful. I thank audiences at the following events: Association for Political Theory annual conferences, 2004 and 2005; American Political Science Association (APSA) annual conferences, 2004 through 2006; APSA workshops on Political Myth, Rhetoric and Symbolism, 2004 through 2006; Political Studies Association annual conference, 2007; Departmental Seminar, Swansea University Politics Department, 2006; University of Puget sound invited lecture 2006; Whitman College invited lecture 2006; 'A Politics of Contingency', Swansea University conference on Butler, 2006; University of Essex, Centre for Theoretical Studies in the Humanities and Social Sciences, invited talk, 2006. Let me note especially my gratitude to the following individuals: Asma Abbas, Paul Apostolidis,

Helen Brocklehurst, Anne Caldwell, William Corlett, Kennan Ferguson, Lilly Goren, Brigid Haines, Noreen Harburt, David Howarth, Kimberly Hutchings, John Nelson, Timothy Kaufman-Osborn, Morris Kaplan, Christopher Robinson, Jackie Stevens and Elizabeth Wingrove. Pieces of the book have also appeared in written form. An earlier version of Chapter 4 was published in *Political Studies* 29.1, and different versions of Chapter 3, 6 and 7 were published in *Body & Society* 13.4, *Politics & Gender* 3.4, and *Political Studies* 55.3, respectively. Deep thanks go to the journals for permission to republish that material here, and the anonymous reviewers and the journal editors – Joseph Peschek and Matthew Festenstein – sfor the comments and criticisms.

For their careful and considered readings of chapters of the book, I note my deep gratitude to the following: Asma Abbas, Rebecca Brown, Anne Caldwell, Lisa Disch, Alan Finlayson, Charles Phillips, Rob Watkins, Daniel Williford, Karen Zivi and my seminar students at Penn State, particularly Elizabeth Ullrich and Ty Henry. Daniel Williford and Charles Phillips earn a second round of thanks for reading the entirety of the manuscript. Other colleagues influenced the book dramatically by way of their own work. Thanks to Diana Coole for the shining example of her writings and for her support of mine. I am particularly indebted to conversations with, and the writings of, Moya Lloyd, whose insights on Butler are quite simply second to none.

Significant sections of this project were completed at four different institutions of higher education, in five different US states and in two different countries. This extensive and rarely chosen travelling – entailing two transcontinental moves and one intercontinental move – makes it impossible not to rely heavily on the kindness, generosity and support of others. In this light, I thank Kim Evans for her eloquence and honesty, and for making a home for us when we were without one. I am similarly indebted to Elizabeth Brown, who allowed us to take over her bedroom and garage, and transform her dining room into a writing space – all while providing the proper support of espresso and Tivo. I want to acknowledge Ryan McIntyre simply for being the same friend he's always been throughout the years – no easy task, that. I owe Michael Riley debts for airport blizzard trips, and a journey across the ocean to help me make a home. Thanks to John Bies for wonderful excursions to places where no conferences were held – St Paul, Buffalo, Columbus and Milwaukee – and for a friendship that now seems timeless. I am deeply grateful to Paul Mariz and Laurie Frankel for their unquestioned commitment, support and love – that is, for being family. And finally, Joel Bettridge is awesome.

Foreigners always need more help than natives, and so the necessary dependence on others seems to double when living in a new country. I owe the following people: Mark Smith for beginning my lessons in British sport; Michael Sheehan for storage, dishes, numerous lifts and the Mondeo; Sarah Gamble for collegiality, friendship, love of *Buffy* and the Micra; and Helen

Brocklehurst for being an exemplary colleague – and for her toleration of dog hair. Keri Finlayson's kitchen feels like a second home; I thank her for her genuine hospitality. And thanks to Jake and Luke Finlayson for letting us crash the party. I am grateful to George Lawson for his spontaneous collegiality and friendship, for introducing me to Premiership football, and for showing me what 'mate' really means.

When it comes to the field of Politics and the study of political theory, all my travelling has led me much closer to home. I thank my colleagues at Swansea University, including everyone in the Department of Politics and International Relations, members of the Centre for Research into Gender in Culture and Society, especially Sarah Gamble, and Dan Healey in the History Department. I am profoundly grateful to find myself in such a supportive environment, surrounded by genuine colleagues. In particular I would like to thank Roland Axtmann for his decency, honesty and steadfast support of my work. And my deepest appreciation goes to Alan Finlayson. Some scholars are lucky to have colleagues who are sympathetic to their own arguments and positions; others are privileged to have colleagues who can offer powerful and substantive criticisms of those arguments; some have colleagues who know the same theoretical sources and share a passion for them; while others have colleagues who have a passionate interest in distinct sources. In Alan I am truly privileged to have a colleague who combines all of these traits, and does so with humour, style and rhetorical flair.

Terrell Carver fits in all and none of the above categories, so it makes sense that he would settle instead into the classification of collaborator (in all its senses) and co-author. The book would not be possible without him, but this statement is true in so many ways that exceed the literal writing of the text. I cannot repay my debt to Terrell for his support of, enthusiasm for and contributions to my work – nor for his ceaseless, unfailing advice and wisdom on both career and life. Although, as a co-author, Terrell proves the exception to the rule of acknowledgements: I *could* blame the errors on him. But I won't.

All those debts incurred during these travels seem massive when piled atop one another, yet they are dwarfed in comparison with the importance of having a partner along the way. I never imagined myself reaching this point in the journey, of being here and now, but I know that I could never have done it by myself. Rebecca Brown read numerous drafts of countless book proposals, abstracts, conference papers and book chapters, all while writing a book of her own and racking up more frequent flier miles than any academic should. It is a good thing that I reject both referential and expressive theories of language, since words will not say here what I need and want to convey. Instead, I turn to a performative: I dedicate this book to Rebecca Brown.

Swansea, UK
April 2007

Terrell Carver writes:

This book began when Sam said – for reasons that were his own – 'I think I'll work better with a co-author'. That was my lucky day. On some of the above events it was my privilege to be there, too, in the firing line or among the questioners. We have gone over every word together, way more than once, not least because I had a habit of taking many of them away and then thinking hard while Sam put a selection of them back, one by one. Some of these words really got us going, and I learned a lot. I hope that our readers have a similarly good experience.

Bristol, UK
April 2007

Introduction
Troubling politics

> Perhaps trouble need not carry such a negative valence. To make trouble was, within the reigning discourse of my childhood, something one should never do precisely because that would get one *in* trouble. The rebellion and its reprimand seemed to be caught up in the same terms, a phenomenon that gave rise to my first critical insight into the subtle ruse of power: the prevailing law threatened one with trouble, even put one in trouble, all to keep one out of trouble. Hence, I concluded that trouble is inevitable and the task, *how best to make it, what best way to be in it.*
>
> (Butler 1999 [1990]: xxvii, second emphasis added)

These opening lines preface Butler's most famous text, *Gender Trouble*, and so it comes as somewhat of a surprise to discover that there has been little or no commentary on them. In the first move of her most important work, Butler images herself as a disobedient and disruptive child who has got into trouble; she places herself in the position of the idle teenager plotting how best to make trouble. In short, she casts herself in the role of *troublemaker*. It seems deeply ironic, then, that Butler prefaced her next book, *Bodies that Matter,* by appearing to *complain* about responses to *Gender Trouble* that describe her in precisely the way she first characterised herself, that is, *as a troublemaker.* Butler writes of 'a certain exasperation' that she hears in responses to the arguments of *Gender Trouble*, and she finds in critiques of *Gender Trouble* 'a certain patronizing quality which (re) constituted me as an unruly child, one who needed to be brought to task' (Butler 1993: ix). Many readers of *Bodies that Matter* found themselves a bit troubled by Butler's comments: why did she take it so personally, they asked?

Perhaps she did not. What if Butler's apparent protestations at being turned into the wayward and disruptive schoolchild were themselves a ruse? What if this is not an unintentional contradiction of herself (and hence ironic), but instead an intentional tactic? Butler might actually mean to tell her readers that in taking her as a troublemaking child who bothered them – someone they wanted to keep in line – her critics had proved her successful. Butler would then be claiming that her critics have established her success at getting into trouble; they have confirmed her to be making just the sort of trouble that *Gender Trouble* describes in its opening pages. Indeed, how else to read the line that Butler leaves on its own as the fourth paragraph of the preface to *Bodies that Matter*, 'Couldn't someone simply take me aside?', than with more than a touch of sarcasm and sass (Butler 1993: x)? What other way to hear this question than as Butler's declaration that she plans to continue getting into trouble, that she never expects to get out of it? While her critics will persist in their desire to force her into line, she will continue to make trouble – and to trouble them. After all, nothing confirms one's status as troublemaker more than being disciplined.

We will never know whether Butler meant to echo the 'unruly child' trope in the prefaces to her books from the early 1990s. (We could ask her – she might even answer – but we'd still never *know*.) Either way, it does not really matter; if the above reading proves even plausible, then it suggests that we take Butler's troublemaking even more seriously as a central theme and strategy of her work. Butler, we shall argue, proves to be a troublemaker of a sophisticated and important sort. Indeed, we contend that the trope of 'troubling' can serve both as a guide to grasping Butler's central interactions with and contributions to contemporary political theory and as a method for putting them to work. *Troubling Politics* therefore names Butler's theoretical stratagems and political conceptions. Butler never relegates the role of troublemaker, and this makes her a careful, difficult and crucial thinker of the political.

Our goal in this book is to explore the types of trouble that Butler has got herself and her readers into, to investigate the manner in which she has made trouble and to track the effects that her troubling has had on politics and the political. In so doing we seek to bring Butler into clearer view as a political thinker – to bring to light her political theory as a politics of troubling and a troubling of politics. Our task in this introduction proves much simpler: to introduce Butler *as* a troublemaker. To do this we will first explore *Gender Trouble*; this means investigating its impact and accounting for its radical nature, but it also means considering the ways in which that very impact has dampened and sometimes hidden Butler's broader contributions to political theory. This leads us to an elaboration of what we mean, and what we think Butler could be taken to mean, by 'troubling politics'. We then finish by mapping out the specific arguments of each chapter as they contribute to the broader claims of the book.

Trouble with gender

Butler will always be best known for the book she published in 1990, *Gender Trouble: Feminism and the Subversion of Identity*. As a title, 'Gender Trouble' names not only a particular problem, the 'troubles with gender' (in perhaps the same way we would read references to 'the troubles' in

Northern Ireland), but also a particular project designed *to trouble* gender. The book has gained its fame (and, in many domains, its notoriety) for at least two reasons.

First, it is a radical text. *Gender Trouble* is radical in the philosophical sense of going to the root, of proposing something utterly new and unexpected. And *Gender Trouble* proves radical politically, in that it suggests possibilities for choice, action and life that one will find nowhere near the mainstream. Both of these senses derive from the book's central claim that gender is not what we have previously thought it to be. To rehearse a story that many readers may already know well, prior to the political and theoretical work of second-wave feminists in the 1960s and 1970s gender did not play a prominent role either within feminism or in common understandings. That is, sex (maleness and femaleness) defined what it meant to be a man or a woman. In the second wave, feminists argued that we should draw a distinction between sex and gender: sex would be taken (sometimes explicitly, sometimes implicitly) as a natural, biological given, but gender should be unhinged from sex and understood as a product of culture, of history, of language and certainly of politics. Gender, on this account, is much more malleable than sex; gender could be learned, practised, shaped.

When Butler published *Gender Trouble* in 1990, the constructed nature of gender had become received wisdom – that which everyone both knew and asserted – within feminism. In response to what everyone already knew, Butler asks a series of far-reaching and deep-probing questions (Butler *loves* questions). Where do we get our notion of what sex is, of what male or femaleness is? How do we have access to this core that supposedly underlies gender? And she goes on to ask the most radical question of all: do we not acquire our idea of sex from the very norms of gender?

Butler argues that gender should not be taken as a simple derivation from sex. On the contrary, gender emerges in the world *performatively*. By 'gender performativity' Butler does not mean to describe gender as something we play at or act out, but rather as something *enacted* – inscribed in daily practices of speech, both expressed and formed through dress, manner and behaviour. But if gender comes to be only through its daily enactments, then – Butler goes on to suggest – our access to, or understanding of, 'sex itself' might be subject to this same gender performativity. In other words, gender might be constructed, 'all the way down'. This means that sex, rather than being the natural ground from which a constructed gender would arise, might be – in some hard to articulate way – *constructed* as well. Better put, Butler suggests that the sex/gender distinction fails to map a clean distinction between a natural realm and a social one. Instead, the sex/gender distinction itself must be thought as a part of the cultural and political domains, for it is only within culture and through politics that we can draw the line between sex and gender (or, for that matter, between the natural and the social, the political and the non-political, etc.).

Nonetheless, everyone knows that radical arguments do not make people famous (even if we confine ourselves to the terribly limited fame of academics). So the second reason for the broad and significant impact of *Gender Trouble* comes in a familiar form, that of context. The book appeared just at the time that a large number of critiques of second-wave feminism (from feminists of colour, from lesbian feminists, from theorists of race, etc.) were beginning to coalesce. It thus contributed to the creation of what some now called third-wave feminist theory, a movement that remains committed to many of the same political goals as second-wave feminism, but which insists that those goals cannot be reached while one insists upon the unity of the category 'woman' as a human subject. 'Third-wave feminism' names an extremely broad, diverse and thoroughly conflicted group of thinkers, but it successfully pulls together those writings that vigilantly question the notion of 'the experience of women' if and when that notion is taken to connote something transhistorical, transcultural or universal.

Moreover, *Gender Trouble* also arrived at the exact moment that – as we now retroactively describe its history – 'queer theory' was emerging in recognisable shape as an interdisciplinary field of study. *Gender Trouble* contributed profoundly, if also unexpectedly, to the central insights of queer theory. David Halperin probably formulated this idea most powerfully and appropriately when, writing five years after Butler, he provocatively defined queer as 'an identity without an essence' (Halperin 1995: 62). An identity without essence calls forth a notion of individual selfhood not founded on a positive cultural or biological fact. This non-essential identity emerges always and only in *relation* to dominant norms. Queer identity therefore must not be confused or conflated with gay identity; it rests not on the ground of a fixed desire for the same sex, but on the position of one's marginal sexuality in relation to the norm of heterosexuality.

Gender Trouble thereby troubles gender, sex, the sex/gender relation and ultimately identity. Many feminists found the text quite troubling; others read it as dramatically empowering. And the trouble it brought to questions of sexual identity helped to form a new field of study. Precisely, then, in the way it troubled current configurations of thought and understandings of power and identity, *Gender Trouble* proved to be a revolutionary and pathbreaking book – one that will always be the most important in Butler's oeuvre. Despite all this, *Gender Trouble* is not (yet?) found in the canon of political theory, and Butler's work plays no central role there. No doubt the idea of 'gender as performativity' will be referenced in politics, but few would argue that Butler has a sustained political theory. Or, if she has one, no one could argue that it has received proper treatment in the field of political theory.

A portion of the explanation for this may lie, paradoxically, with the impact of *Gender Trouble*, in that the significance of that book tends to eclipse Butler's other writings. Since the publication of *Gender Trouble*,

Butler has published nine more books (and she had published one before). Nonetheless, few students of Politics will be likely to encounter in the classroom (if they encounter Butler's writings at all) anything more or other than *Gender Trouble*, or excerpts from it. We suggest that Butler's contributions to political thought may often be *obscured* by focusing only on her earliest work, and this for a number of reasons.

First, in looking only to *Gender Trouble* teachers and scholars take Butler to be a 'theorist of gender' – a label she has consistently and vigorously refused – as if that area were separate from politics or only played a marginal role (that is, when one deals specifically with 'gender issues'). Second, this move also *dates* Butler, and suggests her time has passed, by framing her as a thinker of the 1990s – a frame reinforced by the fonts, colours and layout of the original cover of the book. Finally, the overemphasis on *Gender Trouble* categorises Butler's thought narrowly; it places Butler in the boxes for feminist theory and queer theory – and not, therefore, in the disciplinary box labelled 'Politics'.

Moreover, the framing of Butler as a theorist who speaks mainly to feminist and queer theory and whose work remains lodged in the past proves particularly problematic because it pairs so conveniently, so tightly, with another dominant discourse. Readers will easily recognise this narrative, and for most it will resonate strongly. This is the political frame that has been mobilised mainly by the administration of President G.W. Bush and the American mainstream media, but which has echoed powerfully in other quarters. This political narrative declares that 'we' (a 'we' that often means only Americans, but that seeks to capture a broader 'we' inclusive of 'the West' or 'civilised humanity') now live in a 'different world'. This encourages the refrain repeated non-stop in the US since 9/11: '9/11 changed everything'. In particular, the Republican Party put this discourse into service (and, some would argue, the American mainstream media aided them in this project) to great effect in the 2004 American Presidential election. The result of this was to draw a stark line between a 'pre-9/11 world' and a 'post-9/11' world. Republican strategists successfully forced the Democratic presidential candidate, Senator John Kerry, into the 'pre-9/11 mentality' box, making him the 'wrong candidate' on Iraq and American security policy.

Hence, to make Butler into a theorist of the 1990s, a thinker of 'minor' issues such as sexuality and gender, would be to pre-decide the issue of whether or not she has contributions to make to political theory. When these two different frames come together or collide, the effect is to produce a vision in which Butler has no relevance to politics. In that vision she falls into the large group of so-called 'postmodern' thinkers who 'played around' with language during the Reagan/Thatcher 1980s and the Clinton 1990s. But during the Bush/Blair 2000s, this narrative says, we need serious attention to our new world order. It concludes that Butler's time, if it ever was, has now passed.

Trouble with political theory

We eschew the narrow focus on Butler's second book, *Gender Trouble*, and we argue, to the contrary, that Butler's time may have just arrived. We insist that Butler's thought speaks powerfully and poignantly not only to the concerns of contemporary political theory but also to the questions and dilemmas of politics. In a significant sense, this book seeks to defend a straightforward and direct argument: Butler is a crucially important political theorist in her own right. However, our text itself will neither articulate nor defend that thesis in a direct or sequential manner. We avoid such an approach since, even before one begins to provide evidence for this claim or to build a case in support of it, one can already, and easily enough, point out a whole host of problems with it. In the first instance, and as we would immediately mention to any student who proposed such a thesis, *it is too general*. For this reason it begs a long list of questions: 'What conception of political theory or the political theorist are we working with?' 'Who counts as a political theorist under these criteria?' 'What conditions would Butler need to meet in order to qualify?' These are only the first few questions that come to mind.

Worse, despite being overly broad, this thesis still proves *highly contentious* and politically fraught. First, many scholars working squarely within the established discipline of political science or its clearly delineated subfield of political theory will staunchly resist the idea that a thinker like Butler could ever be granted the status of 'political theorist'. These imaginary critics of the thesis might well grant Butler's importance as a thinker, as a scholar, as a writer, but they would continue to position Butler outside the field of political studies. Thus they seek to locate Butler's significance elsewhere (other than in the domain of Politics), to circumscribe her sphere of influence and to contain the impact of her thought. In this effort they have much evidence to cull: Butler has a PhD in Philosophy, an appointment in 'Rhetoric and Comparative Literature' and her most obvious scholarly contributions have been to the fields of feminism and queer theory. Her work, therefore, might have something to *say* to political theory, but it could never *make her* a political theorist in her own right. Other critics, rather than seeing the thesis as indefensible, will express their outrage that we have not taken it as already proven. In short, they fear we 'protest too much'. These critics (made up almost entirely of scholars working outside the disciplinary boundaries of political science) will loudly insist that Butler is *obviously* a political theorist, and they will therefore reject not so much the locutionary meaning of the thesis, but the illocutionary force. In other words, this group will assume that our intention in posing the claim 'Butler is a political theorist' must be to question it. They will read our defence of Butler as a political theorist (and especially our elucidation, just above, of the many criticisms of this claim) as, in fact, an attack on Butler. 'How', they will ask, 'can you even suggest that Butler is *not* a political theorist in her own right'? And they too have a wealth of support for this claim, since Butler's writings have always been intimately concerned with politics.

Quite obviously, this is a game we cannot win. The more strongly one defends Butler against the first group's criticism that she can never be a political theorist (i.e. the harder one tries to prove that Butler 'really is' a political theorist), the more one enrages the second group. We take the time to narrate the rules of the game here so as to clarify our choice *not to play it*. Butler is not a linear or analytic thinker, nor can her 'post-foundational' thought be merely repackaged as a sceptical critique of political and philo- sophical foundations (thus bringing her into dialogue with the political theory tradition by characterising her narrowly as its critic). She has no systematic or singular 'theory' of politics, and therefore in one sense there is no such thing as her 'political theory', if we take that phrase to resonate the way it does for Aristotle or Hobbes. Further, Butler refuses to work within the confines of any single academic discipline or any single genre of thought. She writes for a wide variety of audiences, including theorists and political thinkers of all stripes, psychologists, feminists, queer theorists, philosophers, activists and artists. Therefore, to treat Butler the way one might treat a more traditional figure in the history of political thought (say, J.S. Mill) would lead to disastrous results. A excursus on 'the political theory of Judith Butler' not only would fail utterly in its attempt to place Butler in the political theory canon alongside the likes of Locke or Rawls (and for all the reasons already outlined), but also would very likely do a great deal of violence to Butler's work – stripping it of its context, trans- forming its untimely encounters into linear principles.

For all of these reasons, we will evade any direct encounters with the thesis 'Butler is a political theorist', and we will resist the possible tempta- tion to play games of categorisation (e.g. 'it's feminist theory!', 'no, it's gender theory!', etc.). Instead, we will work in a non-systematic manner to investigate, elucidate and elaborate Butler's writings as they *relate* (taken in a broad sense) to politics and political theory. The idea here is to fight against the tendency to view Butler's thought from above – that is, an effort to hold it all together as a single theory of politics. Rather, we structure our exploration of Butler and political theory through a series of very specific and focused engagements – starting 'on the ground' as it were, at the level of her textual encounters, and then moving laterally to other encounters rather than seeking a vertical integration of them. It is the detailed ela- boration of these engagements that, taken as a whole, should give the reader a clear sense of Butler's places within contemporary political theory – 'places', plural, since she will turn up unexpectedly, then disappear and emerge elsewhere.

The notion of 'troubling politics' serves to tie this set of engagements together, not into a tightly bound and singular theory of politics, but into a set of encounters with politics, political theory and the political. We should now take the time, then, to say more about our title, and to unravel some of its meanings as they guide our study of Butler's writings over the past 20 years. At the very least, one can produce three important and distinct meanings for the notion of 'troubling politics', and careful consideration of these three ways of reading our title will help to develop and broaden not only its meaning but also the meaning of the book.

We start with the way that Butler's critics conceive of her politics (or putative lack thereof) and why they find it so troubling. Many of Butler's critical readers find something terribly worrisome in her writings, particularly the books from the early 1990s. These critics often give a name to this supposedly troubling dimension of Butler's work; they call it 'the disappearance of the subject' or 'the loss of agency'. Both 'subject' and 'agency' prove to be terribly slippery political and philosophical concepts, around which one finds no intelligible consensus; thus it is not always completely clear what her critics mean when they accuse Butler of robbing the subject of agency or calling for the elimination of the subject. Nonetheless, the troubling dimension of Butler's politics, from the perspective of these critics, certainly has something to do with Butler's consistent challenge to the notion that there could ever be what she often calls a 'ready-made subject'. Butler, like many thinkers influenced by Continental philosophical thought, provides a series of critiques of the sovereign and autonomous individual – one that stands outside culture, moves beyond history or detaches itself from relations of dependency with others. It seems to be specifically here that Butler's critics find themselves troubled – here that they conceive of Butler's politics as troubling.

The critics seem to think, then, that without a philosophically grounded category of the human individual one cannot even conceive of political action. They therefore find themselves very much disturbed by what they perceive as the lack of strong normative foundations in Butler's critical arguments. They read Butler as denying all knowledge claims, and thus they ask Butler to provide epistemological grounds for her conception of politics. When she refuses, it troubles them. In this first sense of 'troubling politics', troubling is an adjective that modifies politics, and does so in such a way as to offer (or at least to suggest) a critique of Butler's project. 'Troubling politics' thus *names* the critique; it tells us that Butler might prove an interesting reader of French post-structuralist theory and that she might even be a provocative literary theorist. Nonetheless, she has a 'troubling politics'.

Second, we have the way Butler would inflect the phrase in terms of the understanding of 'troubling' that we can see in *Gender Trouble*. That is, Butler's most famous book *troubles* gender, by refusing the terms in which it had previously been understood by second-wave feminism. If we take this conception of 'troubling' and transpose it into our own title, we then produce a particular reading of 'troubling politics': to *trouble* politics would be to disturb, to challenge and to question consistently. Ultimately, to trouble politics might be to *transform* our given understanding of politics. Troubling politics in this sense resonates with Foucault's project of problematisation and his conception of philosophy as concerned with the project 'to know how and to what extent it might be possible to think differently, instead of legitimating what is already known' (Foucault 1984: 9).

This second sense of 'troubling politics' takes troubling not as an adjective that modifies an already given understanding of politics, but as a verb that performs an action on that given understanding – perhaps to bring about something new. Thus we can think of Butler's work as 'troubling politics', in that it refuses the static conception of politics. While she rarely conceptualises politics explicitly, Butler clearly rejects the notion of politics as the production of consensus, and she consistently takes her leave of the idea of politics as mere administration of affairs. She insists on a politics of struggle, strife, conflict – a radical democratic politics that is disturbing in that it literally *disturbs* by interrupting the given order. In insistently troubling politics, Butler suggests an untimely politics: 'democracy', she says, must remain 'unknowing ... about its future' (Butler *et al.* 2000: 41).

In dialogue with this second reading, but as an essential supplement to it, we wish to draw out a third sense of 'troubling politics'. We do so in an effort to illuminate Butler's theories of politics and the political. In this book we will press consistently the argument that Butler's politics proves to be *a politics of troubling*. In this more expansive understanding of Butler's theoretical encounters with the political, we formulate 'troubling' as neither adjective nor verb, but rather as a noun (a gerund). In this important sense, then, troubling cannot be merely something one does *to* politics; it turns out to be *its own politics*. In other words, we must locate that thing that we would otherwise be tempted to call 'Butler's political theory' in a subtle understanding of the way she approaches gender, sex and other political norms *through the concept of troubling*. Butler tries to make trouble, to get into trouble and to trouble actively those norms.

However, there is much more to it than this. Our approach to Butler's works abandons the idea that they will contain a linear model of politics. That is, we reject the notion that her politics would somehow be *derived* from a 'theory' that grounds it – the idea that politics only gets under way after normative or epistemological grounds have been established. Therefore, we refute the similarly flawed assumption that Butler cannot be doing political theory unless she has established such grounds. In working outside such a linear model, our approach makes it possible to read Butler's writings for the broader theory of troubling that they produce. This reading of 'troubling politics', and thus this reading of Butler, will demonstrate what it means to take a given norm and trouble it. Part of this process involves denaturalisation, of course. But troubling should not, cannot be reduced to that process since it also involves (as we shall show) a positive conception of human relations. 'Troubling politics' therefore must not be taken as another name for deconstruction, or some other so-called sceptical project, since the process of disrupting and reorganising human relations goes well beyond the notion of doubting their naturalness.

In a similar vein, we maintain that despite Butler's own characterisations of trouble as something we get into as children, her politics of troubling must not be reduced to childishness: even if troubling *can* be thought as the unruliness of a schoolchild, it nevertheless turns out to be an extremely serious, thoroughly grown-up endeavour. Children must *learn* the already-established norms of the society into which they are born, and thus they may have more occasion to deviate from those norms than the so-called grown-ups who know the norms so well. Deviation from norms, however, often proves to be a very weighty affair with grave consequences, and to deviate from the norm can often be a radical theoretical or political practice.

The question of the 'radical' animates Butler's work throughout her writings, and we have raised the issue repeatedly here in our effort to give a skeletal account of Butler's politics of troubling. In the 10th-anniversary preface to *Gender Trouble*, Butler makes an apparently offhand, perhaps even banal remark, when she writes: 'there is nothing radical about common sense' (Butler 1999: xviii). The comment seems little more than tautological, at first. Until, that is, one considers how much effort is spent in the humanities and the social sciences on systematising, codifying and elaborating common sense in an untroubled way. Butler's writings always work against this tendency. This is why they are troubling. This is why they are important politically.

Troubling to come

While arguing for Butler's unique contribution to thinking the political, we have now said repeatedly that she has no singular or linear theory of politics. Thus, in our effort to avoid forcing Butler's work into a prefabricated system, we approach her writings here in somewhat eccentric fashion. As the organisational structure for the book, we have chosen neither chronology, nor problem-solving, nor concepts, nor categories. We reject the model of political theory as problem-solver, and most chapters of the book (while obviously often focusing more heavily on certain texts than others) span various years of Butler's writing; we frequently jump from *Gender Trouble* to texts written in 2004 and 2005. Further, while we seek to uncover crucial political tropes in Butler's writings – to reveal various ways in which she theorises the political, to develop those crucial concepts that she mobilises for her (and our) specific interventions – we resist the temptation to reduce Butler's thought to a series of either concepts or themes. In other words, the various parts of the book do not operate on the same level.

Part I, 'Terms of political analysis', looks more closely at the language Butler mobilises to make her arguments – particularly in her early writings (those most clearly 'on gender'). Our approach here seeks to do a good deal of 'introductory work' by pulling the reader into the contexts in which Butler has operated and surveying the terrain there both before and after her interventions. Nonetheless, while going over ground familiar to many readers, we attempt to survey her work from a fresh angle. Thus, Chapter 1 takes the terms by which Butler's early writings have often been known, 'gender/sex/power', and reverses them, arguing that 'power' is not the term that comes after Butler has done her 'feminist' work with gender, but proves instead (and unexpectedly) to be the guiding principle of her thought, even in the text that made her most famous as a theorist of gender. Thus, by proving that Butler places power at the beginning, we can read her, first and foremost, as a political theorist, and we can do so despite the fact that she does not present herself as such or write in the same language or about the same texts as most traditional political theorists.

Moving beyond the primary terms of our engagement with Butler, Chapter 2 takes up three terms that are famously and particularly associated with her: 'performativity', 'citationality' and 'repetition'. Because Chapter 1 effectively outlines the political character of Butler's theorising *without* using these terms, Chapter 2 can then make a critical assessment of exactly what they add to Butler's political theory, and what they portend for philosophy more generally. This chapter thus revisits the content and conclusions of Chapter 1 in order to explicate what these characteristically Butlerian terms mean, and to indicate precisely what philosophical and political work they are doing for her. This analytical strategy has the advantage of laying out Butler's ideas first in one set of terms and then in another set, thereby deepening the reader's understanding of the 'difficult' material through which Butler herself (particularly in *Gender Trouble*) sails at superordinate speed. Chapter 2 concludes that many of the 'standard' criticisms of Butler that concern materiality and agency, as well as the alleged apolitical character of her theory and its purportedly depoliticising effects, follow from a rush to 'read Butler' on performativity and drag without careful attention to the philosophical arguments (critically derived from both the Anglophone 'analytical' tradition and French 'post-structuralism') through which these concepts are themselves articulated as part of a very general *political* project.

The final chapter of Part I, Chapter 3, addresses 'the body', a topic that Butler's critics have been demanding that she herself address since the time of her earliest publications. We argue that, simultaneously, Butler's critics have misread her and she has misread her critics. The problem deemed 'denying the body' or doing away with its pain points less to the body or materialisation per se, and more toward the problem of fully conflating 'sex' with the terms of gender norms. We therefore set out to prove that while she refuses to use the body as an ontological foundation, Butler neither erases the body nor denies its material physicality. The body enables agency and constrains it. This chapter theorises the body through a reconstruction of Butler's theory of sex/gender, and it insists – sometimes against Butler's own logic and rhetoric – that to think sex as itself subject to gender norms cannot allow us to do away with the specificity of sex. This chapter thus concludes Part I, on 'Terms of political analysis', by offering a fuller theory of the body and by insisting that sex remain an essential element in Butler's lexicon.

'Theories of the political' denominates Part II of the book, comprising two chapters that elucidate specific contributions Butler makes to political theory. The first, Chapter 4, focuses on her concept 'normative violence', a term that Butler retroactively applies to her work in *Gender Trouble*. We demonstrate the validity of Butler's own application by doing the conceptual work with the term that she herself never takes up. More importantly, we then put the concept 'normative violence' to work, to make sense of a number of post-9/11 political predicaments. At first blush, the concept of normative violence sounds either redundant or self-contradictory, but we argue that it proves essential to understanding the power of Butler's theory of the political and to navigating the stormy political waters of today.

In Chapter 5 we move from the study of a particular political concept in Butler's writings to a broader investigation of what we call her *political ontology*. We develop this account for the most part from her later writings, especially her 2005 book *Giving an Account of Oneself*, a text devoted explicitly to ethics and moral philosophy. Many, perhaps including Butler herself, see this book as her definitive 'turn' to ethics. We argue, to the contrary, that if this book offers any sort of 'turn' it is a *return* to the relation between ontology and ethics that has always been at the heart of Butler's writings. Therefore, we deny that there is anything especially new about Butler's supposed first book on ethics. We suggest, instead, that we can understand a great deal abut Butler's broader project, particularly as it relates to politics and political theory, if we conceive it as a political ontology. To illuminate this claim we analyse Butler's later writings in the context of recent work in contemporary political theory that centres on the question of ontology; we claim that Butler makes a profound contribution to these debates and that her ontological work proves to be crucial political work.

Part III of the book also contains two chapters, both devoted in distinct ways to articulating a political theory of heteronormativity. The first of these chapters, Chapter 6, focuses on Butler's politicisation of kinship structures in her reading of the figure of Antigone. Through this linkage, Butler forwards a powerful and novel critique of heteronormativity by analysing the incest taboo as a social force that both maintains heteronormativity and produces a particular configuration of the family. She does this theoretically through her introduction and explication of the concept of (un)intelligibility, and she does it politically through her attention to the 'incest-born' person. We show that the unintelligibility of the incest-born demands a thoroughgoing reconsideration of the liberal framework of tolerance. The unintelligible, we argue, cannot be 'tolerated', as they have not even been granted access to the category of the human. When Butler asks us to reconsider kinship outside the dominant terms of the incest taboo she makes a powerful critique of the contemporary politics of 'the family' and she proffers a distinct and important conception of politics.

Chapter 7 moves from this focused political intervention to a higher level of abstraction, as it considers the possibility (and possible merit) of a theory of subversion. Like the concept of normative violence in Chapter 4, the theory of subversion can be used as a lens through which to view the entirety of Butler's corpus. We argue, contrary to the implicit claim made in the subtitle of *Gender Trouble*, that Butler seeks not the subversion of identity but the subversion of heteronormativity. Butler's understanding of subversion only emerges in relation to her implicit theory of heteronormativity, and this theory can help to illuminate the general problem of normativity for politics – just as it offers a robust response to that problem. We develop Butler's account of subversion through a fuller articulation of the theory of heteronormativity. At the same time, we suggest that the politics of norms found in this aspect of Butler's work proves essential to the field of Politics. Thus we conclude that political theory cannot afford to ignore either the theory of heteronormativity or the politics of its subversion.

If it makes sense to read Butler's work in relation to political theory through the rubric of 'troubling politics', then this is precisely because Butler remains committed to a conception of democracy and politics as always thoroughly *troubled* by theory. She rejects any linear model of politics; she criticises any conception of the relationship between theory and practice that would prioritise one or the other, or that would place theory prior (temporally or logically) to practice. Butler writes of 'the futurity which is essential to democracy itself' (Butler *et al.* 2000: 268). 'Troubling politics', we contend, names one of the many practices by which that futurity can be kept alive. This vision of radical democracy and the future-to-come leads Butler to a crucial commitment – a commitment, we offer, that she makes *as* a political theorist:

> the commitment to a conception of democracy which is futural, which remains unconstrained by teleology, and which is not commensurate with any of its 'realizations' requires a different demand, one which defers realization permanently. Paradoxically... democracy is secured precisely through its resistance to realization. ... [W]hatever goals are achieved... democracy itself remains unachieved.
>
> (Butler *et al.* 2000: 268)

The struggle for democracy demands an openness to democracy's future-to-come, a struggle that must not 'use' theory to constrain or foreclose options in advance. The role of the political theorist must therefore be to join this struggle to shape the political.

Part I
Terms of political analysis

1 Power/sex/gender

Gender is not the obvious place for a political theorist to start, even a feminist one. It is also not obvious that Butler set out in the first place to be a political theorist or even a feminist in some easily recognisable way. Nor did she start with gender as her main category. As Butler says in her preface (1999) to the anniversary edition of *Gender Trouble* (originally published in 1990), she 'understood herself to be in an embattled and oppositional relation to certain forms of feminism', although she also understood her text to have been 'part of feminism itself' (Butler 1999: vii). Understandably and informatively, Butler imbues the anniversary preface (1999) with her concerns, concepts and categories at that time, and she looks back at her 1990 text in that light. For our purposes here it is really more useful to take the 1990 text without this later framing, and to examine quite carefully what Butler says there, and in reverse order of expectations – thus Power/Sex/ Gender. From our perspective what makes Butler a political theorist (perhaps *malgré lui* – intentionality is not an issue here) is precisely her philosophical focus on power, to which sex and gender are adjuncts theoretically and of which they are results in practice.

Political theory, gender and 'Divine'

Butler is in fact an unusually well-focused political theorist with respect to power, because she frames other concepts in power-terms at the outset, rather than working in the opposite direction, as so many others – political theorists, social theorists, feminist and gender theorists, etc. – would generally do. That is, we would 'know' what gender is, 'what' it refers to, and we would then look for power-relations and effects of this 'given'. A term such as gender would be a readily available descriptive universal, an analytical category (with a history, of course) that could be 'applied' (with suitable adaptations) in political studies. The how, when and whether of power-relations and effects would follow on, much as Greek subjects formed a polis or as generic humans contract to legitimate sovereignty – two familiar narratives with which political theorists occupy themselves. In other words, human subjects would be assumed to have bodies and subjectivities, and would be assumed to 'have' gender in some way to be dealt with *in relation to* politics.

Obviously Butler was not 'doing' political theory in the usual way when she launched into *Gender Trouble*; nor was she following an easy pathway in feminist philosophy, as she herself notes in her original commentary on her title. In her original preface of 1990 she explains that she set out to 'trouble' gender, whereas most readers of the title *Gender Trouble* (then and now) would probably assume that she was referring to some conceptual and practical problems already *troubling it* which she could then fix (Butler 1999 [1990]: xxviii). *Troubling Gender* would have been a more accurate title in her own terms but publishers and readers do not respond so positively to this turn of the tables. They are more amenable to overtly positive and upbeat messages about finding something in trouble and putting matters to rights.

As we have already shown in some detail in the Introduction, Butler associates trouble not merely with gender, as in the title, but with herself in an autobiographical sense – linking her current motivations with childhood experiences, subtly re-setting these into contemporary philosophical terms, and foregrounding the concept of power. While Butler's opening trope of herself as 'bad girl', causing trouble and getting into trouble, may seem merely amusing, it aligns almost subliminally with a larger and more disturbing issue, namely her relationship with feminism as a movement. While she makes this explicit in the 10th-anniversary preface, she puts the argument subtly in the earlier text. There, Butler casts herself as feminism's bad girl, suggesting that trouble 'need not carry such a negative valence' (i.e. she's right to cause trouble) and effectively putting feminism in the role of a strict and controlling parent. Having suggested that current 'feminist debates over the meanings of gender' were driven by a desire to remedy the 'indeterminacy of gender', i.e. to stabilise the categories 'man' and 'woman', Butler then notes that those categories are only 'untroubling' when 'they conform to a heterosexual matrix', 'compulsory heterosexuality' and 'phallogocentrism' – concepts with a clearly negative political valence for Butler (1999 [1990]: xxvii–xxviii). In other words, for Butler, feminism's commitment to 'woman' and 'women' was itself imbued with the man/woman naturalising logic of gender and caught up in a regime of heterosexual privilege.

From that perspective any human identity as 'man' or 'woman' already sets 'a common ground' of constraint (as odd an idea as this seems), and in particular it constrains anyone who refuses heterosexuality (e.g. in her phrase 'gay and lesbian cultures'). In short, the 'foundational categories of identity – the binary of sex, gender, and the body' – make trouble for some people, not least Butler herself, and she presents this as a *central* political problem, not an occasion for tolerance, sympathy or therapy within a liberal framework (Butler 1999 [1990]: xxviii–xxix). This is why feminism, as a self-avowed liberating movement of theory and practice, figures in Butler's

original preface as something of a bad parent: 'The prevailing law threa-
tened one with trouble, even put one in trouble, all to keep one out of
trouble' (Butler 1999 [1990]: xxvii). She finds this troubling, and remains
determined to trouble it, i.e. to disrupt it. Butler calls the idea of 'female
trouble' – the notion of a particular female problem or affliction – entirely
laughable, and yet, echoing other feminists, she calls for 'laughter in the face
of serious categories' (Butler 1999 [1990]: xxviii). Here, Butler invokes one
strand of feminism against another. She poses the 'playful' feminism supported by her childhood trope against those feminists who are troubled by
the 'indeterminacy of gender' and who then seek *to secure* feminism by
securing 'woman' – thereby securing gender and gender oppression. From
Butler's perspective, this is all too serious (Butler 1999 [1990]: xxvii, xxix).

While engaging in feminist debates within the movement was not particularly controversial (though in terms of strategy and tactics it was usual, of
course, for sparks to fly), Butler's next move assuredly was. If she had
merely complained as a lesbian or on behalf of lesbians that the movement
was complicit with heterosexual privilege and concomitant homophobia,
there would have been relatively little fuss, and no great troubling of feminism. There have been numerous strongly worded and theoretically grounded lesbian critiques of mainstream feminism, both before and after Butler.
At the same time, however, lesbian feminism is generally taken to be a part
of feminism, just as lesbians are generally understood to be women.
Mounting a lesbian critique would not therefore have made Butler's work
especially radical, or troubling.

However, Butler's opening shot is to write at some length about 'Divine' –
a female impersonator both 'in person' and in an underground camp film –
as an important instance of feminist 'laughter in the face of serious categories'. As her hook, Butler uses the John Waters film that features Divine,
Female Trouble, which might even be the model for Butler's title. And she
also mentions the rather more famous cult classic by Waters, *Hair Spray* –
where Divine plays both the mother of the lead character and the antag-
onistic male police chief – perhaps to make sure we get the point (Butler
1999 [1990]: xxviii). Few feminists would have found the move Butler makes
here particularly funny, and only with the subsequent and consequent
developments in gender studies and queer theory has the scandal died down.
With this step, Butler troubles sex, gender and the body all at once from
what is purported, via laughter, to be a feminist frame of reference. *What
kind of woman was this?* The question applies to both Butler and Divine.

The history of enquiring 'What is woman?' is an old one in feminism;
arguably it is what feminism is all about, or at least it is a central and continuing point of debate (Squires and Kemp 1997). Presumably what sparked
these debates were exclusionary practices and definitions which ostensibly
defined 'woman' as different from, and generally inferior to, 'man' (notwithstanding other exclusions and gradations of hierarchy within those
categories). Feminist answers, or indeed answers that became feminist,

varied, of course, but they did so along fairly identifiable lines, e.g. 'someone who can do all, or most, of what men can do, and other things they can't', or 'someone different from, and indeed superior to, men or most men in terms of virtue'. The latter claims generally related to psycho-biological arguments, particularly but not exclusively concerning motherhood (Elshtain 1987). It would seem then that men made a problem for themselves, and even made themselves a problem, when they defined and devalued 'woman'. Consequently, women made feminism when they sought to redefine and revalue 'woman' in various kinds of theory and practice. Butler undercuts profoundly this entire line of argument, by suggesting that, however this kind of feminism proceeds, it is inevitably a search for *stability* in gender relations. For Butler, this search for stability entails the heterosexual matrix, compulsory heterosexuality and plenty of trouble for those who find those identities, and that form of life, deeply and personally troubling – if not utterly unlivable (Butler 1999 [1990]: xxviii–xxix).

In Chapters 6 and 7 we address in detail Butler's most-discussed and perhaps most troubling concept – the heterosexual matrix. Here, however, we focus on the crucial concept 'naturalisation', which gets rather less explicit attention. Butler gets to this concept by invoking Foucault's account of 'juridical notions of power' that appear to regulate in negative terms, e.g. through prohibition, regulation, control, 'protection'. Although 'juridical systems of power' are founded on 'the contingent and retractable operation of choice', they actually '*produce* the subjects they subsequently come to represent' (Butler 1999 [1990]: 5). As Butler explains, this account differs from the usual or commonsensical understanding of power precisely because power of this kind works through a process which *conceals* its own workings, i.e. the subject-producing practices that are both exclusionary and legitimating 'do not "show" once the juridical structure of politics has been established' (Butler 1999 [1990]: 5).[1] Political analysis, Butler argues, then takes these 'juridical structures' as a 'foundation' for the subject-producing political processes themselves (Butler 1999 [1990]: 5). The 'foundation' metaphor, of course, implies solidity, stability and security in reasoning or argumentation (see Seery 1999), and to that mix Butler adds a concept of 'naturalisation'. Naturalisation describes the way in which subject-construction is concealed, and references the apparently non-malleable, pre-political character of this subject, which can therefore be taken as *foundational*. These threads are drawn together as and when Butler invokes the classic 'foundationalist fable' of political theory in its characteristically modern guise: 'the state of nature hypothesis', which she says is 'constitutive of the juridical structures of classical liberalism' (Butler 1999 [1990]: 5).

Butler's argument is generally and rightly read with respect to the constitution of 'woman' as a gendered subject. Further, this gendered subject is produced through certain political operations, operations that Butler repeatedly invokes but, at this point, does not extensively illustrate. However, Butler actually casts her argument in very general terms about 'the subject' as such. That is, she outlines what it is to be any kind of human person with a subjectivity that is not merely and uniquely individual but also socially intelligible, categorial and ultimately legal under the prevailing juridical system – a system produced and maintained politically. She contends that our 'prevailing assumption of the ontological integrity of the subject' is a 'contemporary trace of the state of nature hypothesis', which she sees as 'the fictive foundation' of the law's claim to legitimacy. In Butler's composite recollection of the contractarian literature, the 'state of nature' presents us with a human subject 'who stands "before" the law' in some fictive or fabulist temporal sense (Butler 1999 [1990]: 4–5). For Butler it is that invocation of a temporal 'before' in classical liberal theories of sovereignty and legitimacy that links the foundational metaphor to nature via a state of nature. What is said to have been 'already' in existence in this state of nature (namely the human subject) is thus *naturalised* through the activity of making this claim convincingly. That is, the subject is ontologically secured in a supposedly pre-political and even pre-social realm. In the liberal fable, these subjects create the social and institute the political 'freely' by means of consent. With that 'foundationalist fiction' the political operations that *continue* to secure legitimacy and the juridical systems that *continue* to constitute the human subject (in diverse categorial ways) are effectively concealed. As Butler says, these operations seem merely to *represent* what had already been constituted elsewhere, whereas on Butler's argument political and juridical power continually produce what they merely *claim* to represent (Butler 1999 [1990]: 4–6). While political theorists might want to take Butler to task on the finer points of her presentation of the social contract, even as a myth, and also on its links to classical liberalism (again, a concept merely invoked but not discussed), the form and content of her discussion – while polemically cast as trouble for feminism – have an impeccable origin in political theory and have broad implications in philosophy.

The 'natural' and 'the Divine'

Following this tactic of argumentative generality, Butler pursues lines of least conciliation in her troubling of contemporary feminism. In her original preface to *Gender Trouble* Butler does not even bother to engage with lesbian identity and liberal tolerance within feminism, never mind society at large. There had already been some questioning and engagement, indeed troubling, of 'woman' as a category by lesbian feminists, especially by Wittig (1973) in her famous claim that lesbians are not women, and therefore stand categorially and experientially outside 'the straight mind'. Butler went a great deal further even than this withdrawal from the category 'woman'. Leaving 'woman' on one side disturbs gender perhaps, and certainly troubles feminists, but it did not trouble the world on the scale that Butler apparently had in mind. Focusing on power, she argues that it cannot be properly understood and analysed as an inter-relation between human *subjects*. This was of course the classic mode of analysis in political theory as well as in commonsensical accounts. Rather, following Foucault, Butler describes power as that which *produces* human subjects (as subjectivities), defines identities (such as 'man' and 'woman') and sets up categories (like 'gender' and 'sexuality'). Accepting all that as 'given' – subjects, identities, categories – leaves little scope for real trouble, according to Butler. If the power structures against which one rebels and by which one gets reprimanded are already presumed to be in place, then the battle turns out to be either long over or inconceivable in the first place (Butler 1999 [1990]: xxvii–xxix). What for Butler could possibly challenge 'the order of things'?

Perhaps choosing Divine as the challenge relates to the name, as well as the character, given the cosmic scale of Butler's enterprise. And it is worth asking at this point precisely what her enterprise is. Certainly Butler seeks much more than justice and respect for gay people, although she has clear concerns with homophobia, intolerance and bigotry in this regard. Perhaps Butler demands the *destabilisation* of gender, and hence the categories 'man' and 'woman'. And with the demise of those two identities, at least in their current configuration, comes the negation of the compulsory part of heterosexuality. However, we insist that Butler sees even more at stake philosophically. She aims to expose the workings of *power* on a large scale by showing *genealogically* how 'what is' has got that way *because of power* – not because anything or everything 'just happened' or 'has always been that way'. On top of that, she wants to illustrate and examine the general mechanism at work here; that mechanism tells us (mistakenly) how we ought to look at society and ourselves: 'designating as an *origin* and a *cause* those identity categories that are in fact the *effects* of institutions, practices, discourses' (Butler 1999 [1990]: xxix). This effort would expose the power-relations involved in *naturalising*, and therefore *stabilising*, categories and relations that have in fact been constructed *historically* and *contingently* with power. Power is then exercised in the present within and through those categories by means of exclusion and devaluation. While Butler probably thought she was merely following in the steps of Foucault, her target was a big one, namely the identity-relations ('man'/'woman') and power-relations (gender and sexuality) that define and constrain every person, everywhere, in every situation. Butler asks rhetorically, 'What happens to the subject and to the stability of gender categories when the epistemic regime of presumptive heterosexuality is unmasked as that which produces and reifies these ostensible categories of ontology?' (Butler 1999 [1990]: xxviii). In asking the question, Butler announces a radical threat to that very stability.

Butler thus mounts a full-scale assault on 'the natural, the original, and the inevitable'. This is an important and quite general *political* strategy. Butler has in her sights any significant conception of 'origins', 'inner truth' or 'genuine or authentic' identity (Butler 1999 [1990]: xxviii). These common discourses provide the common answers to common anxieties.

Power often comes from claims concerning what is original, primordial, natural, inevitable, factual, genuine, real, scientific and the like, typically in a 'founding' or 'grounding' narrative of certainty. This applies to any organising category of identity – national, religious, ethnic, etc. – as well as (much more radically) to the supposedly natural binary categories 'man' and 'woman' that Butler associates with gender and therefore with 'feminine' and 'masculine' subjects. Just to make her challenge to feminism on this point as thorough as possible, Butler announces that '"female" no longer appears to be a stable notion', an assertion that would surely leave her audience wondering why on earth she could think that (Butler 1999 [1990]: xxix). Her conclusion follows, again, from her invocation of Divine as a challenge not just to 'woman' – which has a certain plausibility, given his/her skilled, albeit overtly parodic, impersonation – but to 'being female' in the *bodily* sense. Divine neither was nor pretended to be in any way transsexual or even consistently transvestite, so Butler's elision of 'woman' with 'female' in this case seems either a stretch or a mistake. How could Divine challenge the naturalness of the female *body*? The answer emerges when we see that Butler takes Divine to be a destabilising challenge to 'the very distinctions between the natural and the artificial, depth and surface, inner and outer' through which discourses – particularly binary discourses such as gender – almost always operate (Butler 1999 [1990]: xxviii).

Butler's reasoning here is infamously quick and elliptical. She does not argue that in her/his appearances on film and in person Divine produces a female body, or is taken by anyone to have one – at least not for more than a moment, except by the very naïve. Rather, for Butler Divine *dramatises* not drag (which is itself a dramatisation) but *other practices* as identity-constructing. These other practices need not have anything directly to do with gender or sex, or any kind of sexuality. This general thesis states that *stabilising* discourses are enacted through practices that create the realities, even bodily ones, that we identify and perceive as natural, 'given', inevitable, etc. Drag itself does *not* do this. The trick for Butler is to demonstrate which practices *do* establish certain claims to 'the natural'. Achieving this will render claims about 'the natural' *suspect*, and *could* lead to their destabilisation – though certainly not to their negation or erasure. Such destabilisation can be brought about precisely when one demonstrates that these categories do not refer to 'something' which *is* 'natural' but rather *follow from* contingent, historical, malleable *practices* that could have been otherwise, and could be different in future.

Divine merely *dramatises* this entire process by making us see the 'signifying gestures' through which something both categorial and physical – in this case gender as 'woman' and 'female' – is (elsewhere) made 'natural' and thus seemingly and tendentiously inevitable, unchangeable, fixed, stable and secure. Drag *shows us* the gestures through which we identify someone as a woman – the gestures that allow us to presume, therefore, a body that is 'sexed' as 'female'. Moreover, because it *is drag* (i.e. a dramatic form) it highlights what we take *for granted* elsewhere, precisely because the dramatic and transgressive character of drag tells us that *elsewhere is normality*. Of course the trope of Waters's films is rather different: he uses drag to create an alternative normality that satirises the one we are used to, not to make Butler's point, which centres on dramatisation as a practice which *draws attention* to the putatively *undramatic* world of normality, a world which Butler argues is defined and constructed through *just the same kind of gestures*. We find these gestures within a discursive space we know as 'normal' because it is always said to be 'natural', rather than located within the discursive space presented in Waters's films, which are a self-consciously *fictive* realm of 'camp'. Waters evidently intended to amuse and make money; Butler evidently intends to destabilise the *power* through which the troubling normalities of gender are naturalised (Butler 1999 [1990]: xxviii–xxix; see also Butler 1993: 230–41).

As she recounts in her preface, Butler had for the first edition of *Gender Trouble* taken a good look at dramatic 'practices within gay and lesbian cultures' which 'often thematize "the natural" in parodic contexts that bring into relief' just how something is produced and constructed as 'true' – in this case, 'true sex' (Butler 1999 [1990]: xxviii–xxix, xxii–xxiv). This is truly a visionary moment of insight, but one that, unfortunately, has remained opaque to many, if not most, of her readers. Few readers would do what Butler was able to do, which is to put ordinary 'natural' people *into Divine's place* and thus transfer the insight about him/her *to their own gestures and practices*, that is, the very ones that seem stable, unproblematic, untroubled and secure, such as 'being a man or woman'. This seems so secure for most of us precisely because it seems so self-defining (how could I 'be' otherwise?) and so body-identified (I can see what I am!) and so natural (I was born one way of the two that are 'biologically possible'), and because it seems so instantly and factually *referential* in telling us 'what other people are'. What would it be like to see one's identity in every sense, especially gendered identity, and one's bodily sex and therefore sexuality, as the *product* of contingent human practices? And what would it be like to see the 'facts of human existence' as *humanly produced* historical products rather than as things that are 'given by biology'? In politics and in political theory, those things – bodily sex and gendered identity – are the foundational, grounding assumptions upon which legitimating claims and distinctions rest, and from which *power* flows along lines of inclusion/exclusion and validation/denigration. What would happen if this were reversed? How could politics and political theory operate without assumptions, in particular about humans and their bodies, that are *claimed to be secured* as founding, grounding assumptions in 'nature'?

Butler questions the need for discourses and practices of 'primary identity' generally, and in particular in feminism. Or rather, on our interpretation, she puts this the other way round. Writing within a feminist frame, Butler understandably puts her thesis in those terms of engagement. But shifting the frame to political theory – which we think does no violence to her argument, but rather draws it out – the critical case is more general. Butler herself asks, 'What new shape of politics emerges when identity as a common ground no longer *constrains* the discourse?' And to what extent does the effort to locate a common identity as the *foundation* for a politics '*preclude* a radical inquiry into the political construction and regulation of identity itself?' (Butler 1999 [1990]: xxix, emphasis added). This set of claims marks a thoroughgoing and on-the-move anti-foundationalism in philosophy and social theory that is just as applicable to religious, ethnic, racialised and national identities in politics as it is to gendered ones, whether these are articulated *via* the body (e.g. 'black power'), the mind (e.g. religious commitment), culture (e.g. linguistic traditions) or history (e.g. nationalist politics). Butler's logic also attacks an implicit hierarchy in these things, viz. the nearer one is to bodily biology, such as sex or skin colour, the closer one supposedly is to foundational certainty and categorial stability. Moving up notch by notch from this supposed basis in bodily naturalism, we could cite claims to ethno-national 'descent' from time immemorial, 'continuous' religious traditions supposedly dating from prehistory, more modern traditions dating back a few thousand years, etc., right up to claims that are rather more obviously historical and contingent (Stevens 1999). These could include constitutional moments of 'unity' as nation-states are founded and re-founded, and through which national loyalties and emotional investments are re-engaged and redistributed as political identities and concomitant obligations. Within Butler's framework, all of these current socio-political concerns would be subjected to destabilising genealogies.

Following Butler's argument as we have constructed it, these familiar hierarchies of nature and naturalness, certainty and fixity, stability and importance, collapse into contingent practices which are humanly malleable and in themselves produce no particular hierarchy or value. They are instead human *projections* of hierarchy and value into a realm that is *claimed* to be over and beyond political judgement and change, and therefore *claimed* to be its founding and grounding assumptions. This is why Butler's sees Divine as drawing into question not just 'woman' but 'being female': the practices that Divine dramatises are practices of projection through which meaning is inscribed *into* materiality, e.g. the body. 'Being female' must be thought, then, as a meaning assigned *to* something, not as a material property *of* something. That we normally perceive femaleness as being *in* the body's *materiality* itself demonstrates how inflexible a 'fact' humans apparently *want* it to be. The more it is lodged there, the less humanly produced it is. Or so we are encouraged to think through the logic of naturalisation. Butler has not merely turned the tables on 'the natural' and 'the humanly produced' in an odd way and for overtly political reasons; she has *levelled out* the presumed hierarchies in the logic of naturalisation that one usually takes to lie between the foundationally material and the contingently historical. Humanly produced things are therefore merely that; their reality and value, because these are both *meanings*, are up to us. If something material resists us, so be it, but we have the capacity and the responsibility to *tell it* what it is, and to interpret the situation in our own terms (Butler 1999 [1990]: xxviii–xxix; see also Butler 1993: 27–35, 54–5).

Doubtless Butler did not have all this in mind when she focused her discussion on gender, sex and therefore sexuality. She may or may not have had an interest in pushing the argument in this direction. But it does go there, and we find sufficient nods and gestures along that trajectory within her prefatory and substantial texts to licence the extrapolation. In any case, political theory has a long history of eclectic extrapolation, with oftentimes far less warrant from the authors involved. Our point is that, whether good feminist or 'bad girl', Butler troubled gender in an always overtly political manner. Her philosophical refusal of foundational binaries – not just man/woman but more potently social/biological and natural/artificial – proves thoroughgoing and profound. While the origin of this critique does not lie with Butler, the compressed yet unforgettable imagery of her discussion turned out to be vastly unsettling within and beyond feminism as it was at the time. Clearly she was Divinely inspired.

At the close of her original preface Butler links her childhood trope of 'getting into trouble' with her overall project, which she defines as philosophical, but in a *political* way: 'to affirm those positions on the critical boundaries of disciplinary life'. While at one level this announces a kind of academic politics, at another level it provides us with a metaphor or code for a more profound and troubling political project, namely affirming those 'unintelligible' subjectivities who find themselves disciplined such that they are forced via categorising disciplines outside the boundaries of genuine and valued positions in social life itself (Butler 1999 [1990]: 43–4; see also Butler 1993: 108–24). The political goal for Butler is to radicalise 'feminist critique', but in a way that – as we have seen – many feminists would hardly recognise, and would swiftly criticise

Fables, facts and politics

Gender Trouble makes a troubling link between 'gender' and 'gay and lesbian perspectives', but the third element in Butler's intellectual triad, 'poststructuralist theory', surely proved the most difficult of all for most readers to understand (Butler 1999 [1990]: xxx). At the time, many rejected it out of hand or on the basis of hearsay caricature (or getting a headache on first reading). Many still do. Butler's political programme at this stage – her assault on the very mechanisms through which gender, sex and sexuality *become* natural 'facts' – relies on a complex and challenging redefinition of commonplace concepts and distinctions. Disturbingly, her childhood recollections turn out to be a 'fable irreducible to fact'. More generally, and even more unexpectedly, she goes on to say that 'gender fables establish and circulate the misnomer of natural facts' (Butler 1999 [1990]: xxxi–xxxii). What kind of political programme denies the existence of 'natural facts', and what kind of politics could possibly start from this idea and then go anywhere? How could anyone expect to get people on board politically with a movement through a strategy of not merely ignoring but explicitly denying 'natural facts'?

Butler's practice since 1990 has been consistent with her announcement then: 'to participate in whatever network or marginal zones is [*sic*] spawned from other disciplinary centers and that, together, constitute a multiple displacement of those authorities' (Butler 1999 [1990]: xxxii). Note again the coded pun on academic and social disciplines, the latter deriving from her extensive citation of Foucault, who was notably graphic on the subject, as well as theoretically fecund. Declaring war on 'facts' and destroying the concept of 'the natural' are *political* projects, however, not 'merely philosophical ones'. In terms of political theory and its influence on practical politics, these ideas cannot be dismissed as absurd. Butler has some distinguished predecessors who overthrew concepts of 'divine right', 'absolute monarchy' and all manner of 'theocracy'. These were formerly unshakeable foundations of an orderly world; indeed, they were the very ideas through which that order was, with struggle, secured – or, rather, *claimed* to be secured (Hampsher-Monk 1992: chs I–IV). Denying king, bishop and God caused plenty of trouble in its day; Butler's deconstructing assault on the 'nature' in human nature is no less political and no less impossible as a rearrangement of the concepts that render 'the human' intelligible in the first place. Any critique of Butler and her politics one way or the other – or of gender and sexuality politics since 1990 – needs to take her work seriously as a project in political theory. Perhaps it is only her bad luck that these projects today are largely located in the academy, where they can be neutralised, belittled and – as Butler puts it herself – domesticated (Butler 1999 [1990]: xxxii).

While Butler rightly takes a serious concern with gender and sex (both as concepts and as lived experience) to be much more characteristic of feminists and of feminisms than of others in the academy, she again casts her argument in the broadest terms possible. And we note: she does this whatever the consequences for anyone involved with her project. Rather than work 'to gender' political theory – an ongoing and important project at the time (Pateman 1988) – Butler works the other way round, and derives her now famous reversal of the sex/gender distinction from the naturalising logic she had already identified in her Foucauldian reading of the social contract theory, i.e. the logic through which the 'order of things' is legitimated and secured. As naturalisation works by establishing the ontological integrity of the allegedly pre-social human subject, so that subject in the state of nature also has a securely stabilised 'natural' sex, through which binary notions of 'gendered' behaviour are naturalised and thus made to seem stable and secure. Therefore the fable presumes not just subjects, but 'men' and 'women' with characteristically 'masculine' and 'feminine' modes of behaviour through which social and political exclusions can be articulated, legitimated and enforced – all through the productive capacities of power. Of course, in appearance, the relevant juridical and legal systems seem merely to *reflect* and *represent* the 'natural' in the sense of alleged biological and social normalities – thereby *concealing* their continuing constitutive operations. This general methodology of production, concealment, representation, legitimation and therefore intelligibility (i.e. the common currency of social and legal categories) underpins Butler's troubling of sex, gender and sexuality. Of course this work also relies on Butler's careful reading of previous feminist work in troubling sex and gender, which she cites (Butler 1999 [1990]: 194–5 nn. 7–11). Nonetheless, the philosophical generality, and the methodology derived from political theory, must be established as Butler's own work.

Sex and gender then cannot be located in a pre-social 'nature' that would precede politics and which politics would then merely reflect and represent. 'Nature' and 'the natural' cannot remain immune to serious political discussion, never mind political change. What then follows for Butler? Famously she suggests that the contemporary view that gender as behaviour is in fact individually, socially and politically malleable carries with it the logical implication that gender 'cannot be said to follow from a sex in any one way', or indeed in any way at all (Butler 1999 [1990]: 9–10). Butler gives an impeccably logical analysis, arguing, for example, that the epithet 'masculine' can apply to a female person; a gendered term thus contradicts its supposed sexual logic. Moreover, as culturally constructed, gendered epithets cannot be limited to two – once again contradicting gender's supposed logic in binary sex. Butler's almost insouciant conclusion – 'gender itself becomes a free-floating artifice' – is sweeping and seldom taken with sufficient seriousness and consistency (Kaufman-Osborn 2006). The urge to *stabilise* any claim to 'free-floating' behaviour that can be construed with reference to 'sex' and 'sexual' behaviour is politically rife, and finds its legitimating logic in precisely the naturalising terms that Butler outlined: the invocation of 'nature' as that which political institutions must represent, and that which is foundational and therefore legitimating for power claims (Butler 1999 [1990]: 9–10).

The 'natural' facts of life

Butler deals with the supposedly natural status of sex as a matter of biological certainty in a rather hasty paragraph of questions, opening with 'And what is sex anyway?' She suggests that our knowledge of sex arises through scientific discourses, which themselves have a history. And that history would include the establishment of duality as a 'natural' fact. Flying miles high over any thought of argumentative justification, Butler then links scientific discourses to 'political and social interests', and concludes that they must be just 'as culturally constructed as gender' (Butler 1999 [1990]: 10). The sex/gender distinction was the point from which the political projects of the most important modern strands of feminism had derived their room for manoeuvre. That is, feminists had argued that biological sex did not represent a singular destiny for women, hence gendered structures in society could accommodate women differently and flexibly, contrary to the supposed restrictions that female biology was said to impose. Butler's conclusion – that 'sex' is itself a 'gendered category' – reversed the previous conceptual relationship, and contradicted the view that 'sex' was always and already established as a 'biological' binary in a prediscursive and pre-political realm onto which science was a window. Gender in Butler's view designates instead 'the very apparatus of production whereby the sexes themselves are established'. This encompasses 'the power relations that produce the effect of a prediscursive sex and so conceal that very operation' (Butler 1999 [1990]: 9–11). This then is a powerful and broad methodology for Butler that dissolves the 'foundations' of science and social science, undercuts the claims to security and stability that cite such 'matters of fact', breaks up settled linkages between the concepts through which social policies and political projects are articulated and legitimated, and frees up human behaviour and potentialities to an apparently limitless extent. If the foundations are merely fictive, then so are the superstructures.

Butler then sets up a neat dichotomy between a determinism based on 'laws' of some sort and the 'free-floating artifice' position she has already announced. She reduces the former quite smartly to, in effect, the same old 'biology-is-destiny formulation'. For the latter, she interestingly aligns Simone de Beauvoir with Divine. Butler's reading of Beauvoir ascribes to her position not only individual 'free will' in respect of 'an agent, a cogito' who could choose a 'construction' and effect it, but also the view that the body is a 'situation', i.e. something always constructed by cultural meanings through and through. Butler concludes succinctly, 'there is nothing in her [Beauvoir's] account that guarantees that the "one" who becomes a woman is necessarily female' (Butler 1999 [1990]: 12).[2] Rejecting the free will/determinism dichotomy, Butler sensibly opts for the notion of 'constraint'. Butler suggests that the body only comes '*into being*' in and through 'the mark(s) of gender'. She concludes that bodies 'cannot be said to have a signifiable existence prior to the mark of their gender' (Butler 1999 [1990]: 12–13). Whether 'gender or sex is fixed or free', Butler says, 'is a function of a discourse', the terms of which are set by 'hegemonic culture'. This discourse is 'predicated on binary structures that appear as the language of universal rationality' (Butler 1999 [1990]: 13). Butler hereby avoids one of the paralysing dichotomies of traditional philosophy (determinism *or* freedom of the will), and she reconceives the usual terms of referential and causal language ('universal rationality') in a politicised way, i.e. as effects of *power*. These then become the limiting terms concerning what can be *imagined* about gender. What *is said to be* 'natural' is fixed, solid, foundational, pre-political, non-malleable, an object represented *in* language; what is *actually* 'constructed' is free-floating, fluid, non-foundational, political, malleable, a discursive cultural effect *of* language. The logic of naturalisation sets *constraints*, which referential language *conceals*. Butler's deconstruction makes this process visible and constitutes a revised understanding of referential language.

Finally Butler takes on 'the person', the subject or subjectivity who is presumed, in political theory and commonsensical understanding, to be the mind and body constituent of political activity. Not even this is fixed or secured in 'the self', it seems. Rather than proceed from a conception of identity, and advance from there to 'gendered identity' via descriptions of some physiological, psychological and/or cultural processes through which a 'person' acquires 'attributes' of familiar sorts, Butler reverses direction. The '*regulatory practices* of gender formation and [binary] division', she writes, 'constitute identity, the internal coherence of the subject, indeed, the self-identical status of the person'. Identity is thus a 'normative ideal' (though not Butler's) 'rather than a descriptive feature of experience' that is 'had' or generated by 'a person' (Butler 1999 [1990]: 22–3). 'Identity' only happens in respect of a 'person' through the 'stabilising concepts' of 'sex, gender and sexuality', which are 'socially instituted and maintained norms of intelligibility'. Thus those who appear 'incoherent' or 'discontinuous' in some way become unintelligible as persons, because identity as a person can only be established within the current social 'laws that seek to establish causal or expressive lines of connection among biological sex, culturally constituted genders, and the "expression" or "effect" of both in the manifestation of sexual desire through sexual practice' (Butler 1999 [1990]: 23). The flip side of this is that the cultural matrix of intelligible gender identities requires that some 'identities' cannot 'exist', by which she means that they appear to us only as 'developmental failures or logical impossibilities'. Gender, it seems, cannot but generate disorder, as the laws of coherence will necessarily generate the possibilities for and realities of incoherence and 'failure' (Butler 1999 [1990]: 22–3).

From this cultural matrix one can take a fairly short step to the heterosexual matrix, which in Butler's view provides the internal unity and coherence for the sex/gender/sexuality conjuncture. In other words, the matrix provides a 'stable and oppositional heterosexuality' which secures the concepts man and woman as the only intelligible ways of 'being a person' (Butler 1999 [1990]: 23). Moreover the notion of the 'person' as 'man' or 'woman' as an 'abiding substance' – who might also have minor dissonant gendered features – is itself a fiction, an 'effect' that occurs because we use these apparently descriptive words as *nouns*. Butler argues instead that we are what we do, we do not pre-exist our deeds, and therefore we can 'be a person' only because we are described as such after the fact. Our being does not derive from something innate to ourselves; to think that it does is to fall prey to what Butler calls 'the metaphysics of substance'. This metaphysics

takes as continuing and 'substantial' what are really 'coherences contingently created' through disciplinary regulation (Butler 1999 [1990]: 33).
Although crucial descriptive discourse rests on it, an 'ontology of substances', Butler concludes, 'is superfluous'. Why then is referential discourse,
and the concomitant metaphysics of substance, the very stuff of commonsense and 'universal rationality'? Because of politics, says Butler, with
reference to the particular project identified by Foucault as the regulation of
'sexual experience'. She ventures no further, no doubt fearing the dangers of
finding functionalist causes in politically produced effects (Butler 1999
[1990]: 23–5).

A philosophy and politics of power

One cannot help but be impressed by the care and speed with which Butler
outlines these terms. And one must also note the extent to which Butler
writes under the spectre of Marx. After all, it was Marx who pungently
pointed to 'social relations independent of our will', who exposed the falsely
historical but potently mythical naturalisation of commodity-relations in
the state of nature fables purveyed by Smith and Ricardo, who explained
that the analytical exposure of the mechanism through which commodities
are fetishised would not in itself cause the practice to disappear (Butler 1999
[1990]: 43–4; Marx 1987 [1859]: 263; 1996 [1867]: 81–94).

Butler's project follows a similar logic but maintains a far more general
scope. She thinks about ontology and epistemology in discursive terms that
transcend traditional philosophical dualisms. Far more potently political,
she sets her sights on *all* the categories through which humanity in general
and individuals in particular can be 'signified' and thus made intelligible.
Butler's major political concern, as it develops, lies very much with the
commonsensical and juridical disciplines and regulations, 'unlivability' and
violence, that go with the exclusions and denigrations of hegemonic cultural
and legal discourses. Casting her work in a feminist frame is important, but
this frame neither defines nor confines her work; the philosophical and
political issues raise the question of what really necessitates a feminist frame
in the first place, and what the implications of feminist concerns – and
concerns that are *like* feminist concerns – actually are for philosophical
thought and practical politics. Power remains the crucial category for
Butler, as it literally produces the stuff of the human social world (i.e.
hegemonic social discourse and 'unlivable' lives). And therefore power and
the analysis of its workings provide the only way that the constructed
exclusions and constraints could be rearranged otherwise (Butler 1999
[1990]: 42–4).

While the origins of this position and project lie with Foucault and Marx,
Butler's summarisations must be noted for their extraordinary concision
and focus. Her background in Continental philosophy makes it easy for her
to cast language itself in a 'constructive' or 'constitutive' rather than

descriptive or referential role. It is not easy, however, to explain this to readers in a way that makes *different sense* of the terms of 'universal rationality' through which we 'normally' perceive and experience the world – not least the everyday rationality of political projects like the feminist one, anchored as it was (and for many still is) in the apparently obvious natural securities of sex, and to some extent gender. While Butler was hardly the first to question these securities, her concept of 'trouble' went far beyond the usual framework of 'debates' in feminism or politics generally. Her thinking on power/sex/gender has an unconstrained quality, a refusal to rest within a frame already known to be inhabited by readers who could be expected to be supportive or at least sympathetic. Butler has, in fact, taken on the burden of a certain amount of the trouble that she set out to cause to gender and hence to what was then the major movement in gender politics, feminism.

Butler's political manifesto of contingent 'coalitional politics' was hardly one to please, even though it deduces logically from her philosophical position. One bases a 'foundationalist tactic', she says, on 'the articulation of an identity within available cultural terms', and this in itself forecloses 'the transformation or expansion of existing identity concepts as a normative goal' (Butler 1999 [1990]: 20–2). An 'open coalition', Butler adduces, 'will affirm identities that are alternatively instituted and relinquished according to the purposes at hand' (Butler 1999 [1990]: 22). Butler clearly rejects a 'normative telos of definitional closure', but what exactly is the overarching descriptor of her own normative commitment? Here she ventures swiftly but decisively into the realm of political theory, offering 'the often tortuous process of democratisation' as her normative frame and suggesting that political action does not require as its prerequisite a 'unity' based on 'agreement'. She targets 'the liberal model', which, she says, assumes precisely this, viz. 'speaking agents' who occupy 'equal positions of power and speak with the same presuppositions about what constitutes "agreement" and "unity" and, indeed, that those are the goals to be sought' (Butler 1999 [1990]: 20–2).

Butler's politics may be coalitional, but it is not liberal-pluralist. The foundations of the liberal doctrines of popular sovereignty, individual obligation, personal security, legal rights, limited government and liberty of the citizen look profoundly troubled by Butler's anti-foundationalism. If we describe Butler's politics as one of 'multiple convergences and divergences without obedience to a normative telos of definitional closure', then what exactly survives (if anything) of liberal political institutions? (Butler 1999 [1990]: 22; see also Butler 1993: 226–30). And how could this survival be understood? Or is this a political theory, or approach to political theory, that – like Marx's – offers no 'receipts [*sic*] ... for the cookshops of the future' (Marx 1996 [1872]: 17)?

Butler answers this difficulty by seeking to resolve the political paradoxes of 'radical repudiation' (which necessarily *reproduce* a logic of domination and repudiation) into 'the terms of power itself'. Again, she targets the regulatory practices of political constraint, but her goal is not some 'sexuality' or politics that is 'outside', 'before' or 'beyond' current conceptualisations. Rather, she argues for pastiche and parody in practice, reconstructions that challenge naturalising fictions and displace regulative norms with 'hyperbole, dissonance, internal confusion, and proliferation'. Making her argument seem easier and somewhat less hopeless politically, she notes that the regulatory matrix of compulsory heterosexuality is itself constructed at multiple sites (e.g. biological and medical sciences, religion, psychoanalysis, etc.) and so is itself likely to be self-contradictory, self-subversive and self-deconstructing. Adding her manifesto to Marx's, Butler explains her project:

> To expose the contingent acts that create the appearance of a naturalistic necessity ... a task that now takes on the added burden of showing how the very notion of the subject, intelligible only through its appearance as gendered, admits of possibilities that have been forcibly foreclosed.
>
> (Butler 1999 [1990]: 42–4; see also Butler 1993: 226–30)

Gender Trouble thereby names a *political battle* against naturalising fictions and launches a practical war of the categories. It does not, however, instantiate a utopia. Marx, of course, had an inversion of the marketised world in mind, and a 'given' historical subject in the industrial proletariat. Butler aligns herself with his denaturalising strategy but refuses, for sound philosophical reasons, to posit the stabilising fictions of identity that purport to secure a future society. For her, denaturalising gender could render 'impossible' identities partially intelligible and thus strike at the heart of what we might call oppression. Exposing the 'person' of liberal theory as a regulating fiction would liberate us from the chains of continuity, consistency and the gruesome burden of inflicting hegemonic norms upon ourselves. Here we see a very Nietzschean revolution of and in the mind, which Butler takes to the body and to the realm of power relations – the place where discourse generates effects through practices. The 'possibilities', she insists, are there for us to grasp (Butler 1999 [1990]: 189–90; see also Butler 1993: 240–1).

2 Performativitity/citationality/ repetition

Butler owes her notoriety as the *doyenne* of post-structuralist feminism to the concepts at the head of this chapter. However, Chapter 1 has taken some pains to redescribe her work as a much more general project in politics and political theory. It has shown that Butler sets out to trouble one of the most ubiquitous phenomena in human social history: the production of power through naturalising discourses that tell us *what* we are and therefore *who*. Such a project aligns her with Marx, Nietzsche and Foucault, and perforce places her somewhat self-consciously at odds with the general feminist framework of enquiry and debate. She pointedly criticised most feminisms in *Gender Trouble* for seeking a secure concept of 'natural' sex through which to stabilise the 'social' concept gender, and thus to ground and to represent an 'identity' in terms of 'woman'. Feminist politics before Butler was generally presumed to take place within this 'gendered' understanding of the human subject as 'woman', through which 'biological females' could reinterpret and therefore change what it is to be one. As with her general argument against the 'naturalness' of sex – dramatised in an over-the-top way by her invocation of the transvestite 'personality' and film character Divine – Butler took radical exception to this argument and the attendant political strategy. She declares gender a free-floating signifier, so she exposes as unconvincing those familiar attempts to bring it back into alignment with 'biological sex'. If women, as Beauvoir said, were not born but made, there was nothing in Butler's view that said that a woman (by gender) had to be female (by sex). So much, then, for feminism and its political appeal to women as self-evidently female and variously 'different', supposedly backed up by careful theorisations based on the 'findings' of natural and social science.

Given Butler's view of language – through which meaning is not descriptive and referential, but inscriptive and constructive – these were never 'findings' anyway, however graced they were by the terms science or social science. The *coup de grâce* to the whole of feminism-so-far was then Butler's reversal of the foundational understanding of gender as, in some flexible and variable sense, an *effect* of 'biological' and therefore paradigmatically 'natural' sex, understood as the female/male binary – itself grounded in the supposed imperatives and necessities of species reproduction. For Butler, gender, the newly declared free-floating realm of *linguistic* rather than 'natural' binaries, itself *defines* the need to have a 'sex' binary in the first place, and then goes on putatively to find that binary 'factually' *in* and *of* the body in its 'material' and superficial properties.

Having thus not merely deconstructed the 'basics' of feminism, but also constructed a distinct politico-theoretical project, what exactly had Butler done, other than cause a lot of trouble? There seems little point in anyone backtracking now to make her fit into lesbian and gay studies, since the same arguments apply there. Gay identity politics puts the same binarising strategies to work as those isolated by Butler within feminism, that is, a presumption that a sexuality binary (homo/hetero) emerges in behaviour from a biological or psychological orientation binary, experienced or discovered within embodied individuals who are already sexed biologically. In the case of homosexuality, this comes about without the supposed 'reproductive imperatives' of 'the species' – at least not reproductive in ways defined by and idealised within the heterosexual matrix.

Butler's view of gender as a linguistic realm of binaries was precisely the point through which she argued that the normalisation of 'compulsory' heterosexuality took hold. How could a male/female sex binary be anything other than a reproductive mechanism? Obviously gay and lesbian theorisations and activism argued otherwise, which as various discussions in *Gender Trouble* illustrate, rather makes Butler's point: binaries are what humans want them to be, because they are constructed in and through language. They are not *reflections* of what is already and necessarily there, and their *referential* claims are power's primary ruse *already built into language itself* in its commonplace locutions and commonsensical understandings. Butler was therefore not an obvious hero for gay and lesbian activists, any more than for feminists, not because she failed to share the political thrust of both; quite the reverse, and indeed she supported many mainstream feminist, gay/lesbian and queer positions, as *Gender Trouble* makes clear and voluminous subsequent writings consistently demonstrate. Rather, Butler's project, relentlessly pursued, is a philosophical one about politics, and specifically about power, and she follows it wherever it leads, not shying away from the implications for the political movements in which she was thoroughly involved, and no doubt through which, as she would probably acknowledge, a considerable amount of her individual 'identity' was self-narrated and experienced in relation to others in her public and private lives.

Readers may note that Chapter 1 presented this view of Butler without mentioning performativity, citationality and repetition as such, and that her devastating contributions to feminism and the politics of sexuality appear complete, at least in outline. What exactly then do these three concepts add to the foregoing argument? Conversely, how much confusion and displacement occur when readers and commentators tackle Butler through 'performativity' in the first instance as an obvious 'way in'? More broadly, what does Butler's discussion of these concepts bring to philosophy generally and to political theory in particular?

As Butler says in the original preface to *Gender Trouble*, 'Philosophy is the predominant disciplinary mechanism that currently mobilizes this author-subject, although it rarely if ever appears separated from other discourses' (Butler 1999 [1990]: xxxii). While this is very much as Butler wanted it in her text at that time, the text then and ever since has been read almost wholly *through* those 'other discourses' and within the *context* of those discourses. In other words, while Butler describes *Gender Trouble* as primarily a philosophical work, speaking first to a philosophical context, her readers have taken the text as a project located within feminism, have read it as a part of psychoanalytic literature or have constructed it as a founding text of queer theory. More than that, the reception of *Gender Trouble* has reconstructed a rather non-philosophical context around the book, in the form of the perceived crisis in feminist politics resulting from controversies about what is or is not denoted or connoted by 'woman'.

This chapter frames Butler's contentions within the philosophical interests that she outlines, thereby reversing the direction of most of her own discussions. She characterises those discussions as critical discourses on 'gender hierarchy' and 'compulsory heterosexuality' through which her philosophical claims would emerge (Butler 1999 [1990]: xxviii). We do not seek here to reveal or critique any debts to philosophy that might be traced in Butler, but rather to get hold of the broadest possible theoretical perspective on her ideas in the first instance, and then to demonstrate very clearly and in the most generalisable way her substantial thesis. Butler makes a very wide-sweeping argument in political theory when she shows how 'foundational categories' are 'productions that create the effect of the natural, the original and the inevitable', precisely because these discourses constantly figure in important strategies that both produce and deploy political power (Butler 1999 [1990]: xxix).

For Butler, 'performativity' is not a specialised phenomenon. That is, she calls acts 'performative' when they *constitute the natural* – always in terms of some specific 'thing' – through discursively constrained, but nonetheless signifying, gestures and speech. Power thus operates at this conjunction between human activity and meaning, and it 'produces' in language what the language 'claims merely to represent' (Butler 1999 [1990]: 5; see also Butler 1997a: 2–3). Butler's particular example of a 'thing' happens to be 'woman' as a gendered category. Butler takes 'woman' as but one of any number of existent or possible 'juridical subjects' – albeit an extremely important one, not least for feminists. For her, 'woman' is not only a 'foundational' category for social practices and individual identity, but also, and very importantly, a 'naturalised' one. This means, as previously shown, that the supposedly timeless realm of nature *conceals* the constructed character of woman. With woman safely naturalised, that is, safely lodged within the realm of 'nature', neither society nor individuals can (supposedly) interfere and cause changes. The natural makes up the realm of the 'always and already', the inevitable and unquestionable, the legitimating groundwork for any number of power-ridden constraints. Undoubtedly, such a realm proves thoroughly paradoxical, in that if the natural were truly natural there would be no need to denominate it as such, and the constraints would be unremarkable uniformities (Connell 2002: 3–4). Rather than take 'the natural' as a mere accounting of the obvious and the given, Butler theorises naturalisation as a powerful *strategy* of concealment.

Butler's concern intrigues us, as it has intrigued her readers over the years. Through the concepts that head this chapter, she focuses less on how 'the natural' *appears* in discourse and more on how it is *enacted* in life. This enactment happens in the everyday ways through which the strategy of concealment also takes effect, and 'the natural' then appears unremarkable and obvious. 'Performativity' thus includes an inherent repetitiousness in our activities. That is, there must be some partial stability in what we do in order for our everyday language to work as well as it does in 'referencing' what we see and what we do. Butler proffers, through Derrida, 'citationality' as a discursive shorthand for this (relative) stability in meaning and therefore reference, precisely because the production of these stabilities means that we can refer to them, or cite them in ostensive and allusive ways. Meaning and reference thus always prove circular with our activities: we know what we are doing (even if we are not thinking about it), and we find it unremarkable when others recognise this phenomenon by citing the referential categories through which everyday stabilities are lived (Butler 1999 [1990]: xxix, xxiv, 184–7; see also Butler 1993: 224–6).

Butler of course is keen to demonstrate the political dimension here, rather than the merely everyday one, by choosing a category, 'woman', that appears in both. Because the category of woman is so thoroughly naturalised, it must be forced to become 'the same' in both of these dimensions, and this outcome is achieved through practices of discipline and regulation. This occurs through the operation of the Foucauldian power-processes that link the juridical (i.e. the legislative, legal and judicial apparatuses) with everyday lived experience and 'common sense'. At the psychoanalytic level Butler investigates identity-constitution in the deepest, most personal realms of the consciousness and the unconscious. As a strategy of concealment, naturalisation works remarkably well, in that the strategy itself protects us from the kind of self-consciousness that would alert us to the repetition and citation through which we are ourselves produced, and through which we ourselves produce the same stabilities that offer us 'things' and 'persons' with which to interact (Butler 1999 [1990]: xxix, 171–80; see also Butler 1993: 121–4). Butler's theorising thus proceeds not *in application to* politics, but *out of* the politics itself with which she engages (Butler 1997a: 20, 40).

Performativity and philosophy

This kind of philosophy refuses a number of traditional distinctions and dichotomies which other philosophers take as necessary constituents of philosophy itself. Butler's approach thus effectively rejects and also claims to transcend the matter/consciousness dichotomy, to overcome the 'opposition' between materialism and idealism, and to avoid the freewill/determinism debate. By rendering these traditional points of reference nonsensical, many traditional philosophers worry that Butler has left the dilemmas unresolved. However, Butler's politicised post-structuralism does draw out certain familiar lines in Anglophone philosophising, albeit from a rather different perspective, and one can locate numerous points of contact between her work and Anglophone philosophy.

In particular, Butler develops her understanding of performativity, and its relation to citationality and repetition, using J.L. Austin's (1962 [1955]) classic *How to Do Things with Words* as a crucial resource. She calls on his understandings of illocutionary force (the intention *in* saying) and especially perlocutionary force (the effects *of* saying). Famously, Austin was concerned to question the assumption that language must be *referential* to either material objects or sensory experience – in the sense that it must *refer* – in order to be meaningful, at least in the first instance of establishing facts and truth-conditions. He saw the logical positivist case as overdrawn, arguing instead that at least sometimes language makes meaning not because it refers to a thing (or follows from such referentiality) but because it does or enacts something, particularly as certain words are spoken intentionally in context. Thus, 'I now pronounce you man and wife' enacts a marriage, and is not in that way merely referential to something – not even to the pre-existing institution. Butler understands this kind of enactment as a performance in the sense of ritual participation in discursive practices, self-consciously set apart from the merely everyday (Butler 1993: 224–5, 244 n. 7, 246 n. 9; 1997a: 2–4, 145–59).

While Austin focuses on a speech-act, Butler looks more closely at context. Her concern lies with the juridical realm (e.g. marriage laws and registration) and in particular with both the *citationality* inherent in the practices that constitute this realm and the *repetitions* needed to maintain it (Butler 1997a: 147–50). While there is a certain self-consciousness amongst all parties involved in a marriage ceremony, there is also a certain unself-consciousness generally about the 'trappings' of the institution, particularly one that is so widely regarded as paradigmatic of social stability. Marriage thus involves a fusion of words-as-concepts with bodily, disciplinary and material practices. Examples include signing required papers, rules of divorce and even the imposition of prison penalties for bigamists. Butler's notion of performativity thus has a philosophical background of some subtlety and complexity. It also holds commonsensical plausibility, in that it is fairly easy to see how a familiar institution consists of individuals' activities that are repetitive instances of formulaic phrases linked to disciplinary political and social constraints experienced in both conceptual and material ways. *Gender Trouble* transposes these ideas, in the first instance, from a social institution to a subject (e.g. Divine), and then from the repetition and citationality inherent in that individual's somewhat self-conscious performance to the point of utter unselfconsciousness in the everyday activities of ordinary people. Butler's use of Divine is thus related to, though clearly different from, the Austinian analysis of marriage as a setting for a 'speech-act'. In the second instance, Butler transposes Austin's thinking from the creation of an institution such as marriage (which is inherently conceptual, however material its manifestations and effects) to the creation of not just a 'subject-position' but a *body*. This is somewhat harder to follow, as we generally understand bodies as material, and so created and changed through material processes. How then can an individual's repetitious citation of a concept such as womanhood *produce* the 'material' body of a woman?

Butler's conceptualisation of performativity reveals the 'twist' in language or discourse that conceals the process of naturalisation. We can now describe this process of naturalisation with a richer conceptual language: it consists of the repetitious activities that make individuals and therefore their bodies what they are through unselfconscious citation of ideas, concepts or norms. Sex and gender offer us helpful and primary, but certainly not exclusive, examples of this process. However, from this account Butler draws the remarkable conclusion that '"being" a sex or a gender is fundamentally impossible' (Butler 1999 [1990]: 25). How did she get to that conclusion, and how does it make sense? While her view remains compatible with a Foucauldian account of bodily disciplining practices that from infanthood produce some bodies in some ways (e.g. 'weak' female bodies) and other bodies in other ways (e.g. 'strong' male bodies), she clearly wants to make a rather different point. She focuses on the gestures and other subtle bodily actions that signal to an observer that 'that person is a woman'. This is a view of surfaces, i.e. dress and gesture, rather than a view of depth, i.e. bodily structures and organs, otherwise known as 'biology'. As such, her account marks an interesting philosophical reversal of emphasis in declaring the importance and meaning of a phenomenon. Butler very self-consciously focuses on how something 'seems' – how we initially make sense of it – rather than on how it 'really is'.

Hence Butler's interest in how gender and sex are signalled through activities that are understood in and through language, and are thus in a sense linguistic phenomena (however apparently non-verbal and visibly material they are in practice). The signalling involved is repetitious, citational and mostly unselfconscious, because we are used to the kind of signalling that produces stability in personal identity. That is, we are used to the kind of signalling that resists all those sanctions that penalise inconsistency and uncertainty in this regard. Seeing sex and gender in this way helps Butler to show the extent to which dress, behaviour and gesture always signal sex and gender *together*; the accumulation of these enactments produces a body presumptively sexed male or female.

Cases of ambiguity invite our presumptions, which are really projections of stereotypical behavioural attributes of gender and bodily attributes of sex onto someone else. Or the reverse occurs: other people make a presumptive identification of us. Most anyone – more or less self-consciously, or unself-consciously, or with intriguing overlays of the two – manages their own identification as a gendered and sexed being in precisely the same ways. Butler therefore contests the naïve 'confusion' of gender and sex that has crept into practice in recent years, e.g. the M and F boxes on forms that used to be 'sex' are now labelled 'gender'. She favours a critical analysis of the way the two interact productively to create an *illusion* of stability, certainty, fixity and naturalness concerning the human subject, i.e. the categorial identities 'man' and 'woman'. We recognise these categories in others and we live them in ourselves, and Butler of course has a particular interest in the latter category, 'woman'. Crucially, Butler knows that medical or biological 'facts' cannot *determine* gender, precisely because these 'facts' are themselves contested. This is because a variety of factors are involved, and because the factors deemed to be relevant are so various in their morphology, functionality and use. All of this arises, of course, in cases of deliberate intervention not to 'change' someone's sex to match someone else's but rather to recreate various bodily and psycho-social phenomena in order to produce a workable *reference* to one stereotype or the other (i.e. femaleness or maleness) and thus to begin the familiar patterns of citationality and repetition that *produce* a 'man' or a 'woman'. As Butler says in her preface to *Gender Trouble*, an updating of her discussion would involve more explicit consideration of transgender and intersexuality (Butler 1999: xi–xii, xxiii–xxiv, xxvi).

This way of framing Butler thus explains what she is getting at with her now notorious examples of drag (rather over-commented upon) and of Divine (rather under-emphasised) in relation to performative categories and thus to 'performativity' in general. It seems likely that Butler came to regret her playful invocation of drag and Divine, or at least to feel rueful about it as a didactic move. Her critics read conclusions off it that she later took pains to explain she had never intended, and undoubtedly the twin tropes of drag and Divine displaced an enormous amount of commentary onto subjects on which most of her critics were ill qualified to comment analytically and about which they seem to have been reluctant to do much real research. Note, for instance, that Divine's 'art of drag' doesn't exhaust drag as an unselfconscious art as one witnesses, for example, in Pride or Mardi Gras parades. Nor does it exclude the practice of drag as an individual statement/displacement of 'identity' in public places, which can certainly occur in an artful way without being framed as a work of art or artistry. In short, as a way of communicating with most of her readers this was a spectacularly unsuccessful move. However, looked at philosophically, and staying close to her text, the twin tropes help explain philosophical concepts crucial to her understanding of gender and sex, and thus they fill in the broader theory of naturalisation under discussion here. Finally, they indicate the potential transferability of this analysis to other 'performatives'. Here we note, for instance, Butler's description of the modern liberal subject as 'the contemporary trace of the state of nature hypothesis' in social contract theory (Butler 1999: xxii–xxiv, 5; see also Butler 1993: 230–6).

Nouns and the metaphysics of substance

Performativity describes the process by which juridical power 'produces what it claims merely to represent'. To put this in more specific terms, '*gender* is not a noun' (Butler 1999 [1990]: 3, 24, emphasis in original). As we saw in Chapter 1, Butler identifies herself with a thoroughgoing critique of the 'metaphysics of substance' (derived from Nietzsche and ascribed to Marx). She takes the metaphysics of substance as a philosophical doctrine asserting the existence of a 'true order of things', from which 'simplicity, order and identity' are instituted in terms of ontological truths (i.e. how things really are as a matter of 'being'). The critique endorsed and rehearsed by Butler argues contrarily that these supposed truths cannot be in any sense a representation of 'how things really are'. Instead, they indicate a confusion between, on the one hand, the grammar and other attributes of language and, on the other, the urge to make claims about 'how things really are' in order to license certainties and therefore secure stabilities. These certainties thus drive power-claims in human society, even though the claims themselves may *appear* in language to be 'objective' claims about 'the world' and 'how it really is' (Butler 1999 [1990]: 25–8; see also Butler 1993: 12–16).

As with her use of Austin, however, Butler takes a philosophical interest in language and its relation to a world of knowable certainties, and moves the discussion on to the practices through which such illusions of stability, certainty, fixity and naturalness are *enacted* in everyday life rather than simply *referenced* in everyday language. How then are these meanings produced through signals and gestures that we understand and apprehend as categories of identity? These are categories which we can then talk about, and things we think our language correctly or sometimes incorrectly references. Or, in other words, why do we think that gender and sex are *nouns*? Why do we think that the nouns 'man' and 'woman' stand for 'abiding substances' when – according to the critique of the metaphysics of substance – they are not 'ontological realities' but, rather, what Butler calls 'fictive construction[s]' with very real effects (Butler 1999: 32–3)?

Butler seeks an example that would clarify the everyday processes through which this happens. She does so not by merely reflecting on the way that they are done in terms of everyday concepts (where they appear unproblematic and unremarkable), but by *re-creating* them analytically as a

performance. This move into the remarkable and the problematic (too problematic, as it turned out) begins with Butler's account of Divine's *performance*, which to her is an *ambiguous* impersonation of a woman that
demonstrates something but is not itself the thing – in this case a process –
of 'being a woman'. Divine's performance *demonstrates* the *process* of 'persistent impersonation that passes as the real'. The performance must therefore *not* be conflated with that process; rather, the performance offers an
example of the process. This demonstration, Butler explains, destabilises 'the
very distinctions between the natural and the artificial, depth and surface,
inner and outer, through which discourse about genders almost always
operates' (Butler 1999 [1990]: xxviii). Thus Butler's account relies on her
'critical' (not naïve) understanding of the 'confusion' between sex and
gender referred to above. That is, gendered behaviour cannot in any sense
be an effect of binary sexual difference. This demonstration of a 'persistent
impersonation' only makes this destabilisation *visible* if we understand
Butler's *interpretation* of it; Divine doing what she/he is doing does not
destabilise anything. And understanding it *as a performance* does not
create a destabilisation either. Drag, we might then say, destabilises nothing
at all. This is because drag is a *performance*, because we understand it
that way, and because anyone doing it wants to signal it as such (though
other cross-dressing practices may of course signal other things, such as
genuine impersonation, and thus be understood quite differently). What is it
about drag, then, from which Butler derives this idea of destabilisation?
And how does this idea of destabilisation demonstrate the instability of
identity categories such as sex and gender, which Butler already understands
as 'fictive constructions' (Butler 1999 [1990]: xxviii–xxix; see also Butler
1993: 230–3)?

Butler makes two crucial moves: from 'performance' to 'cultural performance' (and performativity) and from dramatic gestures to 'signifying gestures'. The 'drama' in the dramatic gestures of drag alerts Butler (and
should alert her readers) to look again at the undramatic and largely
unselfconscious world of sex and gender which is *not* a performance. Sex
and gender are not performances precisely when they are not *understood as
performances*, which is to say they are not performances when they are not
signalled as such. Divine gives Butler a way to make the normal into the
problematic – in much the same way that Marx, as Butler cites, works to
make everyday objects problematic as 'commodities' (Marx 1996 [1867]:
81). We take our gestures to be unproblematic because they seem *natural*,
both to us and to the sex and gender we 'are'. Therefore we presume that
they could not be otherwise. Butler's view of drag *highlights* behaviour as
gesture, and likens it to an unselfconscious performance – almost a contradiction in terms. She resolves this contradiction by showing us that we
should be prepared to accept the inherent *instability* of our own gestures
because, in themselves, they cannot be distinguished all that clearly from
Divine's 'hyperbolic' ones. We must see our own gestures as very much like

Divine's, in Butler's view, even though we understand them differently, because they are *framed* differently. Divine's acts and gestures look like performance because of their framing by the dramatic, while our acts and gestures do not because of their framing by the everyday. It follows from this argument that the referential stability we find, both within ourselves and within the language that we use (about ourselves and others), is a product only of *persistence* in gestures that *signify* something culturally: Divine's gestures signify drag queen; ours signify gender and sex together (as 'woman' or 'man'). Butler suggests we take both 'drag queen' and 'gender and sex' as 'cultural performances', even if we never see or experience our everyday gestures as such. No doubt Divine would be amused to have her performance reframed as 'cultural'. Gender and sex can be taken as 'cultural performance' because Butler sees them that way (not because they 'are' that way): everyday gestures are such because they *signify* everyday identity to others and for ourselves; drag is such because it does the same, albeit in a highlighted or 'hyperbolic' manner (Butler 1993: 230–3).

Performativity, as distinct from performance, must thus be located at the very centre of Butler's analysis (Butler 1994; cf. Lloyd 2005a), not in the sense of thinking gender as something one chooses to 'put on' – as many critics have suggested, and which she herself refutes (Butler 1993: 6–12, 230–1). Rather, it proves crucial because it highlights and thus isolates a number of gestures and other surface signs that are repetitious citations of what we understand culturally as sex and gender. These citations will of course be different in different cultures, all the way down, as it were, to different understandings of the sexed body of a person. Butler describes these gestures and other signs as 'a compulsory ordering of attributes into coherent gender sequences' or 'coherences contingently created through the regulation of attributes' (Butler 1999 [1990]: 32–3). Neither coherence nor regulation can ever be complete, since, as Butler says, there are 'attributes that resist assimilation into the ready made framework of primary nouns and subordinate adjectives' (Butler 1999 [1990]: 33). Examples include 'woman' as a noun and 'feminine'/'weaker'/'loving', etc. as adjectives. However, the existence and use of 'dissonant' terms (e.g. 'lesbian' as a noun and 'masculine'/'butch'/'predatory', etc. as adjectives) does not in itself expose this production of coherence and stability as fictive, and indeed any of these somewhat dissonant terms may still work retroactively to redefine the terms of sex and gender. Once the ontology of substances is understood as an 'artificial effect', Butler concludes, it is 'essentially superfluous', i.e. we can live out the knowledge that 'being' a woman or man is impossible, and that these apparent nouns do not refer to anything from which identity arises or to which it corresponds. Gender names not a thing or a substance. Rather, it is 'a doing' and is thus paradigmatically 'performative' in Butler's definition: 'constituting the identity it is purported to be'. Or, to put it the other way round, 'identity is performatively constituted by the very "expressions" [e.g. feminine and masculine gestures] that are said to be its results [e.g. being a woman/man]'. Ultimately, Butler says, we are looking at, and participating in, 'a parody of the *idea* of the natural and the original'. As parody, gender is thus 'the repeated stylisation of the body, a set of repeated acts within a highly rigid regulatory frame that congeal over time to produce the appearance of substance, the appearance of a natural sort of being' (Butler 1999: 40–4; see also Butler 1993: 218–22).

Pronouns and identities

Given that we usually think of woman/man in bodily/genital terms, there seems a certain implausibility here. Why and how did gestures and other signals become so important? Butler may have a point in terms of super-ficial recognition and first-glance assignment of identity (in terms of gender and sex), but surely in terms of more searching inspections and experiences the 'reality' of femaleness and maleness is obvious and indisputable. Surely this is proof of sex-as-substance? Presciently Butler opens up the question of binary sex in the bodily sense, when she writes: 'even if the sexes *appear* unproblematically binary in their morphology (which *will become* a question) ... ' And in *Gender Trouble* she refers in footnotes to pioneering work on transsexuals (Butler 1999: 10, 137–9, 195 n. 9, 211 n. 24, emphasis added). Fausto-Sterling (2000) has since thoroughly exposed binary sex as a fictive construction – and indeed a masculinist glorification of 'maleness' over 'femaleness' – which science and medicine have imposed *on* bodies, rather than observed *of* them. For the importance in juridical terms of 'surface' gestures and other signals of gender, and their regulated coherence in terms of a binary identity constrained as 'man' or 'woman', one need look no further than the UK's Gender Recognition Act (UK Parliament 2004). 'Recognition' requires merely that one 'live in the acquired gender', without necessary recourse to surgery or drugs to accomplish this 'change' in terms that the law will identify and uphold.

As if it were possible to be more controversially deconstructive than this, Butler also takes on human subjectivity itself, i.e. the 'I' of identity, or the 'doer behind the deed'. That is, we would usually think that if gender is 'a doing', then someone must surely be doing it, but this is exactly the 'some-one' as 'substance' that Butler wishes to deny. By 'deny' we mean that through her criticisms of the metaphysics of substance she wishes to reveal such a 'substance' as both fictive and superfluous. If I can't 'be' a man or woman, then man or woman can't be an attribute of an 'I' either. Appro-priating Nietzsche, Butler notes that '"the doer" is merely a fiction added to the deed' and adds her own corollary: 'identity is performatively constituted by the very "expressions" [i.e. nouns, adjectives] that are said to be its results' (Butler 1999: 33–4, 42–4). How could someone who – as a femin-ist – would be presumed to hold or commit to an emancipatory project of social change, possibly deconstruct the subject in this way as a *political move*? What happens to 'agency' and purposive action? Butler resolves the paradox rather quickly at the end of *Gender Trouble* by arguing that, within a metaphysics of substance, agency is necessarily constrained by identity, whereas in her critical view agency emerges precisely because identity is 'neither fatally determined nor fully artificial and arbitrary'. In other words, 'agency' is not something 'I' have, precisely because 'I' is an effect produced by 'generative political structures rather than naturalized foundations'. Construction is not 'opposed to agency' but rather its 'necessary scene ... the very terms in which agency is articulated and becomes culturally intelligible'. Or, in other words, agency is evidenced by what is said and done, not by what 'I' said and did (Butler 1999: 181–8; see also Butler 1993: 121–4).

Still, what could possibly be the point of seeing the world in this apparently reversed way? Certainly Butler's critics, beginning with feminists, have found her critique of the subject, and hence of 'humanism', perverse in the extreme, and they have even suggested that it proves politically debilitating (see Chapter 4). If there is no 'doer' behind 'the deed', how can there be any deeds, they ask? Butler must have been rather puzzled by all the furore, since her conclusion is quite the opposite of the one that her critics were so swift to draw out at length. Butler focuses on constraint, or rather *supposed* constraint, on human activity. Holding a substantial view of the human subject – whether as woman or anything else – that by definition follows from a pre-political notion of substance implies, according to Butler, a commitment to *constraint*. Or it suggests a commitment to presumed *grounds* of constraint, in relation to what individuals might be allowed to do, or be considered capable of doing, or properly do. Butler's argument entails a radicalised freedom in politics – freedom from the constraints 'grounded' in pre-political 'substances' of which 'identities' are supposedly 'expressions'. Clearly, then, her argument does not lead to anti-political paralysis, as is charged by her numerous critics on this point. Or, to put it very simply (and in a way that Butler herself will consistently complicate): 'you are what you do', rather than 'you can only do what your identity allows you to do' (Butler 1999: 183; see also Butler 1993: 226–30).

Butler calls for strategies of 'subversive repetition', i.e. interventions *enabled* by current cultural constructions even as they *contest* them in political practice. These repetitions are thus 'generative structures' – sites of power and change – rather than points of access to 'naturalised foundations', through which pre-political constraints are so often powerfully articulated. The crucial philosophical move in Butler's reasoning here slips by very quickly in her text: she refers to the *terms* in which agency is typically articulated. These terms produce the linguistically malleable character of the deed, through which 'doers' *become* 'doers' and so *are said* 'to have' agency. Butler strongly rejects this account of reason and agency on the grounds that it is both logically constrained and politically constraining. This traditional account of agency leads us to ask the general question 'what kind of "doer" am I', which takes the particular form of 'the woman question' within feminism. However, for Butler questions like this *limit* agency at the outset. In resisting this conception of agency, Butler argues powerfully that pre-political constraints do not reside 'in nature' (e.g. the 'natural woman' she ironically mocks) but in an *idea* of nature understood as founding, fixing, constraining, limiting (Butler 1999: 29–30, 199 n. 34). The power of naturalising discourse comes about because such discourse appears to represent substantial truths – truths apprehended through a metaphysics that takes them to be representations of the real and thereby unchangeable.

Butler intends her critique of this metaphysics to locate her readers in (re)*constructive interventions* unintimidated by naturalised constraints at the supposed outset. Butler calls this the pre-political 'before'. In practice, of course, these interventions would hardly be unaffected by constraints encountered in a human process of struggle. 'Woman' for feminists should thus, in Butler's view, be an effect of struggle, not a 'fact' of nature furnishing something in common as a matter of 'identity'. There have been doubts and problems encountered in feminism precisely because this congruence between people and politics in terms of 'identity' never seemed to emerge unproblematically. Butler's argument is intended to dispel these doubts or, better, to contribute to a process of demystification and reconstruction, albeit along contingent and unpredictable lines. That very contingency and unpredictability is redefined as a *democratising* political virtue by Butler. That is, such contingency defies a logic of *exclusion* as to who 'is' and 'is not' a real or proper exemplar of the supposed identity. At the same time it invites even those who were centred (or perceived as centred) in an identity to reject singularity and exclusivity as a matter of definition and practice and to find other political interests and affiliations (Butler 1999: 181–90; see also Butler 1993: 223–42).

However, to many, Butler's solution looked too much like dissolution. In political terms the results would very likely be similarly regarded by any other 'groups' that employed the very familiar strategy of identity politics that she attacks: that is, seeking a unity 'arising out of' some common factor, and thus 'appealing to' that factor as a foundation for unity. Without unity of that kind, so it is generally argued, a group would simply fail to cohere and thus fail to produce a measurable effect in politics. Certainly Butler's call for repetitious citation of subversive interventions rejects the traditional model of mass politics. Nonetheless, however one feels about this as a strategic move, it is a rather separate question from the validity of her critique of naturalised discourses of constraint (as themselves quintessential instances of the metaphysics of substance). All the strategic essentialisms in the world may be defensible in political terms as political strategies, but they won't put the Humpty-Dumpty world of identity politics back where it was again. Butler's 'off-the-wall' critique in *Gender Trouble* gave it a great big push.

Abjected by success

Butler says in her anniversary preface that her sense of who she was writing *Gender Trouble* for and who might read it was very wide of the mark, given the stormy reception and widespread currency of the work (Butler 1999: vii). It seems highly unlikely that at any level she was writing the book as an introduction to post-structuralist philosophy for feminists, although arguably that is in fact what the book became. The book sharply criticises mainstream feminist assumptions about politics; it even challenges such feminist philosophical icons as Beauvoir, Irigaray and Wittig, none of whom was regarded as particularly easy to understand. Butler swiftly acquired a reputation as an even more difficult philosopher, yet, written at that point in English and from a position in Anglophone feminist culture, her work was in a way more accessible than such classics even in translation (Disch 2008). Oddly, as it turned out, many feminists thus encountered post-structuralist philosophy in a political setting on their own turf when they turned to Butler, yet the almost abbreviated style of argument – which assumes an exceptionally clear command of certain Continental thinkers as the conclusions speed along – works against an easy entry. Butler wrote as she thought, working from her background in philosophy, engaging with the feminist thinkers and problems she had on her mind (particularly psychoanalytic ones), moving along to the philosophical implications and on again to the political ones. And she does all this work at almost breakneck speed – even describing that work as 'thematic' (Butler 1999: ix). For a disturbing and difficult book, *Gender Trouble* did well with an audience that was essentially ill equipped and hostile. Why the success?

Performativity, performance, repetition, citation and drag probably provide the answer, and feminism and sexuality politics – 'identity politics' – provided most of the readership, as there is no doubt that Butler spoke to those people and those issues, even if few wanted to read precisely what she wrote. Perhaps even fewer could find and appreciate the more general philosophical references and implications. Butler's use of these concepts and images, particularly drag, sounded a hard-to-hear note. While drag was readily identified with gay men (in some sense – the connection with male–male sexuality is not obvious or universal), it was then difficult to see what it was doing in a political and philosophical 'intervention' in academic politics by a feminist academic (Butler 1999 [1990]: xiv). What exactly drag was citing about 'woman' was obscure, to say the least, and how repetition figured in the analysis – since any given 'performance' (like Divine's) is apparently a one-off – was far from obvious. Moving from performance to performativity was difficult to understand, given the puzzling and paradoxical definition: how can gender 'performatively' constitute 'the identity it is purported to be'? How can identity be 'performatively constituted by the very "expressions" that are said to be its results'? Worse still, how can Butler argue that this performativity *conceals* the fictive character of 'naturalisation', when – obviously – if *she* sees it, and reveals it, then it's surely there for all to see. What exactly is concealed from whom, with what consequences, and what does it take to make this process visible? Finally, what is the final result? While Butler may have started the book thinking about gender, wanting to make gender trouble and wanting to trouble gender, there seems also to be an inordinate amount of trouble puzzling out what exactly all this trouble really is.

To 'puzzle this out' we first note that Butler's readers were thrown up against someone who had really thought through the philosophy of, and political implications of, a thoroughgoing view of language as inherently *non-referential*. One can certainly reconstruct a considerable background for this approach: either in Wittgenstein's account of meaning as found in language *use* or in Austin's attack on referential views. However, Butler, drawing on Derrida, begins with a view that goes considerably beyond these modest critiques. From Butler's perspective, referentiality is a *fiction*, because language simply cannot be referential to objects, even when it appears to be so in commonplace usage and experience, and even when language simply *is* referential and descriptive as a matter of *grammatical* fact. For Butler, referentiality is a fiction in the sense that its locutions of description and factuality are *features of language*, not effects or representations of a relationship between language and the world. Or, in other words, any referentiality in language is built into language; factual language is simply that, not a sort of 'window' on a material or otherwise 'natural' or 'real' world which provides language with the meanings it expresses.

This view of language does not deny the 'existence' of anything (e.g. the world we know as 'material'); rather, it denies that anything other than language will provide us with meaning. We thus tell the material world what it means. And we do so repeatedly. For those with a different view of language, Austin's speech-act was rather too much about speech and rather too focused on an act. Butler's perspective must not be confused with that found within the purely philosophical debate about whether a thoroughgoing non-referential view of language can be sustained. Rather, her use of this is itself a 'doing' in that she presumes it and then uses it to explain, not natural objects as such, but *naturalised* objects, or, rather, naturalised *objectivities*, such as gender. Gender has apparent objectivity because it is a noun, as Butler notes, and it is widely taken as natural in some sense, either as 'biological' or as feeling natural to those who 'have it'. *Gender Trouble* is thus an assault on, and hence exposure of, that kind of naturalisation of human attributes (i.e. nouns that name qualities that are ascribed 'by nature' to humans as 'beings'). Gender is commonly taken to name 'something', but as Butler writes:

> The dogged effort to denaturalize gender in this text emerges, I think, from a strong desire both to counter the normative violence implied by ideal morphologies of sex and to uproot the pervasive assumptions

about natural or presumptive heterosexuality that are informed by ordinary and academic discourses on sexuality. ... It was done from a desire to live, to make life possible, and to rethink the possible as such.

(Butler 1999: xx)

Butler's contends that gender only 'purports' to name something that is object-like or objective, in the sense of some specifiable property or attribute of humans, particularly something in and of the body. Hence she insists that sex and gender be taken together, because whatever distance or difference might be allowed between the two, there is in practice no coherent way of understanding one without the other. Indeed, gender – the supposedly more variable property – is inevitably understood in sexual terms. Yet gender is a noun, and does name properties ascribed to humans, so what, then, is Butler's problem? If gender is not thing-like in some sense (and thus a 'basis' for identity), what, then, does it name? Butler's solution is not the weak constructionist one, where gender names a 'social practice' in a rather vague way. A 'social practice' has some objectivity and could be named, and from Butler's perspective this would merely reinstate the referentiality thesis, and its corollary, that humans and their activities are constrained by 'things' that exist outside language because they figure as nouns in discourses of constraint. If this is so, as Butler tells us, how then is this also *concealed*? Performativity is essentially a name for this activity of concealment, that is, the production of *referentiality* in language that purports to describe and *legitimise* the constraints that the 'real world' imposes as a matter of *supposed* necessity. What is concealed is the 'supposed' behind the *assumption* of 'necessity', and the consequent language of constraint and legitimacy.

In *Gender Trouble* Butler moves beyond philosophical arguments to an experiential realm where we would be likely to have more difficulties constructing counter-examples and plausible denials to her thesis (see Butler 1997a). Gender certainly names a set of behavioural gestures and signals, according to Butler, but the radical move is to argue that (really) that's all that gender is: a 'stylized repetition' that (somehow) creates the illusion of what is 'natural' to the sexed body and what feels 'natural' to those who are said 'to have it' – but who only 'have it' in the sense that they 'do it'. The *language* of naturalisation *conceals* this knowledge, a knowledge further covered over by the disciplinary processes of repetition and citation through which 'doing gender' becomes an unselfconscious activity – albeit not quite so much for Divine. Butler's argument turns not so much on concealment, however, as on the forces that allow only a *limited recognition of the fictive* (rather than objectively referential) character of gender as a 'basis' or 'attribute', inasmuch as drag is an *open* display of gender as artifice – thus giving the lie to 'the natural'. However, precisely because drag is framed as a performance, and precisely because it is marginalised and suspect, the knowledge that gender is merely a 'doing' (and *not* the name of a 'basis' or attribute) almost never disturbs the discourses of naturalisation. Hence these discourses have a *productive* relation to the constraints deployed by political power.

Butler's concept of performativity, of which gender is an instance, thus rests on a view of considerable philosophical sophistication, and much of *Gender Trouble* involves her explication of it in philosophical terms. Understandably the discussion proceeds, not from first principles, but from her own attempts to pursue this idea through feminist philosophy. This process includes recognising the clues to her own position and the evident shortcomings in selected writers, explicating at the same time a political position that was obviously quirky, and also said to be a consequence of the philosophical questioning and reasoning in which she was engaged. It follows from this that performativity does not represent an easy way into Butler's thinking, because it is not a concept that stands well on its own. In fact, to understand it the reader must absorb quite a number of counter-intuitive propositions ('there is no doer behind the deed'), analytical false-hoods (gender is 'not a noun') and apparent counterfactuals (bodies are not sexed male and female by nature). Butler takes the reader through this, but on her own intellectual and political terms and at her own speedy pace. As if this were not exasperating enough, the whole discussion is framed as the subversion of identity, particularly that of 'woman', the concept through which feminism was obviously supposed to be secured. This is not to mention an overwhelming and familiar weight of social institutions and norms of a decidedly anti-feminist character that were also bent on securing 'woman'. For feminists, gender was perforce the concept that stood for women's oppression, and identity was thus doubly secured: woman represented female oppression. Butler made the supposed 'natural' fixity of sex into an effect of gender, a 'social' feature of humanity and therefore relatively malleable; then she made the factual 'reality' of gender into a fiction and located this – for heuristic purposes anyway – in movies made by a drag queen. Her 'local interventions' in politics did not look very feminist either, and in *Gender Trouble* are really rather unspecific, almost afterthoughts. Subsequently Butler did not attempt to put feminism back together again, but her political engagements have become increasingly specific and her philosophical points somewhat easier to absorb.

3 The body[1]

I confess, however, that I am not a very good materialist. Every time I try to write about the body, the writing ends up being about language.

(Butler 2004b: 198)

This quotation from 2004 easily reads like an admission of guilt on Butler's part, an apology for her failure to 'write about the body' in a way that proves satisfactory to her critics (who have been most vocal on this particular issue). Even though Butler uses the language of confession, however, we think it more appropriate to read these lines as displaying a certain self-awareness on Butler's part about the *way* in which she approaches the body. Even in her most concerted endeavour to 'write about bodies' in *Bodies that Matter* (Butler 1993), Butler contends that the effort to describe matter is always just that: a writing *about* the body, a materialisation *of* the body only in and through language. One can never get at the thing itself – certainly not in writing. And in the preface to *Bodies*, written a decade before the above 'confession', Butler already emphasises that in trying to fix her gaze on the 'materiality of the body' she always finds herself in 'other domains' (Butler 1993: ix). How to get at the body that keeps slipping away, in light of critics' insistence that she should, that she must?

Butler refuses to fix the body as primary, as antecedent to discourse. 'The body posited as prior to the sign is always *posited* or *signified* as prior' (Butler 1993: 30). We cannot have any access to the body except *through* discourse. Yet this does not mean that the body can be reduced *to* discourse. Indeed, the body exceeds discourse, and reworks the very norms that would constrain it. Butler has as little patience with an idealism that would reduce all matter to signs as she does with a materialism that would reductively separate matter from signs. The former ignores the fact that matter cannot be created by discourse; the latter ignores the fact that matter is always and only materialised through discourse. Both remain blind to the simple truth that all signs are themselves material (i.e. made up of either sound waves or physical marks) (Butler 1993: 15, 30).

For Butler, therefore, the body can never serve as an ontological foundation (Stone 2005: 11). The body cannot ground a theory of feminist politics any more than it can ground a theory of gender. Nonetheless, to say this is not to dismiss the body; nor is it to ignore the critics' constant question: 'what about the body?' (Butler 1993: ix). While Butler rejects any theory grounded in an ontology of the body, she still finds something fundamental about bodies: bodies, for Butler, are *vulnerable*. A body is both dependent upon others and subject to violation by another, by others. Through our bodies we always remain exposed to others, and our very vulnerability ties us to others (Butler 2004b: 20, 22). In this sense, and only in this sense, we find something primary about the body, something fundamental, undeniable. This chapter will demonstrate that Butler takes the body just as seriously – and at times perhaps much more seriously – than her critics.

The problem is not the body *per se*. What is lacking in Butler's politico-theoretic project is not an attentiveness to the potential pain and suffering of bodies: Butler has been centrally concerned with this issue from the very beginning of her work. Rather, perhaps Butler's critics ask after the materiality of the body because they are concerned about what Butler's theory of gender does with/to sex. Butler's critics, both implicitly and explicitly, worry most about the primacy and materiality of sex and the epistemological grounding that it provides. More to the point: if sex is really gender 'all the way down', then is there no such thing as sex? And if everything is gender, then does the body no longer matter? We will try to reconstruct this implicit logic of the critics, to illustrate that the criticisms about 'the body' stem from a much deeper concern about the place of sex in Butler's radical theory of gender.

As an answer to her critics, the title *Bodies that Matter* contains within it the straightforward assertion that bodies *do* matter. But the word 'matter' in the title clearly carries a double meaning. In the text, Butler articulates a theory of materialisation: she shows how bodies *matter* in the sense of becoming materialised through discourse. Perhaps, however, what her critics want most of all is to know how, within a radical constructivist theory of gender, the body *matters* in the sense of being *important*, proving *significant* for both theory and politics. Butler was undoubtedly cognisant of the two senses of matter within the title that she herself chose. And yet to answer this question concerning the second sense of matter requires a further exploration than Butler has explicitly provided of the role of 'sex' within a theory that proves sex to be subject to gender norms. If sex no longer serves as the ontological ground that gives rise to gender, then does sex simply disappear? And if it does not, then what role will it play?

Working with both the resources supplied by Butler herself (her writings) and those called on by her (the writings of Foucault and Beauvoir), this chapter will theorise the body by way of reconstructing a Butlerian theory of sex/gender. The key to such a reconstruction will lie in insisting on two points simultaneously: (1) always stressed by Butler, sex is itself gendered and thus sex does not lie outside gender norms or causally produce them, but is instead a product of those norms; and (2) not often emphasised or made clear by Butler, sex cannot be reduced to gender. The category of sex has a crucial role to play even within a radical theory of sex/gender that takes sex itself to be gendered. To gender sex is not to do away with sex. This point can be elaborated and explained within the frame of Butler's project, even if she herself has not always been careful to stress it.

Questioning/the body

Gender Trouble appeared in 1990 and, as noted above, critics immediately objected to what they saw as a 'neglect' of the body in Butler's writings (Tyler 1991; Fraser 1995; see also Rottenberg 2003). Butler herself either missed the irony of this criticism or graciously chose not to highlight it, since *Bodies that Matter* appears to take the charges seriously. But accusing Butler of ignoring the body in *Gender Trouble* might be a bit like accusing Marx of ignoring Hegelian idealism in *Capital*. We make this somewhat hyperbolic claim because in 1989 Butler published articles with the following titles: 'The Body Politics of Julia Kristeva', 'Foucault and the Paradox of Bodily Inscriptions' and 'Gendering the Body'. Why, then, and how, would Butler's critical readers conclude that she pays too little attention to the body?

We hope to unravel this paradox in the following section, by analysing the way in which Butler's particular readings of Beauvoir and Foucault in *Gender Trouble* produce a 'theory of gender'[2] that might be *taken* as an elision of the body. Here we need to lay the groundwork for that argument by first showing how, within the history of philosophical thought, arguments *like* Butler's often prove to be arguments against the material existence of the body. That is, Butler works within and against a philosophical tradition that has often displayed the very 'hostility to the body' that concerns her readers. And she speaks to an audience of feminist scholars who have proven quite adept at challenging such theories; it therefore comes as little surprise that Butler's critics might take *her* to be rejecting the body as well.

Our ultimate objective in this chapter is to refute Butler's critics, to bring to light a sophisticated, subtle and significant thinking of the body in Butler's approach to sex/gender. Yet here we reconstruct a context in which the critics' claims make more sense, not less. Our goal is to show not only *that* Butler is misread, but *how*. This proves to be much more than mere academic research (scholarly reconstruction for its own sake), since it makes it possible to distinguish Butler's writings from those contexts into which she would be most easily assimilated. Butler is not a (simple) Hegelian; she is not merely an existentialist;[3] and she certainly is not a sceptic. To read her as any of these is to lend credence to the idea that she neglects the body. In articulating the centrality of the body to her project we will simultaneously remove her from these folds of thought.

Despite our terse assertions to the contrary, there are good reasons to read Butler in *all* of these ways – as Hegelian, existentialist or sceptic. The strongest claim would perhaps be made for Butler the Hegelian: both her PhD dissertation and her first book centre on Hegel, and throughout her writings she continually returns to Hegelian questions of reflection and desire. Moreover, while many post-foundational thinkers reject what they see as the teleological closure in Hegel's thought, Butler, working in a similar vein, remains a fierce defender of Hegel.[4] Her debate with Ernesto Laclau – staged in *Contingency, Hegemony, Universality* (Butler *et al.* 2000) – demonstrates her commitment here: Laclau and Butler agree on almost every political point and they forcefully reject the Lacanianism of their third co-author, Žižek, yet they go round and round over Hegel. Butler remains a champion of Hegel and insists on the continued significance of Hegelian thought. Why not call her a Hegelian then?

Next we turn to perhaps the weakest case, but a plausible one nevertheless: we might take Butler to be a tacit existentialist to the extent that she takes up Beauvoir's theory of gender. Beauvoir's distinction between sex and gender – her view that sex can be taken as natural while gender must be thought as a social, cultural and linguistic production – serves as her point of departure in *Gender Trouble*. Beauvoir's thinking of sex/gender offers both the frame for Butler's argument and the counterpoint against which, throughout the book, she will work – in order to show that perhaps even sex cannot be 'taken' as natural. Certainly Butler never identifies her work as existentialist, but there can be no doubt that this tradition of thought proves central to Butler's project.

Finally, as any review of *Gender Trouble* will tell us, that text offers a radical, sceptical questioning of the taken-for-granted ground of second-wave feminism: namely, 'woman'. It is easy to read Butler as an epistemological sceptic (see Zerilli 2005). And in *Gender Trouble*, as in all those texts that will follow it, Butler embraces a questioning style. There can be few serious readers of Butler who have not, at some point or another, wondered aloud at her ability to string together rhetorical questions, sometimes for entire paragraphs. And those reading even more closely will know that this style is not accidental, not a lazy default position for Butler (afraid, one might guess, to pose her arguments in more positive terms), but a strategy she actively embraces, a style that she very consciously chooses (Butler 2004c: 326–30). Above all, Butler insists on questioning precisely that which we would take to be ordinary, natural, unquestionable, and in this endeavour her project seems to mirror the sceptical endeavour to question (in the sense of radical doubt) *everything*.

To reiterate, we sketch out these surface links not in order to build an argument for (or against, as the case may be) Butler as a practitioner of any of these particular schools of thought. Instead, we aim to acquire a clearer sense of the case against Butler on the body before offering a defence. And one of the strongest elements of that case proves to be *guilt by association*. In other words, the charges of ignoring or dismissing the body can most certainly be made to stick against the following defendants: Hegel, Sartre and Descartes. In Hegel and Sartre the body most often proves to be precisely that which needs to be overcome, to be transcended. We do not live the body, embrace the body or become it; we seek to move beyond it, to prevail over its limitations. In Descartes, the body must be radically doubted in order to produce a more firm foundation for existence. Descartes insists that he is not his body, precisely so as to prove that he *is*. Nothing, for Descartes' scepticism, proves more doubtful than the body.[5]

Thus, if we can put Butler in their camp she will be found guilty automatically. The relations to existentialism, scepticism and Hegelianism certainly prove important to an understanding of Butler's overall thought. However, we contend that the evidence against Butler here turns out to be completely circumstantial. From the very beginning Butler reads Hegel against the grain: his is not the presumed project of desire transcending the body, but a realisation that the permanence of desire depends upon its enduring ties to the body, on the fact that desire is always embodied (Butler 1987a: 43, 54, 56, 57). And while Butler toys early on with Beauvoir's version of existentialism, her initial argument insists on vanquishing the 'Cartesian ghost' within Sartrean existentialism (Butler 1987b: 129–30; cf. Coole 2008), while in *Gender Trouble* she goes on to insist that neither Beauvoir nor Sartre can ever overcome the mind/body dualism (Butler 1999 [1990]: 17). The 'body' case against Butler can easily be made to resonate in the minds of readers – perhaps even to ring in their ears – and this may go some way to explaining the *longevity* of the critique. But the charges of guilt by association will not hold up to scrutiny.

Far from either ignoring the issue of the body or coming down on the side of a philosophical privileging of mind over body, Butler consistently rejects a mind/body dualism and repeatedly insists on taking the body as a site of theoretical and political problematising. We will argue that the genuine confusions over Butler's thinking of the body (as opposed to trumped-up charges of 'ignoring the body' designed merely to dismiss Butler's politico-theoretical project) arise precisely because she offers a novel and unique theory of sex/gender. By radically reconceiving the relation between sex and gender, Butler calls into question almost all of our everyday assumptions about anatomy – particularly about the importance of genitalia. In so doing, when it comes to the body Butler takes the ground from under the feet of her readers, and she does not always put something else in its place. In other words, we will demonstrate that the implications for conceptualising the body – and especially for thinking about specific parts of the body – are often *under-theorised* by Butler. The next section explicates carefully Butler's theory of sex/gender, so that we can then go on to specify her sometimes implicit theory of 'the body'.

Freeing gender from sex; doing away with sex?

Butler's theory of sex/gender and her conceptualisation of the body are both produced by the confluence of her particular readings of Beauvoir and Foucault. That is, Butler interprets Beauvoir and Foucault in specific ways, but she also goes on to read Foucault into Beauvoir and Beauvoir into Foucault. This intertextuality creates the product that one often sees referred to as 'Butler's theory of gender'. Explicitly in the way it gets named, and implicitly in content, this theory leaves out both sex and the body. Yet these terms are central to the theory from the very start. Our project here will be to reconstruct the theory in such a way as to highlight sex and the body. Going back to, and going back over, Butler's theoretical resources (Beauvoir and Foucault) makes it clear how wrong it is to read sex and the body out of her theory (see Coole 2008).

As noted at the outset, Butler's earliest, pre-*Gender Trouble* articles focus centrally on the body. In 'Gendering the Body' Butler takes up the case for Beauvoir's contribution to feminist and philosophical understandings of 'bodily experience'. According to Butler, Beauvoir's project comes out of the philosophical tradition of Sartre and Merleau-Ponty; as such, her enterprise seeks to reveal what Butler calls 'the structures of embodiment' (Butler 1989a: 253). Read in relation to this philosophical tradition, Beauvoir offers a distinction between the natural body and the historical body; read as a contribution to second-wave feminism, this distinction turns into the difference between sex and gender. Here we see the typical line of argument explained in every Introduction to Gender Studies course: sex is a natural, biological fact, but gender is a cultural, historical and linguistic production or achievement. In standard language: gender is the social construction of sex (with the latter implicitly coded as natural, outside of said social construction). Butler, summarising Beauvoir, puts it this way:

> one is perhaps born a given sex with a biological facticity, but ... one becomes one's gender; that is, one acquires a given set of cultural and historical significations, and so comes to embody an historical idea called 'woman'. Thus, it is one thing to be born female, but quite another to undergo proper acculturation as a woman; the first is, it seems, a natural fact, but the second is the embodiment of an historical idea.
>
> (Butler 1989a: 254)

Up to this point, no second-wave feminist would disagree with Butler's reading of Beauvoir; very few would quarrel on these points with Beauvoir herself. The latter's work proved to be such a powerful force in the women's movements of the 1960s precisely because it revealed to women and men that gender might be something other than a natural given. The logic has been appealing to every sympathetic reader of a 'social constructivist' approach to gender: if gender is not natural, but rather historically contingent, then it can be *changed*.[6] Beauvoir's distinction between sex and gender proves exciting (to feminists, to theorists of gender, to anyone who feels constrained by the norms of gender), because it relegates sex to the category of the natural while bringing gender into the realm of culture and politics. Indeed, the famous feminist slogan 'the personal is political' reflects precisely the transition from the natural to the political – the politicisation of that which was formerly taken to be apolitical – that the distinction between sex and gender makes possible. Beauvoir, says Butler, 'shows us the contingency at the foundation of gender, the uneasy but exhilarating fact that *it is not necessary* that we become the genders that we have in fact become' (Butler 1989a: 257).

Here, and throughout the essay, Butler centres her reading on Beauvoir's existentialist language: our gender is something we *become*. The question, then, twists: *how* do we become our gender? Despite the possibilities for change, Butler argues that to become our gender is not simply to choose it, since gender itself remains controlled and constrained by norms, taboos and expectations, all of which originate outside our selves – in society and in the political domain (cf. Zerilli 2005: 11). As Butler stresses in an even earlier essay on Beauvoir, the choice must be thought in non-Cartesian terms: 'One chooses one's gender, but one does not choose it from a distance' (Butler 1987b: 131). This strips choice of its radical voluntarism and transforms it into a kind of embedded reading: 'to choose a gender is to interpret received gender norms in a way that reproduces and organizes them anew' (Butler 1987b: 131).

In the 1989 article, Butler uses the language she will return to fifteen years later: 'there are punishments for not doing gender right' (Butler 1989a: 255; cf. Butler 2004b: ch. 2). This claim complicates significantly the earlier suggestion – arrived at after the 'discovery' of gender's contingency – that we do not have to become the genders that we 'are', i.e. have become. What other gender besides this one could we possibly ever become? What could it mean to become another gender? If we do not choose our genders because of the abovementioned gender constraints, does this mean that the process of becoming our genders is dictated in advance? To reach this conclusion would be to remove entirely the thrill of gender-construction, and thereby to do away with the significance of the sex/gender distinction. Our gender thus turns into that which we were already, from the very beginning, destined to become – this is the move from gender voluntarism to gender determinism.

And it seems clear how we would flesh out this determinist logic: the destiny of gender would lie in sex. Sex, the natural foundation of gender, turns out to be the cause of gender all along. Beauvoir, of course, does not intend to treat sex as this unshakeable, original ground. While she never states her suspicions in unequivocal terms, Butler may well *suspect* that Beauvoir's sex/gender distinction actually harbours this problematic –

indeed, dangerous – concept of sex. In other words, although Beauvoir's work produces the radical effect of rendering gender contingent, her decision to preserve the naturalness of sex may sap the political strength of her 'constructivist' theory. Butler explains why: 'we tend to assume that if one is a given sex, then it follows that one is a given gender' (Butler 1989a: 258). The reasoning could not be plainer: females become (to use Beauvoir's language) women; males become men. Within this framework of what we 'tend to assume' the converse holds as well: men are males; women are females. (And in this final formulation becoming has been reduced to being, existential choice reduced to natural determinism.)

To save the radical potential promised by the distinction between sex and gender, Beauvoir – or, better, Butler – will have to challenge these everyday assumptions about the relation between sex and gender. Butler must find a way to interrupt the causality that takes us smoothly from one to the other. Gender can only be meaningfully contingent – variable, malleable, subject to the battles of politics – if it proves to be something other than the predetermined result of sex. Thus any far-reaching, significant theory of gender must also entail, or require as supplement, a similarly powerful theory of sex. To find such a theory, Butler looks to the resources of a thinker who said almost nothing about gender, but who wrote a very great deal on the subject of sex. Butler turns to Foucault to flesh out (pun intended) Beauvoir's work on sex/gender. At the crux of her argument, Butler brings in Foucault as follows:

> There is a kind of causality [suggesting] that desire and gender are attributes of sex, that they are expressions of sex, and essential ones at that, ones that make sex known. Sex itself becomes secretive, as Michel Foucault suggests, for *we only know sex through gender and desire*, but they in turn everywhere point back to this core, this essence, this substantial self.
>
> (Butler 1989a: 259, emphasis added)

This quotation requires a great deal of unpacking: Butler calls in Foucault to help explain precisely that which we 'tend to assume' about sex and gender. Foucault, Butler here implies, may show us how and why it is we take sex to be a causal ground for gender (and its concomitant vectors of desire). Butler uses the language of Foucault's *La Volonté de savoir* to describe sex: sex proves to be both the secret of the self and also the genuine essence of a person, the substantial core.

Foucault's own language echoes clearly here. Indeed, if we look to the conclusion of his most famous work on sexuality we can find the passage that Butler was reading (but did not cite[7]) when she made the above claims:

> 'sex' made it possible to group together, in an artificial unity, anatomical elements, biological functions, conducts, sensations, and pleasures,

and it enabled one to make use of this fictitious unity *as a causal principle*, an omnipresent meaning, *a secret* to be discovered everywhere.
(Foucault 1978: 154, emphasis added)

Foucault's arguments concerning the historical emergence of the discursive construct 'sex' provide the missing link in Butler's reading of sex/gender. It is precisely this particular conception of sex (as a discursive, historical construction of the 19th and 20th centuries) that suggests the causal unity between sex, gender and desire, of which Butler speaks in reading Beauvoir. If sex is the secret, substantive truth of the self, then it will always ground and govern gender – and will do so no matter how radically we formulate our readings of the latter term. To maintain that 'exhilarating' potential lodged in Beauvoir's distinction between sex and gender requires a similarly original and creative rereading of sex. Foucault provides exactly the needed argument (the terms of which will be elaborated below).[8]

Butler, however, does more here than just repeat Foucault's conclusions from *La Volonté de savoir*; she repeats him with a significant variation, since Butler wants to apply Foucault's conclusion to Beauvoir's problematic of sex/gender. And that's not all: she overlays yet a third variation, a repeating of both Foucault and Beauvoir (another repetition with a difference) when she suggests that we read the causality backwards. To repeat Butler: 'we only know sex through gender'. This counter-intuitive claim has enormous, perhaps incalculable, implications for how we think sex, gender and the body. Beauvoir does not make this argument; for her, sex is a natural given, a biological fact. Foucault says no such thing either, since his concern lies with the historical production of the discourse of sexuality that includes what he calls 'sex itself'; Foucault never mentions gender (a historical fact for which he has received much criticism; see Sawicki 1991). The combined yet fundamentally transformed thesis that we can only arrive at the construct of sex by way of the contingently produced concept of gender – *this* is Butler's most significant contribution to thinking sex/gender/body. It will serve as the core argument of her most famous work, *Gender Trouble*, and lie at the centre – even if often suppressed, covered over by other more inflammatory rhetoric – of disputes with her critics and their (or so we hope to prove) misreading of Butler's take on the body.

Everything hinges on how we understand 'by way of', how we read the 'through' in 'know[ing] sex through gender'. With this phrase Butler calls on Foucault's conclusions again, by suggesting that we can have no direct access to sex. Sex should not be thought (as Beauvoir sometimes suggests, or otherwise allows us to conclude) as a natural ground that then causes gender; rather, we have no unmediated access to sex. Thus, even if we think sex as a natural ground, we are still *thinking* it. And therefore we are likely to think it, to see it, to understand it through the already culturally produced frame of gender. Butler here makes her same old, but never stale, argument: the prediscursive can only ever be a particular product of a particular discourse. The outside of discourse can always be reconstructed (if we work carefully) as the projection from within a historically specific and contextually locatable discourse.[9]

Thus we can interpret the claim 'we only know sex through gender' as a rejection of Beauvoir's argument that sex remains natural, bodily, ahistorical, while gender becomes weighed down by culture and history. Whatever sex may be, it cannot reside outside politics and culture. Foucault's arguments about sex follow this line of logic, and we will attempt to extend it in the next section, by offering a revised Butlerian account of sex and the body. First, however, it is necessary to delineate Butler's own potential deviation from this path: at times, she herself reads the claim about knowing sex *through* gender as an undoing of sex. To put it bluntly, Butler toys with reading sex *out* of the theory of sex/gender, of reducing sex to nothing more than a particular manifestation of the construction of gender. That is, Butler sometimes keeps the concept of causality but *reverses* it: rather than taking sex as the root cause of a predetermined gender, Butler may suggest that gender causes sex. And in this sense sex turns out to be nothing but a crude ideological abstraction – one that we can wish away.

We have been focusing closely on Butler's early reading of Beauvoir, not only because it is here that we see laid out the core elements of her later theory of sex/gender, but also because it is here that we witness Butler's tendency to reject sex entirely. And, to repeat, the argument throughout this chapter is that Butler's critics challenge her on 'the body' precisely because of her argument about sex/gender. This logic begins with the presumption of Butler's 'rejection of the sex/gender distinction', based upon 'her refusal to distinguish between sex and gender' (Hutchings 2003). And if Butler will not maintain the sex/gender distinction, then sex must not matter at all (Webster 2000). By dismissing sex, as her critics read her, Butler must also be dismissing the body.

Having sketched out the case against Butler, let us call on some evidence. It emerges at the conclusion of 'Gendering the Body', where Butler writes: 'but what if this substantial sex *does not exist*, and our experience of gender, pleasure, and desire are *nothing more* than the set of acts, broadly construed, that *constitute* an identity rather than reflect one' (Butler 1989a: 259, first two emphases added, final one in original). Sex does not exist. Gender is nothing more than our actions. Here we paraphrase Butler, but the sentences themselves can be cut and pasted into any number of Butler critiques.

Once Butler has implied the non-existence of sex – and while the actual quotation says '*substantial* sex does not exist' it will be hard to keep readers from dropping that first adjective – and then 'rejected' this 'fictitious unity' she is free to make bold claims about the enacted nature of gender (which, on this account, is really just sex as well). Butler turns back to the existentialist language of action and becoming in order to theorise the performance of gender. In so doing, she produces much more fodder for critics:

'gender is *nothing other* than the continuous presence of actualizing certain cultural possibilities' and 'the acting is itself the constituting [of gender]' (Butler 1989a: 260, emphasis added). Having removed the impediments of sex, Butler now turns gender into action. This sets up her utopian conclusion, when she hypothesises about the possibilities produced when a man acts in a feminine manner:

> the very meanings of 'masculine' and 'feminine' become fluid, interchangeable, and indeterminate, and their repeated usage in dissonant contexts erodes their descriptive power. Indeed, we might imagine a carnival of gender confusion that not only confuses fatally the sorry cultural institutions that we originally accepted at the outset of this discussion, but institutes a new gender vocabulary, a proliferation of genders freed from the substantializing nomenclature of 'man' and 'woman'.
>
> (Butler 1989a: 260)

From the important and powerful claim that sex has no pre-political, ontological or prediscursive status, Butler has now veered into the very calls for gender pluralism that we will argue should *not* be taken as the crux of her work on gender and sexuality. Perhaps Butler has allowed the exhilaration of contingent gender to carry her away into these grand possibilities of 'new gender vocabularies'.

At some point along the way, Butler's argument has run off the tracks. She has moved from a close reading of Beauvoir – focused on the question of embodiment and the relation between sex and gender – to ungrounded hypothesising about the future of gender plurality. Tomorrow genders will be multiple and sex will be good again. But there seems to be no sex in this future, just multiple, unrooted, enacted gender(s). This possibility, which so intrigues Butler, proves to be exactly what most worries her critics. If there is no sex, then what about the body? If gender is 'nothing more' than its enactments, then can anyone be a woman? And how would we know who really is? In the face of Butler's logic at the end of this essay, one can see that these repeated, not-quite-rhetorical questions from her critics start to retain both traction and critical purchase. A proper response to them will require retracing our steps with Butler, back to the moment she calls on Foucault.

Recovering sex and the body

We argue that Butler's reading starts to run off the rails at the moment she calls on Foucault – at that moment, we will contend, when she misreads Foucault.[10] Recall that Butler draws on Foucault in an attempt to rescue Beauvoir's distinction between sex and gender. She needs, somehow, to find a way to interrupt the causal logic that would turn gender into nothing more than the predetermined outcome of a prior, naturally given, sex. Butler refers to Foucault, claiming that we only know sex through gender and asking rhetorically what it would mean if sex (substantial sex) did not exist. These argumentative moves in this early essay set up Butler's fuller account in *Gender Trouble*. There, Butler completes the logic by once again referencing Foucault: if we can only get at sex through gender, and sex does not really exist, then we have *reversed* the problematic causal logic. Rather than sex causing gender, gender causes sex. Butler writes:

> The tactical production of the discrete and binary categorization of sex conceals the strategic aims of that very apparatus of production by postulating 'sex' as 'a cause' of sexual experience, behavior, and desire. Foucault's genealogical inquiry exposes this ostensible 'cause' as 'an effect'.
>
> (Butler 1999 [1990]: 31)

On this reading, Foucault would save the radical potential of Beauvoir's sex/gender distinction by reversing the causal relation between sex and gender. If gender turns out to be the cause of sex (rather than the other way round), then the malleable, contingent and political nature of gender is not only preserved but significantly heightened. We have moved, on this account, from a small opening up of gender to politics, to the full-scale abandonment of sex and gender to the political realm. And if *both* sex and gender remain fully politicised, utterly contingent (and how could they not be if gender causes sex), then we really have no reason to worry about sex at all – it is nothing more and nothing less than the causal product of gender. Finally, if sex has disappeared one sees no reason to worry about the body.

We will not address the merits of this position on its own: first, because it has more than its share of competent, well-spoken critics (Webster 2000; McNay 2000); second, and more importantly, because Butler herself moves further and further away from this argument as her work develops over the years; and, finally, most centrally, because this reading of Foucault proves untenable. Butler invokes Foucault at precisely the correct moment, i.e. as a supplement and support to Beauvoir's conception of gender. She reads him, however, far too carelessly. Foucault's account of the historical emergence of the discursive construct 'sex' serves to undermine our taken-for-granted notion that sex serves a unifying, causal function. But Foucault wishes to *interrupt* the causal logic itself, *not* to reverse it (Foucault 1978: 154).[11] Butler's move to invert the sex/gender relationship proves unsubstantiated;[12] both in her early essay on Beauvoir and in *Gender Trouble*, Butler mentions Foucault in the texts at the places previously quoted, but in neither case does she cite Foucault.

Turning to Foucault's own texts, one sees perhaps why Butler fails to cite him at exactly those crucial moments of her argument in which she invokes his work. The last half of Foucault's *La Volonté de savoir* meditates on what he calls 'the deployment of sexuality', on, that is, the emergence and expansion of a particular discourse of sexuality in the 19th and 20th centuries. Initially, this attention to the discourse of sexuality provides proof for Foucault's opening argument: Foucault rebuts (if not necessarily refutes) the 'repressive hypothesis' by showing that 'the discourse on sex has been multiplied rather than rarefied' (Foucault 1978: 53). Foucault repeats this point so frequently over the course of the first 70 pages of the book that many readers wind up taking it as his central thesis.

It is not. As Foucault himself emphasises, 'the claim ... is not altogether new' (Foucault 1978: 81). Foucault's central concern, instead, lies with the deployment of sexuality itself, with the historical consequences produced by this discourse. And the most radical claim of the book comes in the conclusion when Foucault challenges our assumption that the 'discourse of sexuality' centres on a particular, prediscursive object that we call sex, i.e the real thing about which we are talking. Foucault returns to the radical nominalism of his earlier writings, particularly in *The Archaeology of Knowledge*, by simply repeating his arguments there that objects of discourse are produced *within* a particular discursive practice or practices. Discourses do not emanate from their objects; quite the contrary: objects depend for their existence upon the discourse. This means that there is no thing-in-itself, as Foucault stresses in the *Archaeology*. Were we not tempted by the secondary literature (Dreyfus and Rabinow 1982; Habermas 1987) to manufacture a vast chasm between Foucault's early (so-called 'archaeological') writings and his later (so-called 'genealogical') works, we would already see the conclusion toward which Foucault is headed. He lays it out lucidly: there is no sex itself. Rather, 'sex' (an object of discourse) proves to be 'a complex idea that was formed *inside* the deployment of sexuality' (Foucault 1978: 152, emphasis added).

Here we see the central reason why Foucault does not invoke gender in his account, since neither it nor anything else could replace sex as the causal principle. *Within a discursive account there is no causal principle.* After all, discourse itself cannot be taken as a cause, since there really is no such thing as 'discourse itself'. There is the historical emergence and transformation of overlapping, intersecting and often conflicting discursive practices, and there are the objects of discourse (and subject positions as well) formed within those discursive practices. As Foucault puts it, 'discourse ... is not an ideal, timeless form, that also possesses a history; ... it is, from beginning to end, historical' (Foucault 1972: 117). This account makes it quite clear that Foucault would never say 'sex does not exist'. Rather, he maintains that 'sex itself' does not exist, and that 'sex' always remains a product of particular discursive practices. But to make this latter claim is, by no means, to deny the reality of sex; it is not to diminish but to *analyse* its historical and political significance. The difference between thesis A, 'sex does not exist', and thesis B, 'sex in itself does not exist', seems subtle, but its importance proves rather dramatic. (Sex exists, but not outside discourse). And one would be hard pressed to deny Foucault's concern not to elide this difference, since he makes his particular argument with the following emphasis: 'it is precisely this idea of sex *in itself* that we cannot accept without examination' (Foucault 1978: 152).

We contend, then, that Foucault's account of the emergence of the discursive construct 'sex' reveals precisely why sex cannot serve as a grounding, causal principle. The unity between sex, gender and desire turns out to be what Foucault himself names it, a 'fictitious unity'. In the face of the commonsense temptation to think sex as a ground, Foucault offers the following counter-thesis: 'sex ... is doubtless but an ideal point made necessary by the deployment of sexuality and its operation'. And given this argument, he goes on, 'we must not make the mistake of thinking that sex is an autonomous agency which secondarily produces manifold effects of sexuality over the length of its surface of contact with power' (Foucault 1978: 155). One of those effects, of course, as we have seen historically, is gender. Foucault thus demonstrates why we would be wrong to take gender as an effect of sex. However, he does not, for that reason, go on to make sex an effect of gender. Sex is neither cause nor effect; rather, it is an essential component of the discourse of sexuality.[13]

And this is also why, far from rejecting or ignoring the body, Foucault's analysis remains centrally concerned with the body throughout. As Foucault is wont to do, towards the end of the book he takes on an alter ego and raises critical questions of his own investigations. And in this case Foucault's self-criticisms closely parallel those directed at Butler over the years. How can you speak of sexuality without sex, Foucault asks himself? Are you suggesting that sex and the body do not exist? 'Does the analysis of sexuality necessarily imply the elision of the body, anatomy, the biological, the functional?' (Foucault 1978: 151). Foucault's lengthy answer demonstrates the centrality of sex and the body to his radical reworking of our understanding of 'sex' and his rejection of 'sex in itself'. And it also provides a number of crucial hermeneutic clues for how we might theorise both sex and the body in light of the radical constructivist account offered to us by Butler's reading of Beauvoir. Below, we argue that what is needed, above all, is a way to think the materiality and agency of the body without reconstructing sex or the body as a foundation – producing, along the way, yet another hypostatised causal unity of sex, gender and desire. How to hang on to a significant, material concept of sex, while insisting, with Foucault, that sex itself does not exist? This will be the question of the next section. But first, as an entrée to that argument, we will close this section by letting Foucault respond to the worry that his account might do away with the anatomical body:

> To this question I think we can reply in the negative. In any case, the purpose of this present study is in fact to show how deployments of power

are directly connected to the body – to bodies, functions, physiological processes, sensations, and pleasures; far from the body having to be effaced, what is needed is to make it visible through an analysis in which the biological and the historical are not consecutive to one another... but are bound together in an increasingly complex fashion... Hence I... envision... a 'history of bodies' and the manner in which what is most material and most vital in them has been invested.

(Foucault 1978: 150–1)

Theorising the body

With this passage from Foucault we conclude that the rejection of sex as a causal, unifying force, far from eliding the anatomical body, instead requires detailed attention to that body. But Butler does not necessarily make this point clearly enough, particularly in her most famous texts from the early 1990s. This explains why Butler's critics can continue to ask after 'the body' in the face of her own continued efforts to write about the body. What Butler has failed to explain is the link that Foucault suggests here. Butler therefore leaves her analysis open to the question 'How can we "do away with" sex and still maintain a focus on the significance of the anatomical body?'

While we will certainly maintain that Butler's critics have misunderstood her on many points, perhaps when it comes to the critique of 'the body' Butler has misunderstood her critics. In *Bodies that Matter* Butler takes her less approving readers to be worried about the pain and suffering of bodies. In response, through the argument over materialisation, Butler demonstrates that she shares just these concerns. But Butler misses a crucial dimension of the critique: namely, that it stems not from the performativity argument per se, but from the notion that sex is actually gender all the way down, e.g. the famous claim in *Gender Trouble* that 'perhaps this construct called "sex" is as culturally constructed as gender; indeed, perhaps it was always already gender, with the consequence that the distinction between sex and gender turns out to be no distinction at all' (Butler 1999: 11). *No* distinction between sex and gender? Sex *just as* constructed as gender? *These* are the sorts of arguments that most bother Butler's critics: the notion that sex is produced, constructed and maintained through gender norms. It is here that they ask: if sex is really gender, then what about the body? They ask this not because of suffering (at least not directly) but because sex is all about the body. As Butler herself admits, '*it is not enough to argue that there is no prediscursive "sex" that acts as the stable point of reference on which* ... the cultural construction of gender proceeds' (Butler 1993: xi, emphasis added). While Butler therefore sees clearly that the sceptical claim 'there is no natural sex' proves inadequate (cf. Zerilli 2005), she does not fully contend with the question that critics most want answered: how can you understand sex as a product of the discourse of gender *without* simply ignoring the body?

Moreover, our interpretations of Butler and Foucault in the preceding section show why Butler's opponents might reach these conclusions: precisely to the extent that Butler *misreads* Foucault. Butler's mistake lies in thinking that once one has revealed the historically contingent nature of 'natural sex' one can then focus solely on the category of gender. Nothing could be further from the truth, since – and as so many commentators have reminded poor readers of constructivism – that which is constructed is no less real for being so (see, for example, Warner 1999).[14] By reversing the causality between sex and gender, and in downplaying the importance of sex (since sex now seems epiphenomenal *vis-à-vis* gender), Butler abets her critics. Nonetheless, Butler does not maintain the thesis that sex is nothing more than gender, and she certainly does not reject, deny, elide or erase the body. On the contrary, Butler carries the focus on the body from her early writings right through to her most recent texts. In addition, and as we seek to show now, Butler's later work offers much more subtle readings of Foucault's conception of discourse, norms, sex and the body.

Throughout this final reading, and in building our own account of the body, we will insist on one central point: to understand sex as *gendered* is not equivalent to claiming that there is no difference between sex and gender. Making this last move amounts to collapsing the distinction between sex and gender so thoroughly that we have nothing left but gender. But while gender is lived through the body (as Butler constantly reminds us) gender norms are not *inherently* bodily. This means that to reduce everything to gender *is*, in a way, to do away with the body. One must hold on to a conceptualisation of sex, so that one does not lose sight/site of the body. In *neither* case, however, does this mean conceptualising either sex or the body as natural.[15] Nor does it imply that we think of sex as analytically distinct from, or *before* gender. *Sex is gendered.* We only understand sex through the norm of gender. These claims prove radical, far-reaching, important. Yet they must be kept distinct from claims that there is no sex. Just as we are born into a world where there are always already gender norms, we are also born into a body (and a sexed body at that).[16]

With this guiding thread exposed, we can now turn back to a reconstruction of a Butlerian logic that theorises the body. One can start with Butler's reading of Beauvoir on embodiment.[17] In the 1987 article, Butler explains the two meanings of 'the body as situation': (1) as situation the body is 'a locus of cultural interpretations', a material location in which the body has already been defined; and (2) as situation the body is 'a field of interpretive possibilities', that is, a place from which one can 'exist one's body' in particular (and particularly political) ways (Butler 1987b: 133–4). Clearly, Butler reads 'body as situation' here in an effort to bypass a voluntarism/determinism dualism. We would put it this way: *the body serves both to constrain and to enable our capacity for action.* This problematic, and its avoidance, will arise repeatedly throughout Butler's writings, most pointedly in her effort to formulate a theory of subjection (Butler 1997b). At this particular point, however, Butler offers the body as strategic solution to the voluntarism/determinism impasse.

In so doing, Butler's essay from twenty years ago resonates with an important recent work on agency. In 'Rethinking Agency' (Coole 2005), Diana Coole seeks to provide a 'novel theory of agency' by making the radical move of disconnecting agency from agents – along the way developing her own theory of embodiment. Coole wishes to accentuate her account of embodied agency by way of contrast with a number of Butler's arguments. This seems a valid and helpful rhetorical tool, as it does indeed throw Coole's account into starker relief. Nonetheless, we maintain that Butler's more fully developed account of sex and the body proves quite compatible with the position enunciated by Coole. Thus we want to reverse things a bit here, drawing out the similarities between the arguments of Coole and Butler, and thereby using Coole's recent work to clarify the terms of Butler's theory on/of the body.

Coole contends that, despite themselves, social scientists remain trapped within the structure/agency debate; they have failed in their concerted efforts to overcome the voluntarism/determinism deadlock. The best-known solution, Coole suggests, probably lies with an interactive, dialectical approach to structure and agency (Coole cites Giddens, Habermas and others), but this turns out to be no real solution at all since it serves to *reify* (by replicating them, even in dialectical fashion) the very terms of the debate (Coole 2005: 135; cf. 125, 137–8). Coole seeks to articulate something much more substantive than a 'middle way' – an approach which so often amounts to little more than a muddling of terms, or an oscillation between them.

Instead, Coole demands 'a more resolutely non-Cartesian social ontology', one that she draws from the resources of phenomenology (Coole 2005: 135). It proves essential, on her account, to take as much distance as possible from the Cartesian *cogito* since this conceptual framework always serves to *link* agency with individuals. In resisting the *cogito*, Coole's strategy rests on the insight that we disentangle agency from individuals as completely as possible. The concept of the Cartesian self will always *reduce* agentic capacities to the actions, choices or thoughts of subjects. Butler offers a helpful comment here: 'as is the problem with Cartesian egos everywhere, their ontological distance from language and cultural life precludes the possibility of their eventual verification' (Butler 1987b: 129). As noted earlier, Butler, like Coole, insists that our thinking of sex, gender and the body work as hard as possible to 'expel the Cartesian ghost' (Butler 1987b: 130).

And like Butler, Coole begins with, and often grounds her account upon, embodiment. Drawing not from Beauvoir, but from Husserl, Coole contends

that 'agency ... is irremediably embodied'. She continues: 'foregrounding
the body means recognising the corporeality of thinkers and hence their
situatedness' (Coole 2005: 127). Coole starts with the body, prior to the so-
called agent, to demonstrate that 'agentic capacities' emerge first in a 'pre-
personal' realm, i.e. in non-cognitive bodily processes (Coole 2005: 128). To
state the point directly, the body itself has agentic capacities, well before the
so-called agent-as-subject. Coole points to both a 'bodily knowing' and a
bodily freedom; the body may 'choose' before 'we' do (cf. Connolly 2002).

Most significantly, given the work of this chapter, this account of the
corporeal level of agency leads Coole to postulate the very *intentionality* of
the body. For Coole, the body is

> *intentional* and *motivated* in its relationship with its environment, which
> it might therefore be said to 'choose'. Although its choices and inno-
> vations will be circumscribed by the accumulated structures and sedi-
> mented habits that lodge within its lifeworld, there is scope for an
> *extemporisation* that brings *change*, while the logic of questioning and
> response suggests at least the possibility of *progress* as a 'crossing out'
> of non-sequiturs; as integration and enrichment.
>
> (Coole 2005: 129)

Compare the above passage with one from Butler:

> The body is not a static or self-identical phenomenon, but a mode of
> intentionality, a directional force and mode of desire. As a condition of
> access to the world, the body is a being comported beyond itself, refer-
> ring to the world and thereby revealing its own ontological status as a
> referential reality.
>
> (Butler 1987b: 130)

To posit the body as intentional, as both Butler and Coole do here, means
to reject as forcefully as possible a 'Cartesian social ontology' (as Coole
puts it), since our standard conception of intention includes the force of a
mind directing the body. The mere construction then, 'intentional body',
does much to undermine any sort of mind/body dualism. The intentional
body rules out the existence (unverifiable, in any case, as Butler wryly
remarks) of Cartesian egos, and shifts us into a realm of embodied agency.[18]

If the body is a situation through which we live or exist our gender, as
Butler contends through Beauvoir, then it follows that *sex* ought to be
thought as a situation through which we live our gender as well. And if the
body itself holds the capacity for intentionality, as Coole demonstrates, then
we simply cannot ignore sex. Two individuals will exist their genders differently (even if their gender is 'the same') when one's situation is different
from the other's, and the difference in situation may be produced by anatomical differences. Put another way, we can say that sex and gender are

both situations, but they are not the *same* situation. One is never reducible to the other and neither can ever be ignored or eliminated.[19]

This argument concerning embodied situations brings us to one crucial problem with theorising the body: the historical production of what Foucault calls 'sex itself'. In addition to being a unifying force that brings sensations, pleasures, anatomies and physiologies all under one umbrella heading, 'sex itself' establishes the conditions for a rather impoverished language, making it difficult to 'get at' the body. To put it bluntly, we rarely talk about our actual bodies (and certainly not in specific terms) precisely because we have very little language with, or in which, to do so. 'Sex' provides the substitute for speaking about bodies, and sex offers the only language *through which* we articulate bodies. No wonder, then, that Butler's critics would accuse her of ignoring or doing away with bodies when she makes the radical claim that sex is not natural, is not the given foundation of gender. But it should go without saying (though it might not) that *we do have bodies* and body parts, and nothing besides current gender norms, rules of politeness, and our structures of discursive practices keep us from talking about a whole host of body parts. Male, female, man, woman are supposed to do the work of talking about bodies for us. In the radical reappraisal of sex/gender that Butler's work calls for, we might need to talk about bodies, and body parts, in much more direct, precise, perhaps even crude ways.[20]

The vulnerable body and the livable life

In order to cash out this work on sex/gender, we close with a reading of Butler's most recent efforts to think the body, link that work with her earlier discussions of embodiment and thus demonstrate the manner in which this theory of the body skirts the earlier trap of negating sex (and implicitly the body). As stated in the very beginning, bodies *do* prove fundamental for Butler, but they can never provide justified grounds for action and they can never serve as the constituent elements for an ontology.[21] Instead, Butler both insists upon the precariousness of politics and focuses her arguments upon the very vulnerability of bodies. Bodies can be violated; bodies are radically dependent. In other words, our bodies constantly insist, despite our protests, on the fact of our being as always a being-with others. Rather than grounding our actions – as a misplaced standpoint epistemology might insist – bodies expose us to others.

Undoing Gender would have been appropriately subtitled 'the livable life'. Butler has never been one for stating concise theses at the outset of her books, but the following quotation from the introduction of that text might serve well as one: 'what is most important is to cease legislating for all lives what is livable for only some, and similarly, to refrain from proscribing for all lives what is unlivable for some' (Butler 2004b: 8). What is a livable life? And how and why could it serve as the central issue in Butler's recent politico-theoretic work? Although Butler never answers the first question directly, she does insist on its broad importance when she claims that 'it is not merely a question for philosophers' (Butler 2004b: 17). And her reply to the second query depends upon the reconstruction of context; Butler argues that 'under conditions in which gender has been constrained, in which certain sexual and gender minorities have felt their lives to be "impossible," unviable, unlivable, then "becoming possible" is a most certain political achievement' (Butler 2000b).

We would submit that a 'livable life' is one which does not require radical deviations from the norms of sex and gender. An unlivable life is therefore one that proves incompatible with those norms. The life of a person who finds herself in a female body, who comfortably self-identifies as a woman, who values the norms of femininity and who desires persons of the 'opposite' sex (who themselves identify with the norms of masculinity), will prove much more 'livable' than the life of a person who finds him/herself in a body that society codes as male, but who identifies more with norms of femininity than masculinity while simultaneously desiring male bodies and masculine individuals. This framework sets the stage for what Butler calls 'the struggle with the norm' (Butler 2004b: 13).

This struggle gets at the very question of the human, of which lives will count as properly human and which will be, somehow, discounted as something less than human. Butler weaves the less-than-traditional philosophical topics of bodies and norms into a discussion of the time-honoured, conventional question of autonomy. Butler, of course, tackles the topic unconventionally, by showing how grief and mourning always work to undo so-called human autonomy; these are processes of transformation, they are feelings that we do not necessarily 'have' as our own, but which, instead, we *undergo*. In grief and mourning we are 'beside ourself', a phrase that, even at the grammatical level, does much to deconstruct the philosophical concept of autonomy. Yet Butler has no wish to offer a theory of grief (or even of desire). Grief and mourning serve as pointers to something more fundamental: being beside oneself derives not from any particular emotion or experience, but from the bodily nature of existence itself. Butler makes the point in what some might call uncharacteristically sparse and direct language:

> Let's face it. We're undone by each other. And if we're not, we're missing something ... despite one's best efforts, one is undone, in the face of the other, by the touch, by the scent, by the feel, by the prospect of the touch, by the memory of the feel. And so when we speak about *my* sexuality, or *my* gender, as we do (and we must) we mean something complicated by it. Neither of these is precisely a possession, but both are to be understood as *modes of being dispossessed*, ways of being for another or, indeed, by virtue of another.
>
> (Butler 2004b: 19)

'Undoing gender', we now see, is not necessarily a deconstructive manifesto, since we are always and already undone by our genders, undone by our own bodies. Butler may, in fact, wish to call forth the further 'undoing' of gender, if by that we mean the struggle with gender norms that would make more lives livable, but she also wishes to reveal the extent to which we are, from the beginning, undone by our gender.

To take the body as that which is most clearly *ours*, this has been a standard approach throughout the history of modern epistemology. It can be traced back at least as far as John Locke, whose ingenious and politically significant theory of private property depended upon this first principle: 'every man has a property in his own person: this no body has any right to but himself. The labour of his body, and the work of his hands, we may say, are properly his' (Locke 1960 [1689]: para. 27). Butler would be unlikely to quarrel with Locke's claim that no one has a right to our bodies but us. She notes without disapproval that 'we ask that the state ... keep its laws off our bodies' (Butler 2004b: 20, quoting a popular bumper sticker). Nonetheless, Butler thoroughly rejects the claim that Locke uses to ground the right to the body, the claim that intuitively resonates with the idea of a right to privacy (i.e. private parts) – the idea that nothing is more intimately our own than our bodies. Butler argues very much the opposite: 'it is through the body that gender and sexuality become exposed to others, implicated in social processes, inscribed in cultural norms and apprehended in their social meanings. In a sense, to be a body is to be given over to others even as a body is emphatically "one's own"' (Butler 2004b: 20). Perhaps surprisingly, Butler's contrary notion resonates intuitively as well, since, just as we think our bodies are always ours, when it comes to our bodies we also constantly worry about others. Would we as individuals and as a society put anywhere close to as much effort, money, time and concern into the appearance and presentation of our bodies if it were the case that our bodies were only our own possessions?

Butler calls this the paradox of bodily autonomy: we fight for rights to our bodies, even as we must (at least implicitly) recognise that our bodies can never be fully ours. 'My body is mine and not mine', writes Butler, 'given over from the start to the world of others, bearing their imprint, formed within the crucible of social life, the body is only later, and with some uncertainty, that to which I lay claim as my own' (Butler 2004b: 21). Yet if the body renders sex and gender somehow 'more than' merely our own, and if bodily autonomy must be fought for with an understanding of its paradoxical qualities, then must we not reconceive the politics of bodies? 'Body politics' must be a politics not merely of rights that attach to bodies, but a politics concerned with the norms that make lives livable.

Bodies undo us because their significance exceeds our reach; their meaning derives from the norms of gender and sexuality, norms that get (re) articulated in culture, in society, in politics. Butler's politics centres on the operation of the norm, not because she ignores bodies, but precisely because she recognises the role that norms must play in any body politics: 'When we struggle for rights, we are not simply struggling for rights that attach to my person, but we are struggling *to be conceived as persons*' (Butler 2004b: 32). And the struggle to be conceived as persons – that is, the struggle to make possible a livable life – cannot take the body for granted. While such a politics will grant that the body is 'ours' (i.e. that one has rights to it), this politics must insist that the body also proves to be 'not ours'. And such a politics must focus attention on those norms that make life livable in some bodies and unlivable in others. Butler puts it this way: 'when we speak about sexual rights, we are not primarily talking about rights that pertain to our individual desires but to the norms on which our very individuality depends' (Butler 2004b: 33). This is how Butler can contribute to a political cause that lays claim to sexual rights while simultaneously declining to take the political subject as given (and certainly refusing to conceive it as a starting point for politics, since politics must also be about the production of that subject).

This consistent insistence on the relation between bodies and norms brings Butler to what we might call her closest definition of the body: 'the body is that which can occupy the norm in myriad ways, exceed the norm, rework the norm, and expose realities to which we thought we were confined as open to transformation' (Butler 2004b: 217). However, it should come as no surprise to readers of Butler if we argue here that the last thing Butler would seek is a *definition* of the body. The body offers the site for Butler's politics; theorising the body proves essential to Butler's theory of sex/gender. Nonetheless, the body's unruly relation to the norm makes it, at one and the same time, both absolutely essential to Butler's project and that which her readers will never be able to locate simply, to pin down or fix within her writings.

Part II
Theories of the political

4 Normative violence

This chapter makes the transition from 'terms of political analysis' to 'theories of the political'. It focuses less on those terms in Butler's work already familiar to most of her readers and it offers more specific and targeted engagements with contemporary politics and theory. Here we articulate the content and demonstrate the importance of Butler's concept of normative violence. Doing so requires rereading *Gender Trouble* through the lens of normative violence, an exercise that proves both counter-intuitive (since the term does not appear in the text itself) and productive (since this reading reveals afresh the impact that *Gender Trouble* should have upon political theory). Beyond this 'contribution' to the field of political theory, however, lies the power of Butler's concept of normative violence to grasp and elucidate contemporary political phenomena. Thus, just as we read normative violence *back* into Butler's famous text, we also read it *forward* into politics today.

Violence after 9/11

'The world is a more violent place today'. This received, post 9/11 wisdom echoes on the right, is consistently conveyed by the Bush administration and even has its adherents on the left (see, for example, Kolko 2002). The evidence suggests it is not true (Human Security Centre 2005), but we know that the truth or falsity of conventional wisdom never proves as important as either its political mobilisation or its political entailments (Hay 2004). In any case, 9/11 was taken by most Americans as a *pure* act of violence – an act of violence above all else, violence plain and simple. As such, it both helped to mobilise and served to legitimate the moralised response to 9/11 on the part of the US. In other words, the idea of 9/11 as an act of pure violence underwrote the response to 9/11 as a response to evil. It should go almost without saying, then, that our need to make sense of the terrorist acts of 9/11 and our need to understand the responses to those acts – in the form of the wars in Afghanistan and Iraq and the detention of potential terrorists and 'enemy combatants' in the US, Europe and at Guantánamo Bay – necessitate further inquiry into concepts of violence.

Such a path of inquiry has certainly been followed in political science by way of increased attention to the empirical study of violence (e.g. Heitmeyer and Hagan 2003), through the emergence of numerous centres of 'conflict study' (in the UK, the Americas and Europe) and in the form of another round of works on the question of a 'democratic peace' (e.g. Keane 2005). In this chapter we eschew this path and take a rather counter-intuitive approach to this question. We both propose and defend here the relevance and impact of the study of *normative violence*. Normative violence points not to a type of violence that is somehow 'normative', but to the violence of norms. Moreover, and more controversially, normative violence can be thought of as a primary form of violence, because it both *enables* the typical physical violence that we routinely recognise and simultaneously *erases* such violence from our ordinary view.

This chapter elucidates the concept of normative violence and then elaborates its broader political significance. Butler suggests provocatively in the preface to *Gender Trouble* what we will contend she demonstrates in the book: that gender norms themselves can do a certain violence to those bodies that would (necessarily) violate such norms. We will argue that the problem of normative violence serves as *the* political problem of *Gender Trouble*. Rereading Butler's text as a response to and a critique of this material predicament throws into stark relief the contribution that Butler makes to political theory. While closely interpreting *Gender Trouble* within its context, as a work of feminist and queer theory, this chapter refuses to cordon it off from the broader field of politics. We reject the temptation to confine the text to feminist theory or gender studies, and instead produce here a reading that reveals *Gender Trouble* as a book of political theory, one that needs to be reconsidered broadly for its impact upon our thinking of the political. To cash out on that promise we close this chapter by showing how deftly Butler wields the concept of normative violence in her recent *Precarious Life* (Butler 2004a), an effort to intervene directly in the political debate over US foreign policy, civil liberties and homeland security since 9/11.

Gender Trouble and the violence of the norm

Almost twenty years after its initial publication, the significance and impact of Butler's *Gender Trouble* both to debates in feminist theory and to the emergence of queer theory seems indubitable. However, as to the question of the book's contribution to the field of political theory, the jury remains out. Here we use the occasion of Butler's 10th-anniversary preface to *Gender Trouble* as a site for reassessing the politics of the book. The new preface reconfigures the political context of the book; it shows that the question of 'opening up' the possibilities of gender must be understood not in terms of a feminist 'gender pluralism' (the crude idea that there should simply be 'more' genders) but in relation to the problem of heteronormativity and the lived existence of non-normative sexuality. When thought in terms of the illegibility and illegitimacy of so many queer lives, the question of gender 'possibilities' is anything but utopian (as might be envisioned by the misreading of *Gender Trouble* as a liberal pluralist tract). Butler links this framing to a newly introduced concept, one that can be located retroactively in the text of *Gender Trouble*, namely normative violence.

Many readers of Butler have commented, and a large number of them have complained, that her works come across as extremely impersonal, that the author remains distant if not invisible in them. When Butler does use the first-person singular in her texts, she usually does so not to fall back to the solid ground of personal experience, but rather to decentre the 'I' and to ask after its conditions of possibility (Butler 1997a, 1999). Butler's texts often read as if they seek Foucault's goal for writing – to make the author disappear (Foucault 1977b, 1981). Her preface to the 10th-anniversary edition of *Gender Trouble* comes as somewhat of a surprise, then: it starts in the first person and it stays there. Butler uses the I not only grammatically, but also personally, situating the text in the context in which it was written, including the circumstances of Butler's own life. Rather than experiencing the disappearance of the author behind a web of discourse, in this short text an image of Butler herself emerges: 'sitting on Rehoboth Beach, wondering whether I could link the different sides of my life' (Butler 1999: xvii). Here we see that *Gender Trouble* served very personal and very much political ends, just as it concomitantly contributed to academic debates.

The context that Butler reconstructs in this preface is very much a *queer* one. And this is not because of a simple identity politics equation – traced back to Butler as a person, or to Rehoboth Beach as a place – but because of Butler's explicit aim to challenge the presumption of heterosexuality. On the first page of the new preface, she writes: 'I was most concerned to criticize a pervasive heterosexual assumption in feminist literary theory' (Butler 1999: vii). Butler shows that her goal in the book had little to do with outlining a better ideal of gender and everything to do with expanding the possibilities of lived genders. Within feminist debates, many have criticised this purported aim in Butler's text, taking it as advocacy for some sort of 'gender pluralism' in which males and females simply choose what gender they ought to 'try on' (Benhabib 1995b; Fraser 1995, cf. Butler 1995a). This area was never Butler's focus, and the argument about 'wearing' genders, or making them up as we go along, was never one she made (see Lloyd 2005a: 137; cf. Lloyd 1999). Butler's concern lies with the very possibility of gender 'intelligibility', with the capacity to live one's life *as* and *through* one's sexuality and gender. This project resonates as powerfully political once we read it within the context of queer struggle: 'one might wonder what use "opening up possibilities" finally is, but no one who has understood what it is to live in the social world as what is "impossible," illegible, unrealisable, unreal and illegitimate is likely to pose that question' (Butler 1999 [1990]: viii). *Gender Trouble*, then, does not centre itself on the usual subject of feminism – the lives of women and the choices they make, the possibilities they have as given subjects, *as women*. It turns instead to the more originary question of the very possibility of a lived life.

The possibility of a 'lived' life hinges on the notion of intelligibility, on the capacity to be recognised as a subject, an agent. A lived life is only possible as a recognisable subject, and this notion of recognisability/intelligibility might be thought through the idea of a 'received' subject. This concept points to a rather quaint (and perhaps quite French) sense of the term 'received' (L. Disch, email to author SAC, 9 October 2004). A received subject is one who, when he or she makes a social call at the proper time, is allowed into the parlour. To be allowed entry, to be 'received' in this sense, entails a recognition of one's humanity; it produces the intelligibility that makes a life livable. The subject who commits a social scandal – for example getting pregnant out of wedlock – will no longer be 'received'. Indeed, his or her identity may lose its very intelligibility. And it proves important to stress here that in Butler's sense of intelligibility there can be no subject before the reception. Being received *makes* one a subject; it makes a lived life possible.

Butler calls the heterosexual presumptions that police gendered lives 'violent', and she describes *Gender Trouble* as an effort to uncover that violence. The exposure and critique of normative violence therefore serve as the focal point of Butler's critique, and in it resides the central political value of the text. It is here as well, in the articulation of and challenge to normative violence, that *Gender Trouble* links Butler's life of activism with her academic pursuits. Butler closes the preface as follows:

> this book is written then as part of the cultural life of a collective struggle that has had, and will continue to have, some success in increasing the possibilities for a livable life for those who live, or try to live, on the sexual margins.
>
> (Butler 1999 [1990]: xxvi)

The question of normative violence is a question centred on the problem of unreal and unrealisable lives. The concept of normative violence draws our attention not to the violence done *to* a pre-formed subject, but to the violence done *within* the formation of subjectivity. To be more than a catch-phrase, to make sense at all as a viable political concept, normative violence must be located prior to subjectivity; it must be thought through discourse. One might call this the violence of the letter.

As a political concept 'normative violence' may, at first, appear paradoxical. That is, on its surface the phrase might be taken to be self-contradictory. To the extent that we typically link the concept of violence to a juridical understanding of power, one in which one subject wields force to harm another, it makes no sense to modify violence with the term 'normative'. Physical violence might 'become the norm' (e.g. in a lawless land) but there could be no such thing as 'normative violence'. To explicate normative violence as a political concept will first require unravelling this potential contradiction. Jacques Derrida invokes the same sort of apparent paradox when he titles section 1 of part II of *Of Grammatology* the 'violence of the letter'. 'Violence of the letter' and 'normative violence' both seek to name a counter-intuitive understanding of violence. In using these turns of phrase, Derrida and Butler demonstrate how much more varied and complex violence can be. At the same time they emphasise the part that language plays in violence. In describing the close relationship between the literary and the political, Anne Norton calls this 'the violence at the heart of language' (Norton 2004: 26). Normative violence would not be thinkable were it not for this violence of language, and Derrida makes a bold effort to articulate what goes on here, 'at the heart'. In a crucial passage from this section, he writes: 'Anterior to the possibility of violence in the current and derivative sense ... there is, as the space of its possibility, the violence of the arche-writing, the violence of the difference, of classification, and of the system of appellation' (Derrida 1974: 110).

The 'derivative' sense of violence that Derrida mentions here proves to be precisely the juridical, force-related sense. This sort of violence operates by way of legal punishments, military operations and physical altercations. Intuitively, we take this sense of violence to be the 'proper' one, and for this reason Butler's phrase 'normative violence' strikes us as odd. Norms, we think, have nothing to do with this intuitive sense of violence; thus 'normative violence' makes no sense at all. But Derrida claims here that what we think of as the proper sense of violence turns out to be the 'derivative sense'. Before this violence can be derived, there must first be an originary sense of violence.[1] Derrida calls this 'the violence of the letter', and he explains it through his quasi-concept[2] of *arche-writing*. Arche-writing creates the trace that precedes the very distinction between speech and writing. And violence is contained *within* this trace, such that arche-writing constitutes the conditions of (im)possibility (both their cause and their limit) of not only the speech/writing distinction but also our 'proper' sense of violence.

We submit that with the concept of 'normative violence' Butler offers us a better way of thinking what Derrida calls the 'violence of the letter'. In his effort to counter the privileging of speech over writing in the history of philosophy, and perhaps in the history of the West (though Derrida really only ever *argues* for the former claim, he sometimes *asserts* the latter), Derrida implies, through the phrase itself, that he wants to make writing (i.e. *arche-writing*) into the instrument of violence. 'Violence of the letter' means that the text does violence, conjuring fantastic images of alphabet strips on US grade school walls that attack schoolchildren from the shadows. The metaphor (and certainly the ridiculous images that we have culled from it) comes up short, however, since in Derrida's own sense *writing cannot be an instrument*. There cannot be a violence *of* the text, since the text can never be a 'thing' in that way.

However, there can be violence *in* the text. Or, better, there can be violence in discourse, since by 'text' Derrida never means to denote a discrete object containing words on paper, but, rather, he seeks to convey a much broader sense of language – language as speech, text, sound, gesture and style. Thus there can be a fundamental violence produced by the construction of discourse and the circulation of discursive practices. Butler illuminates this idea with the notion of 'normative violence', a violence done 'before' the proper sense of violence.[3] To say that normative violence happens 'before' our proper (i.e. derivative) sense of violence is to suggest two phenomena at once. On the one hand, normative violence proves to be primary violence in that it may *enable* the secondary violence that we then think of as typical. On the other hand, and perhaps more significantly, normative violence may be primary in that it serves to *erase* such typical violence. In other words, normative violence done 'before' everyday violence makes such everyday violence invisible, illegible, non-existent. *Gender Trouble* might be read, then, as an effort at unmasking the operations of normative violence so as (1) to interrupt its capacity to enable other violences and (2) to render them visible when they do occur.

Normative troubles with gender

Butler introduces the concept of normative violence toward the end of the 10th-anniversary preface to *Gender Trouble*. 'I grew up', she writes, 'understanding something of *the violence of gender norms*: an uncle incarcerated for his anatomically anomalous body ... gay cousins forced to leave their homes ... my own tempestuous coming out at the age of 16' (Butler 1999: xix, emphasis added). We would typically think of these examples as violence, or perhaps merely inconveniences, done to sovereign individuals *because* they have violated gender norms. Butler describes the situation quite differently by attributing the agency of the violence not to outside forces, but to the norms themselves. This is 'the violence of gender norms', not the violence of bigots – *normative violence*, not simple (yet no less horrendous for that) gay-bashing.

Normative violence thus helps us to show how radically Butler reconceives agency, and such a reading serves to answer those critics who have been centrally concerned with the question of agency. Alison Stone, for example, offers a sympathetic defence of Butler on agency (Stone 2005). Stone seeks to show how subversive agency could be possible in Butler's account (Stone 2005: 2), responding to those critics who charge Butler with doing away with agency entirely (Nussbaum 1999) or with constraining it severely (McNay 2000). Even Stone, however, reduces agency to the capacity of an agent – 'a capacity that subjects may exercise to subversive effect'. Instead, as described in more detail in Chapter 3 (through dialogue with Coole's work), we see again here that Butler conceives of agency beyond the agent. Butler offers a thinking of agency much broader and much subtler than Stone's definition will admit, since Butler allows for the possibility that agency may not be exhausted as a capacity *of* a subject, but may involve the prior *formation* of subjectivity. Agency thus cannot be reduced to the idea of 'performative agency', as many critics would have it (Webster 2000).

Butler goes on to explain and unravel the counter-intuitive nature of her description of normative violence, and she suggests that only retroactively can one see normative violence clearly. This retroactive seeing likely applies both to Butler's description of her time growing up, 'understanding something' of normative violence, and to her redescription of the work of *Gender Trouble* in the terms of normative violence. In either case, the difficulty lies in making such violence visible. Butler continues: 'it was difficult to bring this violence into view precisely because gender was so taken for granted at the same time that it was violently policed' (Butler 1999: xix). The work of denaturalising gender thus does not serve the end of making gender completely 'fluid' and thereby utterly meaningless. Rather, the denaturalisation of nature seeks to 'bring ... this [normative] violence into view'. Thus we see a shift from a narrow reading of *Gender Trouble* that would (confined by a frame of standpoint feminism) take Butler to be arguing for an expanded (but unhelpful) sense of women's agency, to a more general political and theoretical (as well as queer) context in which Butler offers a radical rethinking of agency itself. Butler seeks to expose prior conditions of possibility for agency as found within norms, not merely to call for a 'choice' of more genders.

Butler's description of the challenge posed by the task of rendering normative violence perceptible and observable must be further scrutinised. Again, her account can be read as a post hoc description of her experiences growing up, in which the naturalisation of gender masks the very violence of gender norms. However, if 'gender was so taken for granted', it seems obvious that the same can be said of sexuality. Even Butler's examples above make it clear that these violent 'gender norms' are always and already norms of sexuality as well: each of the examples goes beyond a betrayal of gender norms to a deviation from the norm of heterosexuality. Norms of gender, as both the examples here and the book as a whole illustrate, always remain underwritten and overwritten by norms of sexuality, and particularly by heteronormativity. Thus we catch a glimpse here of what we will argue in Chapters 6 and 7: Butler reworks gender within the context of her queer critique of heteronormativity.

Butler draws these links herself on the very next page, at the place where she first uses the phrase 'normative violence'. We see the concept emerge not merely as a supplement to the lexicon already introduced by *Gender Trouble* – and then advanced and refined by Butler's other texts. Instead, Butler, retroactively, places normative violence at the very core of the text, as the central political concept. Butler writes: 'the dogged effort to "denaturalize" gender in this text emerges, I think, from a strong desire to counter the normative violence implied by ideal morphologies of sex and to

uproot the pervasive assumptions about natural or presumptive heterosexuality' (Butler 1999 [1990]: xx). Thus, the task of exposing the thoroughly constructed nature of gender – that is, the effort to show that gender
is anything but natural – can never be dissociated from the challenge to
heteronormativity. Until the presumption of heterosexuality is 'uprooted'
gender could never be 'denaturalised'. And, looking at it from the other
side, we can say that Butler denaturalises gender precisely *through* her critique of heteronormativity. The 'naturalness' attributed to women's 'nur-
turing' qualities, the pathos of male–female relations (where women are
relation-oriented and men are autonomous), all this was what we might call
a 'gift' from the heterosexual matrix. Thus the normative violence of which
Butler speaks and to which she seeks a response must be understood as
always involving the norms of sex, gender and sexuality at the same time.

We are trying to show here that Butler's account of normative violence –
highlighted in the preface, but latent in the book – serves as an answer to
the most pointed, the most repeated, the most vociferous charges of her
critics: 'the writing of this denaturalization was not done simply out of a
desire to play with language or prescribe theatrical antics. ... It was done
from a desire to live, *to make life possible*' (Butler 1999: xx, emphasis
added). The first half of this claim obviously speaks to critics of post-
structuralism broadly, critics who would describe the work of radical con-
structivists as mere play with language (see Benhabib 1995a, 1995b); it also
offers a rejoinder to the specific criticism of *Gender Trouble* as a call to turn
gender into theatre (Hawkes 1995; cf. Lloyd 2005a). The second half of the
quotation comes across much less clearly: what does it mean 'to make life
possible'? On its surface, the claim might echo as hollow, as a merely
rhetorical response to critics – balancing the seriousness of 'a desire to live'
with the frivolity of 'play' but without substance to back up the rhetoric.
Quite the contrary: the concept of normative violence provides the substantial grounding for this claim.

When read within the framework of normative violence, the effort to
'make life possible' comes to light as a serious politico-theoretical effort.
The denaturalisation of our reified notions of sex/gender serves the political
end of resisting and countering normative violence. To *expose* the workings
of normative violence is the first step in challenging it. One could read, for
example, the modern history of 'gay liberation' over the past 35 years as a
claiming of rights (and a struggle for them) by already-constituted political
subjects. This is the standard story, presumed by the mainstream gay
movement that makes gay marriage the final and ultimate achievement in
this progressive history. But recently queer writers have been trying to tell a
different story; authors such as Michael Warner (1999) and Butler herself
(Butler *et al.* 2000) have challenged the dominant narrative, showing that
'gay liberation' had its roots in an alliance against normative sexuality, an
alliance formed by gays, lesbians, sex-workers, transgendered people, people
with AIDS, family and friends of those with AIDS, and a whole host of

others that could never be subsumed by an 'etc.' or encompassed within today's mainstream gay movement. This alternative narrative can be read powerfully as a battle against normative violence.

After all, the so-called 'origin' of modern gay liberation lies, as everyone knows well, in the pools of blood outside the Stonewall Inn. Gay liberation emerges from violence – of course it does. Moreover, the gay activists and the movements for sexual liberation that they started, groups that came together initially as a response to Stonewall, were not merely challenging juridical violence. Indeed, what one must remember about Stonewall is that police raiding a 'gay' bar in Greenwich Village was par for the course. The raid on the Stonewall Inn was a routine act; what set it apart was the resistance put up by the patrons of the bar (D'Emilio 1992). This resistance transformed the invisible normative violence practised every day against non-normative sexualities into an act of violence in the intuitive sense of force wielded by one subject against another. Foucault understood something of normative violence when he tacitly suggested that we not let the police get away with exercising it: 'it is the cop's job to use physical force … anyone who opposes cops must not, therefore, let them maintain the hypocrisy of disguising this force behind orders that have to be immediately obeyed' (Foucault 1975, quoted in Eribon 1991: 265). We have no evidence to suggest that Foucault was thinking about Stonewall when he gave this quotation – he might well have been reflecting on his own physical battles with police – but the description applies quite nicely nonetheless. The Stonewall riot started because of a refusal to allow the cops to hide their exercise of normative violence behind orders that must be obeyed. It was an act of resistance that rendered the normative violence visible by forcing its translation into a juridical violence.

And like most other political examples in *Gender Trouble*, drag must be read as a site of potential resistance to normative violence. Within the context of normative violence, and building on our previous discussions of drag, we would emphasise the following points. First, the meaning and significance of drag cannot be understood outside the terms of heteronormativity. The naturalisation of gender and gender differences does not occur on its own. *Heteronormativity produces and maintains the naturalisation of gender*. Only 'through the regulatory fiction of heterosexual coherence' can gender appear to be natural. Thus the resistance to that naturalisation, the challenge to the regulatory fiction, must operate by way of a primary challenge to heteronormativity. Gender cannot be exposed as performative through drag unless drag also undermines 'the law of heterosexual coherence'. If the law of heterosexual coherence, heteronormativity, remains undisturbed, then drag does little to challenge the naturalisation of gender. In other words, if a male dresses as a woman in order to express his desire for a male, then perhaps he really only attests to the power of heteronormativity. However, if a drag queen appears before us, performing a certain somewhat recognisably feminine gender, but in such a way that both his/her sex and his/her desire remain unclear or unrecognisable, then the core foundation of presumptive heterosexuality begins to crack. Without that foundation, we can no longer resuscitate a notion of either sex or gender as natural, since the natural must be based upon something.

Second, Butler makes it clear that to be subversive drag must denaturalise gender *and sex*, and thereby call into question their relation. The difference between drag as subversive and drag as imitative hinges on where we locate the application of drag's parodic force. If it applies only at the level of gender, then, as its critics charge, drag may simply serve to ape pre-given, naturalised gender norms. However, if it works at the level of presumptive heterosexuality, then drag calls into question the fundamental relation between sex and gender. It undermines that core element of the heterosexual matrix that links gender to sexuality and sexuality to gender. If drag performs only gender, then it can be said to consolidate a certain given sex. But if drag performs both sex and gender at the same time – if neither variable can be fixed – then drag critically challenges the idea of naturalised gender or sex. And our arguments in Part I of the book already make it very clear that Butler always takes up the *relation* between sex and gender; in isolation, she has no theory of either. None of this is to say that drag will *necessarily* be subversive – and Butler rightly refuses to offer a metric for subversion (Butler 1999: xxi) – but merely to suggest that the subversive potential of drag is renewed when we make clear the expansiveness of the field of application for 'performativity', i.e. the field reaches all the way down from gender to sex.

We need to rethink drag through the terms Butler lays out in the preface. This leads us to ask not whether drag is necessarily radical (or not) in the abstract. Instead, we should consider the question of whether performances of drag can make certain sexed and gendered subjects' lives more livable, make their existence intelligible. This is to ask after the potential of drag – or any other practice – to counter violence at the level of discourse, to contest the 'violence of the letter' by opening up a space within norms for more and other subjects to appear. Reading drag as a resistance to normative violence proves once more that Butler's project in *Gender Trouble* (and after) is the queer project of struggling against those norms that render some lives unintelligible. To make life livable, to create a possible space of existence for those whose lives prove unintelligible within the terms of dominant norms of gender and sexuality, all of this amounts to an important struggle with the norm, a challenge to normative violence within the context of a radical, untimely politics.

Drag must therefore be reread within the context of Butler's avowed goal for the book, 'to make life possible', but, more importantly, so must the other concepts in the book. The heterosexual matrix, the politics of subversion and the engagement with psychoanalysis all come more clearly into a *political* light when read in these terms – a point we will elaborate in Chapter 7. Rather than working back through other concepts or theoretical devices in the text of *Gender Trouble*, we want to follow through on our argument about the political importance of both the concept of normative violence and the project of the book as a whole by turning to another text of Butler's – her recent engagement with post-9/11 politics.

Normative violence, 9/11 and *Precarious Life*

American political discourse today consistently marks 9/11 as a breaking point, a paradigm shift. We are now, it is said, in a 'post-9/11' world; '9/11 changed everything'. Rules, procedures, strategies and interpretations that made sense before 9/11 now, it is often claimed, no longer apply. This epistemic shift from 'pre-9/11' to 'post-9/11' could easily be attached to the question of violence, and with predictable results. That is, most Americans would take for granted that the horrible events of 9/11 and the terrible deaths that resulted from them were about violence plain and simple. 9/11 marks the first act of (foreign) terrorism on American soil, and such terrorist acts are not merely an example of direct, uncomplicated, physical (juridical) violence; they *epitomise* such violence. Thus, in much the same way as politicians today refute their opponents with claims like the following, 'but we live in post-9/11 world today, and you are invoking a pre-9/11 mentality', one might similarly dismiss our investigation into 'normative violence'. The critical argument appears obvious: if today's political problems centre on the war on terrorism, if our biggest fear must always be the detonation of a biological or nuclear weapon in a global city or tourist locale, then our concern must lie exclusively with the question of physical violence. Now is not the appropriate time for an investigation into the question of 'so-called' normative violence; it is a waste of time. Only out of touch academics would even contemplate such a project. Call this the *concrete dismissal*.

Butler herself has often been accused of being an out-of-touch academic, locked in her ivory tower – ignoring real-world pain and suffering in order to explore abstract, meaningless and often unreadable theories (Nussbaum 1999). But not even a casual reader will doubt that *Precarious Life* is a political text, and a highly readable one at that. Throughout, the book remains centrally concerned with, and focused upon, questions of law, foreign policy, practical politics and political agency. Of course, it would prove hasty and perhaps even dangerous to try to draw from the fact that Butler has written a book on post-9/11 politics the conclusion that her corpus is somehow now 'politicised'. One could easily suggest, instead, that Butler's recent shift to the role of political commentator reflects nothing more than a sign of the times. In other words, the critique might run as follows: given the dire straits of the American and world political situation, Butler finally abandons (or, at least, puts to the side) her abstract philosophising and her so-called radical thinking of gender, and turns instead to practical matters of policy and politics. Moreover, and along these lines, one finds little new or 'radical' in *Precarious Life*: the critique of the Bush administration's policies, both domestic (encroachment on civil liberties) and foreign (neo-colonialism through unjust pre-emptive war), will sound quite familiar to anyone who has read anything coming from the putative left over the past few years. Call this the *general dismissal*.

This final section takes both of these dismissals quite seriously. It elaborates responses to both the specific rejection of an investigation into normative violence as inappropriate to a post-9/11 world and the general denunciation of Butler's recent work as simultaneously unoriginal and disconnected from her earlier project. Taking the latter critique first, we stress that our argument is *not* that the appearance of *Precarious Life*, in and of itself, somehow legitimates Butler as a political theorist. However, we also refute the notion that this text marks a redirection or disjuncture in Butler's work. Butler's engagement with post-9/11 politics, far from constituting an abandonment of her previous work, instead relies upon and further elaborates her previous theoretical position. *Precarious Life* offers a linked continuation of Butler's politico-theoretic project; it is of a piece with her earlier writings. More specifically, the conceptualisation of political agency that first emerges in the conclusion of *Gender Trouble* (1990) provides the framework and the conceptual resources for Butler's contentions concerning agency within *Precarious Life*. In addition, and much more to the point, the argument about normative violence that we have been advancing throughout this chapter is further illustrated by Butler's engagement with American domestic and foreign policy. The concept of normative violence ties this recent book to Butler's larger project.

In reply to the primary dismissal of normative violence: just as we can use Butler's phrase 'normative violence' as a hermeneutic clue to reread the politics of *Gender Trouble*, we can also use it as a concrete political concept in order to understand the violence mentioned in the subtitle of Butler's more recent book. To put it partially in the language of our spectral (but very real) critic from above: rather than providing the grounds for ignoring normative violence, the 'post-9/11 world' *requires* an understanding of normative violence. At the same time as 9/11, in fact, offers us the opportunity to witness normative violence, an appropriate response to 9/11 *demands* an attentiveness to normative violence. Butler puts it this way, in the preface to *Precarious Life*:

> That we can be injured, that others can be injured, that we are subject to death at the whim of another, are all reasons for both fear and grief. What is less certain, however, is whether the experiences of vulnerability and loss have to lead straightaway to military violence and retribution. There are other passages. If we are interested in arresting cycles of violence to produce less violent outcomes, it is no doubt important to ask what, politically, might be made of grief besides a cry for war. One insight that injury affords is that there are others out there on whom

my life depends, people I do not know and may never know. This fundamental dependency on anonymous others is not a condition that I can will away. No security measure will foreclose this dependency; no violent act of sovereignty will rid the world of this fact.

(Butler 2004a: xii)

Butler reads the violence of 9/11 and its aftermath through and with the lens of normative violence. Thus rendered, the terrorist acts of that day cannot be *merely* acts of physical violence (although they most certainly are that as well); they must be situated in the context of a prior human dependency. They are both expressions of that dependency – to the extent that Al-Qaeda saw itself reacting to suffering caused by America – and manifestations of it, since the lives of US citizens have now been destroyed by 'others'. In pointing to 'other passages' available as responses to loss, responses to suffering, Butler suggests that violence be thought more broadly. The prior human dependency that 9/11 exposes shows us that 'cycles of violence' cannot be measured solely by overt acts of terror or war. The war in Afghanistan and the war in Iraq constitute obvious and not so obvious, respectively, responses to 9/11, but only at the level of physical acts. Butler reveals here the possibility of responding to our prior dependency, to working within the terms of normative violence – a possibility we pursue in Chapter 5.

One can thus read normative violence as the central concern of both *Precarious Life* and *Gender Trouble*. Normative violence binds this recent text back to Butler's earliest, breakthrough book. To make this case we turn again to *Gender Trouble*, this time to that point in its conclusion where Butler offers some of her most criticised remarks on agency. It is here that Butler calls gender 'a performance', and it is almost always here that critics turn when they seek to dismiss Butler's account of agency as either deterministic (we are 'trapped' in language) or voluntaristic (we 'perform' whatever gender we please) (Benhabib 1995a). However, Butler's remarks are framed – and this is the frame that the criticisms elide – by (1) the problem of normative violence and (2) an alternative account of agency. Each of these framings re-emerges in stark and politically powerful terms in *Precarious Life*. We will take them in turn, starting with the problem of agency.

Much to the consternation of so many of her readers, Butler consistently and stubbornly refuses to reduce the question of agency to the question of the 'I' who acts. To do so would be to conceive of an 'I', an actor, an agent, somehow outside the language *in which* he or she acts. But 'the question of agency is not to be answered through recourse to an "I" that preexists signification ... the enabling conditions for an assertion of "I" are provided by the structure of signification' (Butler 1999: 183). As shown in Chapter 2, that 'structure of signification' – what we would call the set of discursive practices in which we find ourselves – conditions the 'terms of intelligibility' by which an 'I' will be recognised and/or legitimated. The 'I' that appears in deviant gender, racial or sexual form may not be allowed to 'appear' at all.

Butler's theory of agency can be clarified by condensing the problematic to the relation between agency and language. The critiques of Butler's account of agency as voluntarist or determinist depend upon a mis-understanding of that relation. Taking Butler's account as determinist turns language itself into the actor, such that it blocks the action of the indivi-dual; presuming a latent voluntarism in Butler's position simply flips the coin and assumes that agency involves making up names and words and changing what things mean. Butler's position may be subtle, but it can be stated quite lucidly. There is no agency *of* language, and agency is not denied *by* language; agency is *in* language.

The clear statement also sounds somewhat abstract, but it need not be. In *Precarious Life* Butler demonstrates that we tell the stories of 9/11 through a specific and ill-formed conception of agency. Butler argues that our frames for understanding violence are shaped by the narratives that circulate around 9/11. In the first case, most of those narratives are first-person stories that begin on 9/11 itself; the violence of that day propels the narrative. According to Butler, the only narratives that start before this point yet are still taken as 'legitimate' are first-person narratives of the pathologies of the hijackers or of Osama bin Laden. These stories tell us where those individuals went wrong. This type of discourse 'works as a plausible and engaging narrative in part because *it resituates agency in terms of a subject*' (Butler 2004a: 5, emphasis added). The knee-jerk reac-tion on the left – that says that the US has reaped what it has sown – invokes the same model of agency, only now the US itself becomes the sole subject that matters. This story, though critical of US foreign policy, thus elevates the primacy of the US as either actor or victim to the same level as the dominant narrative about the personal responsibility of the non-state terrorists.

Given the contemporary political situation, Butler invokes the same con-ception of agency that she articulates late in *Gender Trouble*. First, she insists that 'conditions do not "act" in the way that individual agents do, but no agent acts without them' (Butler 2004a: 11). Thus conditions can never 'determine' an actor's choices or actions fully (agency is not denied by language), but neither can an agent act external to conditions (agency is always within language). Butler's approach to agency here, rather than mystifying, reifying or abstracting from reality, serves to cut incisively across current debates concerning US foreign policy. In facing the difficult choices of today's US foreign policy, we must retain the crucial concept of 'responsibility'. But we cannot simply place blame, nor assume, as President Bush prefers, that 'you're either with us or against us'. Butler concludes by elaborating, not dismissing, a notion of responsibility: she insists that 'those who commit acts of violence are surely responsible for them' while also reminding us that 'these individuals are formed' and thus their acts never emerge *sui generis* (Butler 2004a: 15). Just as the 'agency' of gender always operates within the given terms of gender, so the individual responsibility for acts of violence works within the context of collective responsibility for normative violence. The act of violence cannot be understood outside the terms of the 'violence of the letter', since, as shown above, normative violence conditions and enables the 'derivative' violence – no matter how extraordinary, no matter how tragic – that we think of as everyday violence.

This move returns us, then, to *Gender Trouble* and the question of normative violence as it is raised there. The problematic of 'performing' gender only emerges within the frame of normative violence, and the problem of post-9/11 political agency will be seen to operate within that frame as well. In *Gender Trouble*, Butler writes: 'gender is a performance *with clearly punitive consequences*. Discrete genders are part of what "humanizes" individuals within contemporary culture; indeed, we regularly punish those who fail to do their gender right' (Butler 1999: 178, emphasis added). To do our gender 'wrong' is to open ourselves up to normative violence because we mark our gender and sexuality as potentially non-normative. To do our gender 'right' is to remain unmarked within societal gender norms, and thereby to remain outside the sphere of normative violence.[4] Of course, gender is not simply something we do; it is often something done to us. Gender norms produce viable and unviable genders prior to any choice we might make about 'doing' our gender. The agency of gender is both enabled and constrained by gender norms. And it should be stressed that the 'choice' to do gender right or wrong may only be available to some. It becomes easy to do normative violence to gender deviants, precisely because they are dehumanised through their non-normative gender or sexuality.

In *Precarious Life*, Butler uses a similar framework to demonstrate with great perspicacity the manner in which the violence of US foreign policy depends upon rendering the other somehow less than human. This process depends upon the workings of normative violence; understanding this process demands an attentiveness to normative violence. And this attentiveness goes well beyond the question of exclusion:

> I am referring not *only* to humans not regarded as humans, and thus to a restrictive conception of the human that is based on their exclusion. It is not a matter of simple entry of the excluded into an established ontology, but an insurrection at the level of ontology, a critical opening up of the questions, What is real? Whose lives are real?
>
> (Butler 2004a: 33)

If a prior normative violence renders a life somehow less than real, then it erases beforehand the violence that would then be done to that so-called 'life'. Here we see the violence of discourse, discussed in detail above: 'on the

level of discourse, certain lives are not considered lives at all ... their dehu-
manization occurs first, at this level' (Butler 2004a: 34). More to the point,
their dehumanisation at this level enables and erases their 'treatment' at the
next level.

One can illustrate by way of a stark example. The subject position 'enemy
combatant' – used to describe what we would ordinarily call 'prisoners' at
Guantánamo Bay – must, by definition, exist outside the human (Butler
2004a: 89). It is the very dehumanisation of those who are 'potential terrorists' that makes it possible to suspend completely all human rights. A
terrorist is worse than a murderer, somehow less than human; this prior
dehumanisation, this violence of the letter, serves both to enable and possibly to justify any violence done to individuals at Guantánamo – or, as we
see even more clearly, at Abu Ghraib.

Indeed, the terminological battle over 'torture' versus 'abuse' centres on
the same normative framework. The torture of a human being involves a
severe and shocking violence done *to* that human being, but in a perverse
way 'torture' itself also *humanises* its victim. That is to say, only a legitimate, livable life can be subject to torture. To describe a set of a practices
or acts as 'torture' serves to undo any prior attempt at dehumanisation of
the subject in question. A tortured subject is, by definition, a human subject; it is precisely their legitimate humanity that torture violates. 'Abuse', on
the other hand, invokes no such fundamental violation, and thus a dehumanised creature, someone somehow less than fully human, could *only* ever
be abused, not tortured.[5] The US insistence on the 'abuse' of Iraqi prisoners
thus serves to maintain their potential *dehumanisation*. 'Abuse' preserves
normative violence, even though – no, certainly *because* – it denies genuine
juridical violence (i.e. the physical harm done to a human subject). To
accept directly the physical harm done to the Abu Ghraib and Guantánamo
prisoners by naming it torture would be simultaneously to undo the normative violence that both enables and erases such physical violence. When
we name the violence done to them torture, we undercut the framework of
normative violence that made that 'secondary' violence possible in the first
place.

In the face of so much overt physical violence done to and by Americans – from the attacks of 9/11 to the wars in Afghanistan and Iraq, from
the deaths of American soldiers and citizens in Iraq to the abuse and torture of prisoners at Abu Ghraib – normative violence cannot, must not, be
reduced to a secondary concern. Instead, Butler shows that any rich or
sophisticated understanding of the current political situation *demands*
attentiveness to the normative frame that surrounds and conditions all this
violence. The 'violence of the letter' – discursive violence as we have been
calling it here – is not something to be cast aside when 'real violence' makes
its ugly and painful emergence on the scene. 'Normative schemes of intelligibility establish what will and will not be human, what will be a livable
life, what will be a grievable death' (Butler 2004a: 146). The politically and

ethically appropriate response to 'real' violence depends upon our careful treatment and assessment of normative violence. From the challenge to heteronormativity in *Gender Trouble* to the critique of dehumanisation in *Precarious Life*, Butler offers us a political theory extremely well suited to carrying out this essential analysis.

5 Political ontology

Butler never ceases to write within what one might call 'the shadow of Hegel'. Yet a strong case can be made that from the first book to the most recent Foucault remains the most important thinker in Butler's work. And, like Foucault, Butler has made a recent, late 'turn' toward the question of ethics and, perhaps, away from her earlier, more polemical political critiques. Some would say that Foucault turned to ethics to answer his critics – those who saw significant gaps in his more critical writings, those who ceaselessly accused Foucault of 'doing away with the subject' or at least robbing it of 'agency'. Close attention to Foucault's late works indicates that he offered a coherent, tenable response to those criticisms. However, the fact of such a reading does not seem to have solved the problem: many, if not most, of Foucault's critics continue to hurl the same charges at him, and many, if not most, of Foucault's followers continue to rely more on his earlier works for formulating their own political arguments.

The path taken by Foucault raises a number of interesting questions for those following Butler's trail; it broaches particularly important concerns for readers of, *Giving an Account of Oneself* (Butler 2005). This is the text that loudly announces on its dust jacket that it will mark Butler's own definitive turn to ethics – 'her first extended study of moral philosophy'. It would appear to provide the location for Butler's own response to her critics, to the general criticisms about Butler's 'normative framework' that have lingered for a decade since Butler made her specific responses, in *Bodies that Matter* (Butler 1993), to the critiques of *Gender Trouble* (Butler 1999 [1990]). Will this putatively ultimate response to *her* critics serve to silence them, or will they continue to make the same accusations? Will those who derive their political critiques from Butler's early work find similar resources in her recent writings on ethics and ontology, or will they, too, continue (merely?) to reread *Gender Trouble*.

Our argument here will begin by denying the premises. That is, we will contend that Butler's early writings already have an ethics lodged within them. Sometimes this ethical orientation remains implicit; at others Butler articulates it directly. Yet even in the former case we find evidence to argue that Butler's recent 'turn' is really no turn at all. Throughout her works

Butler has articulated an ontological position that entails a particular set of ethical orientations. She does this again in *Giving an Account*. While this text makes its moves more obviously and does so within a frame clearly marked as 'ethics', we will nevertheless insist that the 'moves' themselves are nothing radical. They are more refined, more subtle and oriented differently (sometimes quite differently), yet we would be wrong to read this text as some kind of break. The ethical argument that *Giving an Account* lays out proves to be a reformulation of arguments Butler has made previously and an activation of arguments that remain latent in her earlier works.

We will defend this set of claims, despite what others have suggested about Butler's lack of ethics in her earlier writings and despite the fact that Butler has implicitly confirmed those suggestions by framing this new book in the way she has. Here we find another interesting analogy to Foucault: Butler, like Foucault, denied the validity of the 'normative grounds' critique for years, but she subtly confirms it by responding so directly to it in this text. That is, one can quite obviously contend that *Giving an Account of Oneself* orients itself toward ethical questions in a way unlike any previous text: the book has been consistently promoted and advertised as Butler's first real foray into ethics. This might seem like a minor point, a fact one would rightly dismiss in a younger, less well-known author. In Butler's case, however, it seems reasonable to assume that this 'marketing' of the book was approved of by Butler herself, that the 'spin' applied to the text proves to be a bit more than spin.

In our principal argument we will insist that Butler's turn to ethics amounts to a (re)turn to ontology. Butler's 'ethics' is always derived from and consistently recurs to a way of understanding human existence in relation to the world – what Heidegger would call being-in-the-world and what Butler often describes in terms of the subject's relation to norms. To put it more succinctly than one should: one's responsibility *for* the other always already depends upon one's ontological relation *to* the other. In developing this argument we will also show, secondarily, that, there is no turn to be found in Butler's oeuvre since ontological questions (and their ethical implications) have always dominated Butler's thinking. Finally, we also will broach the question of whether this so-called turn to ethics is itself, or somehow produces, a turn to politics.

Ontology and ethics

The dust-jacket blurb and the publisher's account both describe *Giving an Account of Oneself* as Butler's first systematic foray into moral philosophy. Each pitches the book as Butler's turn to ethics, with a narrative that suggests to would-be readers that '*this* is the book where you will find the *answers* you've been looking for' about ethical questions and worries. This narrative carries with it the implicit suggestion that Butler is not a moral theorist, that her work has not centred on ethics, that her own interests have consistently fallen outside the sphere of 'systematic moral philosophy'. And perhaps this is all true. Certainly if one defines moral theory as *systematic* and limits its study to a focus on a *specific set* of thinkers and questions, then one cannot question the choice to place Butler's concerns elsewhere.

All of these seemingly logical steps, however, would add up to a prior decision on the question of ethics. They would presume from the start what ethics is and must be, rather than allowing the question of ethics and the ethical to be the relevant subject matter. What if, following a certain Butlerian style of questioning, we inquire as to the conditions that constitute the ethical or moral realm? What if the question of ethics – of ethical relations, of the moral sphere – depends upon prior metaphysical or ontological considerations? What if 'ethics' as we traditionally, systematically conceive it always already assumes a particular conception of the subject, a particular configuration of the ontological realm? Butler both asks and answers questions of this sort in her most recent, most explicit entry into the field of moral philosophy. But Butler has *always* posed just these types of queries. *Butler has raised questions regarding ethics throughout her writings.* She has consistently shown distinct and considered concern with the way in which a theory of subjectivity, or an ontological formulation, shapes, enables, constrains or produces particular sorts of ethical relations.

More to the point, Butler's questions have always implicitly contained a critique of those individualist assumptions that lie at the centre of traditional approaches to, conceptualisations of, and theories about ethics. Butler has consistently sought to displace the liberal individual by way of closer attention to the norms in relation to which that individual must be constituted and reconstituted.[1] For this reason, this chapter seeks to illuminate the manner and extent to which Butler's 'political ontology' carries with it a critique of 'sovereign agency'.

Butler articulates the constitutive relation between ontology and ethics very early on in her writings; this relation emerges in the introduction to her first book, *Subjects of Desire* (1987a), a text she refers to simply as a 'revision' of her 1984 PhD dissertation (i.e. these ideas go way back). Butler begins by tracing her topic, desire, to the area of moral philosophy. She insists, even here, on the link between moral philosophy and ontology. Moral philosophy, she says, 'has assumed a moral ontology, a theory about what a being must be like in order to be capable of moral deliberation and action, in order to lead a moral life and be a moral personality' (Butler 1987a: 5). She concludes that moral philosophy always presumes 'a more general ontological scheme' (Butler 1987a: 5). Butler will centre her own theoretical efforts, not only in this text but also in each of the nine books to follow, on precisely this ontological scheme – including its enabling conditions, its limits and its effects.

Butler continues the account of the relation between ethics and ontology in specific terms: in order to get its project under way, moral philosophy presupposes a theory of a 'unified subject'. It must secure a 'metaphysical place' for the subject before it can investigate the requirements of moral choice, moral action, moral life. Butler describes her entire project of investigating the subject of desire both in the work of Hegel and in his French reception back to 'the question of the metaphysical place and *moral efficacy* of human subjects' (Butler 1987a: 5, emphasis added). Here we see the question of moral philosophy placed at the beginning of Butler's corpus and linked to the study of ontology.

While the explicit language of 'moral philosophy' recedes into the background in the much more famous texts of Butler's to follow, the central concern with ontology (and implicitly, then, with its relation to ethical orientations) never recedes, never wanes and certainly never disappears. Butler opens the preface to *Gender Trouble* by asking at the beginning of the second paragraph how we might 'question' an 'ontological regime' (Butler 1999 [1990]: xxviii). And this challenging of ontological regimes remains linked to the question of 'metaphysical place', as Butler called it in her first book, of the category of 'woman', as Butler will refer to it here, of 'intelligibility' and 'the livable life', as she will describe it in texts from 2004, and finally of the 'I' that gives its account, as she will articulate it in her most recent text (Butler 2005).

The fundamental relation between ontology and ethics serves then as the framework for investigating the impact and analysing the implications of *Giving an Account of Oneself*. This framework, however, does not need to be created anew in Butler's latest text, as it is carried over from her earlier writings and reworked here. The emphasis on this relation in Butler's earlier texts gives us a hermeneutic hint at how to read the new book. It tells us, already, that Butler's account of morality will always be preceded by or implicated in an account of ontology. And Butler's onto-theoretical framework, just like anyone else's, has an implicit ethical orientation (Connolly 1995). This is why phrases like 'moral ontology' and 'moral philosophy' prove (perhaps illustratively) redundant; *ontos* implies *ethos* and no philosophy can be amoral.[2]

Reading the Butlerian 'turn'

To insist, as we continue to do here, that Butler's political ontology carries an ethics lodged within it is by no means to deny that it is right that we read Butler's most recent work as a work *of ethics*. It makes good sense to centre an account of 'Butler's ethics' upon a close reading of this text (as we will do below). But we would be very wrong to take this text as somehow separate or distinct from, or in contrast or conflict with, Butler's earlier writings. This text takes up similar themes, repeats old arguments (even if in a new key) and often reaches similar conclusions. *Giving an Account of Oneself* makes a crucial and significant contribution to Butler's established body of writings, but this contribution does not appear in the form of a supplement (at least not in any simplistic sense) that would fill a gap in Butler's 'coverage'. Rather, this text proves significant precisely because it *elaborates* upon already established themes, because it carries forward arguments that Butler began long ago and because it reaches certain conclusions (and eschews others) that Butler has been working toward for two decades.[3]

At this juncture one might quite reasonably ask: why all the fuss about this? Why spend so much time insisting that this new book isn't all that new, when you plan to talk mostly about the new book anyway? Our answer depends on showing how much more than classification proves to be at stake in calling *Giving an Account* Butler's first turn to ethics. To let that claim stand – that is, not to make all the fuss we have been making here – would be to ignore the normative force of this seemingly descriptive claim. This is the case because the suggestion that Butler has never really discussed ethics until now carries with it an implicit critique; it suggests simultaneously that there has been no normative force to her early writings. This framing implies that it is only now, with this new book, that Butler has got serious, that she has finally turned to the solemn and weighty business (as opposed to her earlier flights of fancy) of normative arguments. In the background – undeveloped, to be sure – one can locate a whole series of implicit claims about the worthlessness (because it lacks normative grounds or legitimate normative force) of Butler's previous work. We refuse to let those arguments stand, even if they do remain off stage. One cannot praise this book as a break without making an implicit condemnation of her earlier books, and *that* would be a terrible mistake indeed.

For this reason, among others, this chapter does not read Butler's latest text as a response to her critics. If *Giving an Account* can be construed as a 'response' it is only in a very limited way. It is not a response in the sense that it takes her critics' claims as valid and therefore offers a correction of her previous project – either by abandoning that project or filling in its gaps (this move, as we have shown, would indict Butler's early work). It is only a response in the circumscribed sense that it offers a redescription of Butler's project, a reworking that demonstrates the very consistency of Butler's writings (thereby validating her early work), even while it reformulates that project using texts perhaps more familiar to her critics and others. This amounts to a redescription in a language more accessible to her critics (and, given the dust-jacket blurb, perhaps also to her publishers).

We can therefore conclude that Butler's so-called turn to ethics must not be taken as either condemnation or dismissal of her twenty-year project. Nonetheless, we must still insist on asking: *is it a concession?* What might Butler be giving up when, rather than patiently demonstrating the ethical and political stakes of the political ontology that has always animated her work, she instead seeks to use the language of 'moral philosophy' to prove her ethical mettle? What is lost when the textual resources, the animating framework, and the language of the argument all change? (And why, then, have many long-time devoted readers of Butler been so disappointed with this book?)

These questions prove particularly pertinent when one recalls what Butler herself has said about 'the turn to ethics' prior to the publication of this recent book. In an interview with William Connolly, published a few years before *Giving an Account*, Butler responded to a question about ethics in the following manner:

> I confess to worrying about the turn to ethics. ... I tend to think that ethics displaces from politics, and I suppose for me the use of power as a point of departure for a critical analysis is substantially different from an ethical framework.
>
> (Butler 2000b; cf. Lloyd 2008)

Where, then, has this worry gone? And can Butler 'turn to ethics' yet somehow avoid the displacement of politics? Do Butler's earlier concerns serve as a critique of her recent ostensible shift to ethics, or has she managed to make the turn in a way that avoids the pitfalls?

The following sections of this chapter will put forward a two-sided reading of Butler's *Giving an Account of Oneself* – picture this reading like one of those texts in translation that provides the original language on the left-hand page and the translation on the right. On the one side, and primarily, we will read Butler's text in an effort to demonstrate its consistency with her larger project and in an attempt to excavate her political ontology (including its ethical orientation and implications). On the other side, and less prominently, we will read Butler's text in order to trace the displacement of politics, to discover what may be lost in taking the subject of 'moral philosophy' as a central concern.

Moral philosophy and (the impossibility of) giving an account of oneself

The opening to this text is striking: Butler inquires 'how it might be possible to pose *the* question of moral philosophy' (Butler 2005: 3). She sees the question lodged within the title of this book – i.e. *'how can* one give, *how does* one give, an account of oneself' – as absolutely central to the domain of moral philosophy, a domain she has never before entered explicitly. On the one hand, 'giving an account of oneself' has always been central to Butler's project in that she has studied the *terms* in which any account must appear and through which any account must be given. These are the terms of gender and sexuality; this is the power of heteronormativity to shape one's account. On the other hand, Butler has never worked on this project using the texts of moral philosophy, and she has never described it using the framework of moral philosophy.

Thus the title, the sources and the initial framing of the argument all have important implications. Even though they do not mark a rupture in Butler's thinking, they are not arbitrary either, and thus they should not be ignored. Butler frames the discussions in all three chapters of the book with the title. She directs her energies toward the title and in so doing toward the questions, the problems, the history of moral philosophy. Her central author in this endeavour is Adorno. She cites him first (though she cites Foucault last) and places his text front and centre throughout the book. The shift to Adorno as a central theoretical resource for Butler holds significance, however, for reasons that far exceed categorisation (i.e. Adorno as 'moral theorist'). Adorno allows Butler to reframe questions that have been central to her since the beginning; Adorno is a resource from which Butler borrows in order to advance a position that is strikingly consistent over the course of her writings. Adorno makes it possible for Butler to *reformulate* crucial concerns from her recent writings; thus Butler has not somehow 'discovered' Adorno and seen the 'moral light'.[4]

Adorno's distinction between ethics and morality offers a perfect example of a resource that Butler uses to effect a two-way translation between her terms and those of more traditional moral theory. Butler reads the distinction, through Adorno, as follows: '*morality* [suggests] that any set of maxims or rules must be appropriated by individuals "in a living way" ... *ethics* [suggests] the broad contours of these rules and maxims' (Butler 2005: 5, citing Adorno 2001). Ethics, then, studies, analyses, perhaps even promulgates rules and maxims, but morality always considers the lived existence of those rules. This means that morality must also and always concern itself with the 'livability' of a rule or maxim. Here Butler articulates Adorno's ethics/morality distinction while at the same time translating his terms into her own conceptual framework. In her books from 2004, Butler introduces the notions of '(un)intelligibility' and 'the livable life'. These map, in their own way, quite nicely on to Butler's particular presentation of Adorno's account of the difference between morality and ethics.

Certain norms make life 'intelligible'; they are the conditions of possibility for the being appearing before us to be taken as human, to be recognised as a subject. Moreover – and as we will explore in a great deal more depth in Chapter 6 – certain other norms render one unintelligible, making it impossible for one to appear in this way (cf. Butler 2004a: 146; Butler 2004b: 30). Butler continues precisely this train of thought when she expounds on the effects of Adorno's distinction: 'an ethical norm that fails to offer a way to live or that turns out, within existing social conditions, to be impossible to appropriate has to become subject to critical revision' (Butler 2005: 5–6). And this argument demonstrates why both Butler and Adorno 'prefer', as it were, morality to ethics, since the critical revision enacted or performed upon ethical norms always proceeds by way of moral considerations – it centres on the questions of how an ethic could be *lived*, on how ethics may make life livable or unlivable. Ethics becomes violent,

Butler suggests, when it ignores moral conditions, that is, 'the conditions under which any ethics might be appropriated' (Butler 2005: 6). And, as we can see lucidly from Chapter 4, the violence referred to here is undoubtedly *normative violence.*

Butler frames the problem of how to 'appropriate' an ethic, how to square ethics with morality in the domain of intelligibility, as the problem of how to give an account of oneself. Butler herself brings the language of (un)intelligibility to bear: 'the question of ethics emerges precisely at the limits of our schemes of intelligibility' (Butler 2005: 21). Moral philosophy asks how, or *if*, we can give an account of ourselves, an account compatible with the norms of intelligibility. To make life livable at the limits of intelligibility will require an account of oneself that calls for ethical critique, that demands alteration of the norms that govern intelligibility.

Thus, 'giving an account of oneself' is never just that. Having initially, perhaps, disarmed her readers with a seemingly straightforward approach to the problems of moral philosophy, Butler has now altered the question in significant ways by showing that 'my' account is always linked to something much bigger than me (and this 'something' points toward relationality). Specifically, to give an account of oneself is to give an account *to* another and *in* a language that is not our own:

> An account of oneself is always given to another, whether conjured or existing, and this other establishes the scene of address as a more primary ethical relation than a reflexive effort to give an account of oneself [here we see the gesture toward ontology]. Moreover, the very terms by which we give an account, *by which we make ourselves intelligible* to ourselves and to others, are not of our making. They are social in character and they establish social norms.
>
> (Butler 2005: 21, emphasis added)

To give our account is to present ourselves to an other or others and to do so in an intelligible way, which means not only that the account must somehow be coherent but that we as human subjects must *cohere* in terms of the norms of intelligibility (Butler 1997a, 1997b; cf. Lloyd 2005a). To make ourselves intelligible means to *conform* to *prior* terms of intelligibility; the account proceeds within terms that both precede and exceed our use of them. In one sense this seems intuitive enough: my account has an addressee (even if only implied) and is given using the discourses available to me. However, in another sense, and as we will now demonstrate, these facets of giving an account prove quite radical.

They lead Butler, in the middle of her first chapter, to deconstruct the very title of her book. Butler rehearses Foucault's understanding of subjects as beings who exist only through the taking up of subject positions, where subject positions are (always and already) constituted and reconstituted by prior discursive practices. Butler paraphrases Foucault as follows: 'what I can "be," quite literally, is constrained in advance by a regime of truth that decides what will and will not be a recognizable form of being' (Butler 2005: 22). Butler describes the antecedent constraints on oneself: they manifest themselves whenever one attempts to give *any* account, but they most certainly appear whenever one offers an account of *oneself*. In this paraphrase of Foucault we see also the ontological entailments of Butler's argument (which we will discuss in more detail below), since the account-giving broaches the question of being. Butler wants to extend Foucault's argument and link it more directly to her project on moral philosophy. This entails increased consideration of 'the other' (neglected by Foucault, says Butler) to whom one must give an account, and it demands fuller understanding of those norms within which one does one's accounting (Butler 2004b). Foucault proves essential to Butler's argument, however, in that he sees the reflexive relation between any challenge to a 'regime of truth' (what Butler would call the social norms that constitute conditions of intelligibility) and the subject position from which one makes such a challenge (what Butler would call the conditions for a livable life). To put it in starker terms: when one calls a set of norms into question one always runs the risk of calling the self into question.

This brings us to Butler's most dramatic conclusion. Ultimately, it seems 'an account of oneself' is precisely that which cannot be furnished by the subject. The language in which we give our account will always disorient us, will always decentre us and undermine the sovereign authority with which we seek to make our account. Thus an account of *ourselves* proves to be the most difficult account to provide. Butler contends that once I recognise that the language of accounting is never mine to possess, then I find myself 'dispossessed by the language that I offer' (Butler 2005: 26).

There will always be an unbridgeable gap between the self and the identity within discourse that it claims; this is the gap between the individual that we can never know and the 'I' who speaks to us in language (Butler 1997a). Once we 'make out' this gap (we can never fully locate it or take its measure) then we clearly see that 'any effort to "give an account of oneself"' will have to fail in order to approach being true' (Butler 2005: 42; same formulation as Butler 2000b). Here Butler not only completes her logic by showing that 'an account of oneself' names the impossible but also embraces the performative contradiction by saying that the account must fail so that it may 'approach being true'. The failure of the account derives not from a weakness within it. The failure proves systematic, and necessarily so. *The failure is constitutive.* The 'I' is that which, by definition, could never give its own account. The 'I' is performatively invoked prior to any story that it might tell about itself. The 'I' is enacted and put to work well before it can give its account; thus the 'I' can never fully account for itself, can never capture this excess in which 'it' is precisely that which is doing the accounting. Butler explains: 'I am giving an account of myself, but there is no account to be given when it comes to the formation of this speaking "I" who would narrate its life'. And then she concludes: 'the "I" ruins its own story, contrary to its best intentions' (Butler 2005: 67). Thus we can see clearly why Butler *positively adopts* the performative contradiction in her earlier formulation: performative contradiction proves intrinsic to the fundamental structure of 'giving an account of oneself'.[5] The 'I' must always be presupposed before it can be proven; its proof always fails because of this prior presupposition.

From this logic one must conclude that 'giving an account of oneself' cannot name a project to be positively filled in or fleshed out. Unsurprisingly, the book contains neither Butler's own account of herself nor her instructions to others on how to give their account. 'Giving an account of oneself' names, instead, an impossibility. But it must do more than that. Of what is this impossibility constitutive? What limits does it impose? But, more importantly, what are its productive effects? These are the questions we turn to next.

Butler's ontology: the primacy of relationality

Clearly, the notion of 'giving an account', the theme that drives this book throughout, proves productive for Butler in that it links her project to more traditional concerns of ethics while translating some of her conceptualisations into the language of moral philosophy. In addition, and as we want to demonstrate here, the very constitutive impossibility of 'giving an account of oneself'[6] points, for Butler, to a particular ontology. This ontology, in turn, forms the ground for Butler's most important contribution to ethics and moral theory. Drawing on other sources in political theory that work more explicitly with ontological conceptions, and drawing directly from Butler's recent arguments, we will draw out a Butlerian ontology centred on what she repeatedly, perhaps insistently, names 'the primacy of relationality'.

Stephen White has devoted the past decade to a project on ontology in political theory (White 1997, 2000, 2005). He has even used the earlier writings of Butler as a case study – a site for working out the terms of his theory of ontology while assessing Butler's arguments within the framework of that theory (White 1999). White seeks to demonstrate that the conditions of our 'post-metaphysical' world require a rejection of 'strong ontology' – claims for foundationalist essentialism, denial of human finitude or preservation of the sovereign subject. In a move that we want wholly to support, White insists that we cannot do away with ontology altogether. He goes further, however – in a move about which we remain much more ambivalent – calling for the affirmation of 'weak ontologies', which embrace two tenets: 'all fundamental conceptualizations of self, other and world are contestable, and ... such conceptions are nevertheless unavoidable' (White 1999: 156). White leverages this starting point to accomplish two distinct but related tasks: he first yokes together a diverse set of contemporary theorists (from Kateb to Connolly to Butler) under the banner of weak ontology, and he then evaluates the work of these theorists according to the terms of a metric that 'weak ontology' supplies.

While White insists on weak ontology over strong ontology, he goes on (at the risk of mixing his metaphors badly) to make a second distinction: 'just as with soups', says White, a rich, thick ontology is better than a thin one (White 1999: 158). According to White, most post-structuralist thinkers fall short of certain ethico-political standards because their desire to reject metaphysical foundationalism leads them to produce a rather thin broth of ontology. White finds Butler's thought exemplary for his account. When Butler refuses to 'thicken' her ontology – when, for example, according to White, she refuses to give an account of human finitude – she opens herself up to the standard critiques;[7] when, by contrast, she theorises 'loss' as a condition of being, she enables 'a contestatory ethos of self-cultivation and political commitment' (White 1999: 177). In other words, her thin ontology cannot sustain an ethics or a politics, while her thick ontology can. As he does, then, with so many of the contemporary theorists that he addresses within his 'weak ontology' project, with Butler White simultaneously *identifies her as* a (potential) weak ontologist and *calls on her to become* a more thoroughgoing and consistent weak ontologist – by enriching her ontological soup.

We would contest whether Butler is as keen to reject ontology as White sometimes makes her out to be.[8] As others have duly noted, the problem with White's account lies in the tendency of its generous affirmation to result in a form of disengagement (Dean 2005). As we clearly indicated above, White aims to produce a 'theory of' ontology, a type of meta-level analysis that can categorise thick and thin ontological works, distinguish between them and sort them out. The problem, as we see it, is that such an account does very little ontological or political work of its own. White's reading of Butler seems generally sound and sometimes certainly illuminating, but White's concern lies much more with seeing how well Butler measures up to the criteria of weak ontology – and how helpful her project can be in elucidating the framework of weak ontology – than it does with engaging with the ontological or political concerns that animate Butler's writings. Therefore, while White's project proves very helpful in shedding light on the importance of ontology (especially as regards Butler), it does not take us much further than that.

Instead of a survey of ontological commitments taken from above, what is needed is an engagement with those commitments at the level of ontology. To be fair, Butler herself has pursued those engagements much more fully in writings published after White's most important work on weak ontology. In *Precarious Life* (Butler 2004a) Butler writes of a dependency that lies at the heart of the human condition; she repeatedly describes the human 'exposure to violence' and our primary vulnerability to others (cf. Watkins forthcoming). Here we hear a lucid account of human being, and we see the emergence of the language of ontology. In an interview given at the start of the Iraq War, Butler describes the ontological condition as 'the general state of fragility and physical vulnerability that people – as humans – live in' (Butler 2003). It might at first seem odd that Butler feels the need to modify the word 'people' with the phrase 'as humans', but this awkward elaboration gestures toward ontology. 'People – as humans' might be heard to echo Heidegger's use of *Dasein* ('there-being') in the place of 'man'; in both cases the shift in language urges a shift from the ontic to the ontological.[9]

The explicit language of ontology flashes more frequently in *Giving an Account*; more importantly, a lucid set of ontological claims (ones that will animate and nourish Butler's conception of ethics) begins to emerge here as well. The argument of the book finally gets underway when Butler turns to a reading of Foucault's own 'turn' to ethics. Butler concludes that reading with a maxim in Greek and French: 'there is no *poeisis* without *assujettisement*'. Butler translates for us: 'there is no making of oneself outside a mode of subjectivation' (Butler 2005: 17). This contention implies an ontological account, since it suggests a fundamental relation between the possibility of human agency, on the one hand, and a certain understanding of the human condition, on the other. Butler herself uses the language of ontology to describe this relation, first when she refers to the 'ontological horizon within which subjects come to be' and later when she quotes Foucault on a 'mode of being' and its link to a 'moral goal' (Butler 2005: 17, 18).

Butler wants to show that a theory of the subject as 'ungrounded', as opaque to itself, does not – contrary to the intuitive assumptions of a linear or foundationalist account – lead to a disavowal of responsibility. It does not lead us to vacate the territory of ethics. To prove this, Butler must build an alternative ontological account and link it to a distinct moral theory. In her words, this requires 'showing how a theory of subject formation that acknowledges the limits of self-knowledge can serve a conception of ethics, and indeed, responsibility' (Butler 2005: 19). What would it mean, though, to 'acknowledge the limits of self-knowledge' as an ethico-political tactic? Is this just another attempt by Butler to 'play' with the language of ethics without actually doing ethics? Is it another variation on her consistent theme, telling us that a recognition of the constraints on subjectivity does not do away with but rather enables agency?

We want to maintain that, in one sense, yes, this is indeed another attempt to express an argument that Butler has made consistently going back at least to her well-known essay 'Contingent Foundations' – originally given as a conference paper in 1990 and published in 1991. There, Butler contended provocatively that 'the constituted character of the subject is the very precondition of its agency' (Butler 1995a: 46). Butler has always insisted that the limits to the sovereign subject do not translate into limits on agency. Here, she appears to turn that argument into a new-found concern for ethical responsibility. However, our argument is that Butler's critique of sovereign agency has always been bound up with a set of ethical concerns, and this is why there is no radical turn here, why this is not really the long-awaited answer to Butler's critics or a filling in of normative grounds.

Nonetheless, this transformation of an older claim comes coupled with a new set of arguments, because the assertions about the limits of self-knowledge are twinned to a much more robust ontological account – an account that can 'serve a conception of ethics'. To shore up this contention, it may prove prudent to look outside Butler's framework, since other writers have convincingly made a case for linking the limits of the sovereign subject to ethico-political concerns. The recent work of Patchen Markell proves exemplary on this point. Markell writes consistently against what he calls 'sovereign agency'. In applying the concept of sovereignty to individuals rather than states,[10] Markell attempts to capture the idea of 'an independent, self-determining agent, characterized by what Hannah Arendt calls "uncompromising self-sufficiency and mastership"' (Markell 2003: 11; quoting Arendt 1958: 179). 'Sovereign agency' goes beyond the notion of a sovereign subject (autonomous, isolated); it gets at the idea of a wilful subject, one that masters its action, controls its fate, predicts its future. Markell seeks to prove that – despite the fact that it largely eschews the 'sovereign subject' – 'the politics of recognition' harbours the latent goal of attaining or preserving sovereign agency. The politics of recognition rejects a liberal contract model of sovereignty based upon individual choice, but resurrects sovereign agency nonetheless by grounding it in knowledge. Markell writes: 'the ideal of recognition ... preserves ... the aspiration to be able to act independently, without experiencing life among others as a source of vulnerability, or as a site of possible alienation or self-loss' (Markell 2003: 12). And in this account one can already hear echoes of Butler's repeated refrain in her post-9/11 writings – her insistence on our primary vulnerability to others, on our exposure to potential violence.

As an alternative to the politics of recognition Markell proposes a 'politics of acknowledgement'. Crucially, however, the 'acknowledgement' that lies at the heart of this political theory is *not* an acknowledgement of the other. It is an acknowledgement relating to oneself, an acknowledgement of human finitude within the human condition of plurality (Markell 2003: 35). This, then, is political theory as political ontology (cf. Cavarero 2002: 513). Markell himself embraces this framing of his project, and, in the face of criticisms of exactly this point, he has recently rigorously defended the centrality of ontology to his political project (Markell 2006). Markell defines ontology in a way that already inflects it toward the political register: 'an implicit or explicit interpretation of the fundamental conditions of life in the social and political world, the kinds of things that exist [in that world], and the range of possibilities that [that world] bears' (Markell 2003: 195).

It should be clear from this definition that Markell seeks to use ontology in a way quite distinct from philosophical or other treatments of ontology – treatments that might take ontology as a separate subfield of study devoted to abstract meditations on being or so-called 'first principles'. In inquiring into the 'fundamental conditions of life', particularly the fundamentally intersubjective nature of the human condition, ontology always already directs itself to political concerns. Markell makes this connection explicit in his recent defence of his ontological project. He describes what we might loosely call his ontological 'method' as follows:

> This is an engaged, interpretive approach to ontological issues, which folds ontology back into history and practice rather than serving as [their] ground, and which stakes the persuasiveness of an ontological perspective on its capacity to illuminate a range of different concrete situations.
>
> (Markell 2006: 30)

Here Markell references in a footnote White's work on weak ontology, citing not only White's use of the term 'fold' but also White's concept of ontology as an inspiration to Markell's own. Placing to one side the importance of acknowledging scholarly debts, we would submit that the differences between their two approaches to political ontology prove stark. Both make a certain case for the centrality of ontology to ethico-political concerns, but Markell's resonates quite differently than White's. Above, we criticised White for remaining above the fray of politics, for using his 'strong' and 'weak' categories to assess political ontologies but not engaging in political work himself. Markell's own ontological engagements provide further support for our previous claims. His is not a political theory *of* ontology, but political ontology *as political theory.* Of course, according to the general account of political ontology that we are trying to draw out here there really cannot be a political ontology that is not a political theory. An ontological account brings with it, necessarily, a set of unavoidable political claims. Our formulation here therefore serves to emphasise this point (by making it redundantly), but it also seeks to emphasise the difference between doing political ontology (as Markell does) and merely offering a meta-theory of ontology (as White does).

Markell fills in the content of his political ontology – that is, he draws out the contours of his politics of acknowledgement – as follows: 'acknowledgment is directed at the basic conditions of one's existence and activity, including, crucially, the *limits* of "identity" as a ground of action, limits which arise out of constitutive vulnerability to the unpredictable reactions and responses of others' (Markell 2003: 36). In moving from the limits of identity as a ground for action, to our fundamental exposure to others, Markell not only provides a clear statement of his political ontology but also offers the beginnings of a genealogy of Butler's work. After all, Butler's recent notion of 'primary vulnerability' derives from her earlier arguments against certain visions of feminist politics, in which she insisted that the identity 'woman' would not serve as the ground of political action. In *Giving an Account* Butler continues to develop this narrative, and as she does so we suggest that she also lays out her own political ontology (one that resonates strikingly with Markell's).

In the last half of her opening chapter, Butler's ontology begins to take proper form. Here one can discern a significant, if subtle, shift in Butler's language. She moves from a discourse – common in most of her early works (and particularly in the *Psychic Life of Power*) – that mixes together the terms of Foucault with those of psychoanalytic theory, on to a new and distinct language of ontology. Butler marshals this alternative vocabulary in order to stake a claim for the primacy of relationality:

> The opacity of the subject may be a consequence of its being conceived as a relational being. Perhaps ... self-preservation is not the highest goal, and the defense of a narcissistic point of view not the most urgent psychic need. That we are impinged upon primarily and against our will is the sign of a vulnerability and a beholdenness that we cannot will away. [It is the sign of] a difficult and intractable, even sometimes unbearable relationality.
>
> (Butler 2005: 20, 100)

The limits to self-knowledge thereby do not derive from a fault within the self. They cannot be overcome. The primacy of relationality occurs both against our will and in such a way that we cannot will it away. Thus the pursuit of sovereign agency can only ever fail, since wilful self-mastery can never be achieved. The alternative to the project of trying to know the self that cannot be known lies in articulating the very relationality that *always* limits our capacity for self-knowledge. This entails an *affirmation* of the other – an other who both cannot be known and who makes full self-knowledge impossible (Butler 2005: 31). Butler characterises this relationality not within a particular historical/political time or space, but as a *fundamental dependency* on the other' (Butler 2005: 33, emphasis added).

Within Butler's emerging ontology, the human being is a being exposed to others, *essentially vulnerable*. Butler places '*this* exposure that I am' at the centre of her account of the human condition (Butler 2005: 33). Again, this apparently awkward way of putting matters actually serves an important purpose as it furthers the difficult move toward the ontological. We call that move difficult, since any attempt at simplifying ontological claims – of formulating them in less awkward plainer language – will always run the risk of expressing those notions in a way that reduces them to the level of the ontic. Hence Butler writes: '*this* exposure that I am' – a formulation that does not describe a particular relation but describes the human condition *as relational*. She writes: '*we are constituted in relationality*: implicated, beholden, derived, sustained by a social world that is beyond us and before us' (Butler 2005: 64, emphasis added; cf. Watkins 2008). Thus our contingent dependency on the other is not itself contingent; it is ontologically fundamental. Moreover, to call such contingency 'ontologically fundamental' means also to insist that such dependency is not universal in the sense that it transcends history or appears the same always and everywhere; the ontological must not be confused with the transcendental.

Thus 'giving an account' is always something we do, something we are called on to do; it is not an a priori structure. As Butler begins to fill out her ontological account she simultaneously shifts her description: now, giving an account is always 'giving an account *for another*' (Butler 2005: 35, emphasis added). And our relation to the other cannot be translated into the simple ontic presence of another autonomous subject. The relation always proves more fundamental than either of the potential subjects (the 'you' or the 'I'). Thus Butler will suggest that the 'I' comes to be only in its very address to 'you'. We call this a *primary relationality*, because that language evokes an ontological condition that undoes any pretensions to sovereign agency.

In elaborating Butler's ontology of relationality, it may prove helpful to contrast it with a much more well-known idea in political thought, one quite famous within feminist theory. Butler's account differs fundamentally from, yet sounds a bit like, the notion that some human beings (perhaps women, perhaps caregivers) may prove to be more 'relational' than others. This argument seeks to conceive of (some) individuals not as autonomous and separate beings who are distant and detached from one another, but as beings whose relations with others could never be exhausted by the concept of consent. Upon this conception, certain authors have made the case for fundamental differences among men and women due to differences in childhood development, and based on this they have described the different 'moral voice' of women compared to men (Gilligan 1982). Other writers have advanced more subtle and significant arguments for a full-blown alternative moral theory based upon the ethic of care (Tronto 1993).

But even in the case of Joan Tronto's deft articulation of an ethic of care, her understanding of 'relationality' bears little or no resemblance to Butler's. In Tronto's understanding of caring, the 'other' is always a concrete, knowable and intelligible other. She writes: 'that "others" matter is the most difficult moral quality to establish in practice' (Tronto 1993: 130). Butler, however, does not focus her attention on intelligible others (those who would then be cared for, be granted rights, be recognised), but on the very processes that render 'them' unintelligible. To put this another way, and to once again borrow Heidegger's language in an effort to get to the level of ontology: Tronto's account concerns itself solely with actual 'beings' and not with the Being of those beings. Butler's 'relationality' not only precedes but also *undoes* any so-called 'ethic of care'. Thus, in describing Butler's political ontology by way of highlighting the 'primacy of relationality', we are at the same time, and in no uncertain terms, rejecting any variant of *individualised* ontology.[11]

As Butler puts it, 'I am mired, given over, and even the word *dependency* cannot do the job here' (Butler 2005: 82). Dependency proves inadequate to capture this ontology of primary relationality since neither subject depends on the other; rather, both depend upon the relation. Thus no individual could be rightly described as 'relational' (or even 'non-relational') within the emerging terms of Butler's political ontology, since *relationality precedes the subject*. Butler aims to produce a thoroughgoing, relentless critique of sovereign agency, not merely to question the extent to which 'consent' can capture ontic human relations. And thus, she writes, provocatively: 'In the beginning *I am my relation to you*' (Butler 2005: 81). This is a productive oversimplification on Butler's part, especially since the language used here resonates easily on the ontic register. The ontological formulation would prove both less reductive and more obscure: in the beginning there is relationality. Or there is no beginning; always and already, there are networks of relations, there are norms, there are discursive practice in which and only through which I may find myself, but which will always prevent me from knowing myself. Butler's own more ontological account goes like this:

> The self that I am yet to be (at the point where grammar does not yet permit an 'I') is at the outset enthralled, even if to a scene of violence, an abandonment, a destitution, a mechanism of life support, since it is, for better or worse, the support without which I cannot be, upon which my very being depends, which my very being, fundamentally and with an irreducible ambiguity, *is*.
>
> (Butler 2005: 81)

Here, once more, one sees the critique of sovereign agency, one witnesses a fundamental rejection of the subject who would be 'the master of its own destiny' (a favourite cliché of professional athletes). And this argument also demonstrates clearly that the ontology Butler lays out can never be individualised. Relationality could never be the possession of a subject, nor could it translate into an ethic of care.

In the interview she gave during the first few days of the Iraq War, Butler contends that 9/11 brought to light a primary vulnerability, a primary dependency beyond dependency, that the militarised response of the war in Iraq seeks (vainly) to deny. An alternative task would be 'to figure out what we can do in light of that very condition of vulnerability' (Butler 2003). The first step in this project, as shown repeatedly above, consists in an acknowledgement of relationality, of the primary tie that binds us to others (Butler 2005: 40). We see, then, a consistent and persistent return to '*the primacy of relationality*' that lies at the heart of Butler's ontology (Butler 2005: 53, emphasis added). Moreover, this ontology always holds an implicit ethical orientation, one that Butler begins to explore as she makes the transition between the second and third chapters of the book. She writes: 'there is, as it were, a sociality at the basis of the "I" and its finitude from which one cannot – *and ought not to* – escape' (Butler 2005: 75, emphasis added). White urged Butler to make a clear case for human finitude; here, she does much more. She not only acknowledges our finitude but also goes on to claim that we should not seek to overcome it. This case illustrates once more what, following Markell, we might call Butler's critique of sovereign agency. Furthermore, within this ontological critique lies Butler's ethical vision: the forceful articulation of Butler's ontology of primary relationality leads her directly to a radical account of ethical responsibility. We now turn to that account.

Butler's ethics: responsibility

Butler opens the third and final chapter of *Giving an Account* by laying out the stakes of the book in the starkest terms. She makes plain the necessity of using the ontological account of the first two chapters as a bridge to the central question of ethics that she wishes to tackle. Thus, in Foucauldian style she begins with a question to herself: 'according to the kind of theory we have been pursuing here, what will responsibility look like?' To respond to this query, she says, 'the very meaning of responsibility must be rethought' (Butler 2005: 83). What, then, does responsibility mean? What meanings has it been given by moral philosophy, and how might one use Butler's ontology in order to transform its meaning?

Above all, Butler seeks to overturn the understanding of responsibility as *individual accountability*.[12] It is in direct response to the question of holding ourselves accountable for our actions that Butler demands a new meaning for responsibility (Butler 2005: 83). This is why she places 'giving an account' at the centre of the book: it provides a pivot point around which she hopes to transform the meaning of responsibility. How, she asks, might 'giving an account' be more than, or other to, a simple taking of responsibility for one's actions? This rhetorical and ethical question pulls together into the same frame two typically separate strands of social and political thought – one playing out the issue of moral responsibility and one exploring the narrative production of the subject. The challenge for Butler – one she sometimes fails to live up to – will be to sew these strands together successfully. She will make the attempt by way of *reading together* distinct theoretical resources. Here we argue that when reading Nietzsche and Foucault together Butler misses her mark of transforming the meaning of responsibility, but that she strikes quite close to her target with the reading she offers of Adorno and Levinas.

In the first chapter, Butler opens the first substantive section of the book with a short reading of Nietzsche. In chapter 3, Butler ends the book with a long reading of Foucault. In both of these interpretations she suggests that Foucault takes up and continues the project that Nietzsche never completed: Foucault moves from the production of a subject *by* history to an understanding of the *self-reflexivity* of the subject *within* history (Butler 2005: 16–18, 133). Butler hopes to link the Nietzschean understanding of a responsible subject with the Foucauldian turn to ethics and accountability.

This seems a laudable, if daring, project to undertake. However, and as we will show below, Butler fails to pull it off, and for this reason the reading together of Nietzsche and Foucault fails to carry Butler's project forward. The attempt to force Foucault and, especially, Nietzsche into the frame of moral philosophy only tends to dull the political force of their historically situated and politically contextualised critiques.

Perhaps in order to make the linkage to Foucault possible, Butler offers a narrow and constraining reading of Nietzsche. Not only does she seem to miss the point of Nietzsche's arguments about morality and responsibility, but she construes them in ways that are non-productive, i.e. this is not a creative misreading. Butler summarises Nietzsche's argument in the *Genealogy* by saying that he 'offers a controversial account of how we become reflective at all about our actions and how we become positioned to give an account of what we have done' (Butler 2005: 10). This characterisation of Nietzsche's work makes it seem as if he is working exactly within Butler's project (hence her opening the book with it). She goes on to say that on Nietzsche's account 'we become conscious of ourselves' and we take responsibility for our actions only after suffering has occurred. The core of her interpretation reads as follows:

> It is in the interest of meting out a just punishment to the one responsible for an injurious action that the question is posed and that the subject in question comes to question him or herself. *'Punishment,'* Nietzsche tells us, *is 'the making of a memory.'* The question posits the self as a causative force, and *it also models a specific mode of responsibility.* In asking whether we caused such suffering, we are being asked by an established authority not only to avow a causal link between our own actions and the suffering that follows but also to take responsibility for these actions and their effects.
>
> (Butler 2005: 10; quoting Nietzsche 1967: essay II, section 13; emphasis added).[13]

Based on this reading, Butler can find her way to a number of conclusions about Nietzsche's argument. Butler asserts that 'I begin to give an account, if Nietzsche is right, because someone has asked me to' (Butler 2005: 11). This means that the question of responsibility depends upon a prior accusation of blame and that moral accountability arises out of fear (Butler 2005: 11). Butler's criticisms follow naturally from these conclusions, and lead her, quite logically, to take her leave of Nietzsche. First, according to Butler, we can conclude *from Nietzsche* that 'giving an account takes a narrative form' but, quite obviously, 'Nietzsche does not fully take into account the scene of address' (Butler 2005: 10, 11). Second, collapsing her reading of Nietzsche into the frame of Freud, Butler argues that one might be forced to 'arrive at a fully cynical view of morality and conclude that human conduct that seeks to follow norms of prescriptive value is motivated less by any desire to do good than by a terrorised fear of punishment and its injurious effects' (Butler 2005: 16).

As one step within her own project to build up a positive account of ethics, we would hardly wish to contest Butler's decision to move away from Nietzsche. Nietzsche, it is no doubt true, does not wish to give his readers supportive reasons 'to follow norms of prescriptive value'. However, we must query Butler's decision to start with Nietzsche in the first place. And this leads us to ask why, in doing so, does Butler drastically distort Nietzsche's arguments concerning responsibility? We question Butler's reading of Nietzsche, then, because we worry it leads her away from the very work on responsibility that she herself says will provide the ethical payoff of the book; we offer this critique to demonstrate the displacement of politics about which Butler herself had previously fretted. Butler makes a number of missteps that take her in this wrong trajectory.

First, Butler *imposes* the framework of 'giving an account' and 'scenes of address' onto Nietzsche's writing. Nietzsche says nothing at all about the 'narrative form' that 'giving an account' would take; despite this, Butler presents her reading of the *Genealogy* as if these were Nietzsche's own terms. Second, Butler remains focused throughout this book on how *I* give an account, how *I* am implicated in responsibility. However, Nietzsche shows little or no interest in this area, both in the *Genealogy* and elsewhere. For this reason, Butler's opening sentence in her interpretation of Nietzsche proves very difficult to make sense of. She speaks of Nietzsche's 'account of how we become reflective at all about our actions and how we become positioned to give an account of what we have done'. But Nietzsche's project in the *Genealogy* is not to pose the question of how to give an account, of how to become responsible for our actions; his goal is to challenge that very notion, to offer a historical critique of the entire idea of 'accounting for our actions' or 'taking responsibility for them'. *This* notion of responsibility belongs to 'slave morality'; it is the notion he wishes to reject, and from which he insists that he and those of his readers who are 'free spirits' should take their distance.

Butler seems to have lost all sense of the *pathos of distance* that drives Nietzsche's writings. This may be a product of the fact that Butler only ever addresses brief sections from the second essay of the *Genealogy*, failing to place it in the context of either the book as a whole or his larger project. This project is not to build a moral account, but *to question the value of values,* to offer a critique of moral values. And this, in turn, may help to explain how Butler can take a description that Nietzsche himself wishes to subject to the harshest critical scrutiny, and present it in a neutral light. Nietzsche steadfastly rejects the idea that an individual should account for his or her actions, or take responsibility for them. Perhaps another reading of the famous parable of the lambs and birds of prey will help to focus this point. In the first essay, Nietzsche gives his initial sketch of the historical transvaluation of values. This is the shift from a system of good/bad –

wherein good means strong, noble, fierce and savage, and bad simply means its opposite (base, common) – to a system of evil/good. In the new system, 'evil' becomes the primary term and is applied precisely to the strong and noble, while good then retroactively attaches to all those who 'refuse' to act out of strength – and to do so, Nietzsche tells us, precisely *because they are weak.*

The parable of the sheep and the birds of prey carries critical force because it captures three crucial dimensions of Nietzsche's historical story: (1) it reveals, from the perspective of the sheep, the logic behind the idea to declare strength evil; (2) it shows, from the perspective of the birds of prey, how ridiculous it would be to accept such a perspective; (3) it demonstrates the enormous historical force that would be the achievement of a transvaluation, a transvaluation wherein the birds of prey came to accept the terms and valuations proposed by the sheep. Nietzsche writes:

> That lambs dislike great birds of prey does not seem strange: only it gives no ground for reproaching these birds of prey for bearing off little lambs. And if the lambs say among themselves: 'these birds of prey are evil; and whoever is least like a bird of prey, but rather its opposite, a lamb – would he not be good?' there is no reason to find fault with this institution of an ideal, except perhaps that the birds of prey might view it a little ironically and say: '*we* don't dislike them at all, these good little lambs; we even love them: *nothing is more tasty than a tender lamb*'.
>
> (Nietzsche 1967: essay 1, section 13, final emphasis added)

Nietzsche has two senses of responsibility, the first of which we see here: he finds logical, powerful and ridiculous (all at the same time) the idea that the strong should be held accountable, should be made responsible for actions that express their strength. The transvaluation of values both brings about and depends upon this concept of responsibility. By making a subject accountable for its actions one then has the grounds to reproach expressions of strength. Nietzsche, therefore, *never* proposes the idea of 'giving an account of oneself' as something that 'we' – Nietzsche's readers, his 'new philosophers', his 'free spirits – should do. It is the weak, the lambs, who recommend *to us* the idea of giving an account of ourselves. To accept that proposal is to lose the pathos of distance, to be reduced to the mediocrity of the timid European.

Nietzsche therefore rejects the very approach to responsibility that Butler ascribes to him. But we are not setting out to reproach Butler merely for the sake of labelling her a poor reader of Nietzsche. What we are calling her misreading of Nietzsche proves significant to *her* work on responsibility, and this for two reasons. First, Butler fails to attend to Nietzsche's own alternative account of responsibility, his proposal to resignify the term outside the context of the slave morality's effort to force us to 'give an account'.[14]

And, second, by doing so Butler limits her project when she turns away from Nietzsche and toward Foucault. Butler closes the book with a 25-page section on Foucault, containing an extended reading of Foucault's work on giving a critical account of oneself. It is a powerful, lucid and we would say brilliant reading that eloquently and powerfully ties Foucault's earlier writings on the history of reason to his latest writings on care of the self, critique and *parrhesia*. However, the intelligence and persuasive force of this reading will not allow it to overcome one crucial weakness: despite appearing in the long concluding chapter of the book, the chapter that Butler clearly describes at the outset as devoted to *rethinking* 'the meaning of responsibility', this reading of Foucault says close to nothing about responsibility.

Our claim, then, is that in her effort to formulate a new concept of responsibility – a concept at the core of her development of a moral philosophy – the resources of Nietzsche and Foucault often prove less helpful than they should. Our suggestion, in turn, is that the two problems are linked: were Butler to provide a more subtle and attentive reading of Nietzsche, she might be able to develop Nietzsche's alternative thinking of responsibility within her insightful writing on Foucault. Nietzsche's idea of 'responsibility' as the achievement of a strong, free spirit whose very autonomy consists in rejecting the 'morality of mores'[15] might be worked into Foucault's account of ethics as *necessarily* bound up with critique (see Butler 2005: 124; Foucault 1989: 254). The reading established here indicates a possible alternative trajectory for the development of a theory of responsibility that takes its cues from Nietzsche but builds the argument through Foucault. Butler often implies that this is her exact goal, but her reading of Nietzsche ignores his novel ideas on responsibility while her reading of Foucault simply fails to fold responsibility back into the account.

Our critical reading here does not aim to undermine the project of *Giving an Account of Oneself*; our thesis is not that Butler fails entirely to rethink responsibility. Instead, we are making two weaker claims. First, we are showing that the resources of Nietzsche and Foucault are not fully mobilised in this book toward the end of rethinking responsibility, but that there is an untapped potential within those sources. Second, by tracing these paths *as dead ends* in this book, we are arguing that her account here proves somewhat limited. This limitation is one of the pitfalls of the so-called 'turn to ethics'; it emerges in the form of the displacement of politics that Butler warned her future self about. Butler misses precisely Nietzsche's historical account of power in the form of his comments on liberal institutions; by forcing his broad-ranging remarks into the narrow and constrictive frame of 'moral philosophy', Butler blunts the political force of her own project. Finally, however, we make a third claim by insisting that Butler does *begin* the project of rethinking responsibility and that she does so quite effectively.

From 'responsibility for' to 'responsibility to'

This effective and productive work appears in the form of her readings of Adorno and Levinas. Here, we find Butler's attention focused specifically on the concept of responsibility, and thus it is here that we see emerge a promising line of argument – one that follows through on the bold claims with which Butler opens chapter 3. In meditating on the problem of responsibility, Butler turns to a topic that Connolly has recently argued is absolutely central to our political concerns in a post-9/11 world: 9/11 powerfully highlights the 'problem of evil' that has always haunted ethico-political concerns, and this 'problem of evil' can be described as a drive toward fundamentalism that animates a part of every 'existential faith' – a term Connolly uses in order to blur intentionally the line between secular beliefs and religious ones (Connolly 2005: 35, 27). The discourse of 'responsibility' dovetails with the problem of evil as follows: in the face of tragedy there appears a drive to make evil the responsibility of an other, and to sanction acts of vengeance in the name of vanquishing that evil. Connolly himself does not proffer a distinct, alternative concept of responsibility, but his project runs in parallel to Butler's because both seek to overcome the 'problem of evil': Connolly, by seeking to attenuate this drive to evil; Butler, by reconceptualising responsibility.

The seeds of Butler's theory of responsibility have been sown in the same soil as Connolly's recent work on pluralism. Connolly opens his book by telling his own 9/11 story (where he was on the day, what he did, what he felt). In the interview given at the start of the Iraq War, Butler articulates the following question: 'What are the conditions under which we find that we are responsive to other human beings?' (Butler 2003). It is in trying to answer this question that Butler develops the ontological account one finds in the first two chapters of *Giving an Account*. Butler consistently ties her theory of responsibility to this ontology; hence her claim: 'I cannot think the problem of responsibility alone, in isolation from the other' (Butler 2005: 84). The primacy of relationality undergirds every logical step in Butler's rethinking of responsibility.

Of course, if one wishes to 'think responsibility in relation to the other' the obvious move is to call on Levinas, and Butler sees no reason not to make it. Levinas insists throughout his writings on a point similar to the one that Butler often repeats: to ask after the subject or self who chooses or acts, we must first ask after the formation of that subject, the conditions of its possibility (Butler 2005: 86). Our standard approach to responsibility seeks to discover how, why or in what way an agent may be responsible *for* the actions or choices that he or she makes. But this means that a typical theory of responsibility does not start at the beginning: it takes up its line of questioning supposedly 'after' the formation of the subject. However, as Butler and Levinas would both contend: the 'formation of the subject' is never a project that can be artificially brought to a close or that can naturally reach an end. 'Subject formation' names an ongoing process, one thoroughly dependent upon reiteration, one always opening on to a future that has no end. This means that to ask how or why a subject will take responsibility *for* its actions is to occlude inquiry into the *prior and continual* formation of the subject.

Butler would certainly say something like the following: I *act*, and my actions are somehow *mine*, but the conditions of my acting are never of my own making. Thus one must surely be considered responsible for one's actions, but that sense of responsibility cannot be allowed to exhaust its meanings. If we allow 'responsibility for' to comprehend our sense of responsibility, then we implicitly deny the truth of the claim that we did not create the conditions of our acting. If responsibility means 'responsibility for', then we pretend that the self is 'ready made' – pre-formed and pre-packed and ready to act (Butler 1995a: 46; Butler 2005: 97). Yet we know that there is no 'ready-made' self, as this is an idea upon which diverse strands of social and political thought from the last 50 years all seem to converge. This is why we must rethink the meaning of responsibility.

What if we were to relocate responsibility at the level of subject formation? What if were to consider the ontological roots of responsibility? To entertain these imaginative possibilities would be to reject the narrow account of responsibility as 'responsibility *for*' and to open it up to a wider sheaf of meanings. Levinas's writings assist greatly in this process of 'opening up'. In this vein, Butler writes:

> We are used to thinking that we can be responsible only for that which we have done, that which can be traced to our intentions, our deeds. Levinas explicitly rejects this view, claiming that tethering responsibility to freedom is an error. *I become responsible by virtue of what is done to me, but I do not become responsible for what is done to me.* ... I am *not* primarily responsible by virtue of my actions, but by virtue of my relation to the Other that is established at the level of my primary and irreversible susceptibility.
>
> (Butler 2005: 88, first emphasis added)

This passage must be clarified by stressing that 'what is done to me' points not to the ontic acts *of* others but to a primary ontological *relation to* others (or the Other, in Levinas's account). 'What is done to me' names 'my' fundamental dependency on and exposure to others – with *my* placed in quotation marks to emphasise that the relationality proves primary, more fundamental than the self.

We are therefore arguing, in a language that neither Butler nor Levinas uses explicitly, for a shift from the concept of 'responsibility *for*' to the notion of 'responsibility *to*'.[16] Butler insists that the ontological 'impingements' of others upon us ought not be taken as a constraint upon the self that would undermine its capacity for responsible action. Instead, she suggests that this primary vulnerability to others must be read as an ontological condition that '*heightens a sense of responsibility*' (Butler 2005: 97, emphasis added). We are made more responsible by our primary dependence on others. Or, better, we have the potential to take up a wider and deeper sense of the responsible precisely because of what we want to call a primary responsibility *to* the other.

Butler argues that the rethinking of responsibility necessarily requires a distancing from more familiar accounts. Thus her sense of responsibility is not 'a heightened moral sense [produced through] an internalization of rage'; nor is it 'a sense of guilt that seeks to find a cause' (Butler 2005: 99). She then asks: 'is there a theorization of responsibility beyond' these? (Butler 2005: 100). Frustratingly, Butler either neglects or refuses to answer her own question *within the language of responsibility*. In the next paragraph, however, she asserts the following: 'that we are impinged upon primarily and against our will is the sign of a vulnerability and a beholdenness that we cannot will away' (Butler 2005: 100). We contend that this is Butler's answer to an alternative account of responsibility. It describes, further, the sense of 'responsibility *to*' that we have named above. We are not only responsible *for* our actions, but always and already responsible *to* the other (or others) in a way that not only *expands* but also *transforms* our prior concept of responsibility. Thus, to be responsible *to* the other certainly means to broaden our sense of responsibility, but it also means to challenge any simple account of 'responsibility for' as the deeds of a wilful and purposive sovereign subject.

Thus 'responsibility to' names Butlers rethinking of responsibility. It takes its critical distance from traditional accounts of responsibility, but, crucially, it does not take its leave of them. Rather, it remains in critical dialogue with standard theories of the responsible moral agent, while expanding our very understandings of that agent. Furthermore, 'responsibility *to*' consistently invokes Butler's political ontology: it links the question of ethical action to the scene of primary relationality.

Above all, Butler continually contends that we must conceive the human 'in its fallibility' and in its finitude. Any ethical theory that hypostatises either the sovereign subject or sovereign agency will break with the ontology of primary relationality and project an impossible or undesirable political worldview (one of sovereign mastery, wilful action or spiralling violence). Butler never denies the need for individuals to *be* responsible (to *take* responsibility) for their actions; 'those who commit acts of violence are surely responsible for them', she says (Butler 2004a: 15). Yet this conception of responsibility, however necessary it may be to maintain it, cannot be allowed to exhaust the meaning of the term; it cannot be allowed merely to spur us to more violence in the face of suffering and loss. Responsibility to the other is the only thinking of responsibility that can do more than lay blame for violence, for loss, for tragedy; it can also stop the cycle of violence.

Butler attributes to both Foucault and Adorno – though, significantly, she fails to attribute to Nietzsche (who made the argument earlier and louder) – the insight that 'to act ethically … we must avow error as constitutive of who we are'. She extrapolates from this position her own logical conclusion to the question of responsibility: 'what conditions our doing is a constitutive limit, for which we cannot give a full account, and this condition is, paradoxically, the basis of our accountability' (Butler 2005: 111). A new understanding of responsibility emerges from the very admission that one can never give a full account of oneself. The project of 'giving an account of oneself' must be undertaken. We must give an account in order to take responsibility for our actions, and to locate ourselves in the world. But we must also give an account in order to discover the limits to this project. These limits, Butler emphasises, are constitutive. This means that they constrain our account, just as they simultaneously make it possible. *We would not be able to give an account, were it not impossible to give an account*. And in giving this impossible account we may come to grasp the meaning of our primary relationality. We may also come to grasp a broader, more enriched understanding of responsibility as a primary responsibility to others that we can never avoid, never evade and never will way. The question of how we negotiate that undeniable, unavoidable responsibility is both an ethical question and also the question of politics.

Political ontology, the political, and politics

This chapter seeks to preserve a productive ambivalence about the status of politics in Butler's critical and theoretical work, particularly with respect to her recent writings on ethics. On the one hand, it reinterprets the 'turn' to ethics as but another return to ontology, and it argues forcefully and repeatedly for a notion of '*political* ontology', suggesting that to do a certain sort of ontological work is precisely to engage in the work of political theory, i.e. ontology *as* political theory. Thus in one sense the chapter can be read as asserting that even in her turn to ethics Butler is never really *not* engaged in a political project. Her account of the political, like that of numerous others within contemporary thought, refuses to cordon off the political from other domains (Chambers 2006a); in her conception of politics, she will never allow it to be segregated from the ethical sphere or to be hived off from the broader ontological realm. Butler's politics always emerges from and remains in dialogue with her ontological accounts. Her theories of politics cannot be dissociated from her always already political ontology.

On the other hand, this chapter has recurrently criticised Butler in political terms, arguing that her incessant focus on 'moral philosophy' and the ethical realm leads her to both poor readings and political blindspots within the project she names 'giving an account'. Butler's earlier worry about the turn to ethics producing problems for politics turns out to be justified: in general terms, *Giving an Account* probably proves to be the least political text Butler has written. It maintains less dialogue with feminist political theory, the new gender politics or radical democracy than Butler's other work (though there can be no doubt that Butler's thinking is still nourished by those resources). It would be not only premature but also unjustified to conclude that Butler's recent work on ethics marks an abandonment of politics, particularly since we have demonstrated that so much of this work remains thoroughly consistent with Butler's earlier projects. Nevertheless, something is lost here.

Perhaps this shows that the turn to ethics cannot help but risk the displacement of politics. However, the solution to this dilemma cannot arrive in the form of a mere avoidance of ethics. A better response to this ever-present danger has to be a certain vigilance in its face; in other words, we must make certain that ethics is not all that we do. This means insisting that political theory can never be logically derived from ethical theory. There can be no doubt that an ethical position is never free of political implications, but to grant this important point is not the same as presuming that politics could be *deduced* from ethics. One must therefore maintain that politics will not logically derive from ethics, while also insisting that to stake out an ontological position is also to take up a certain ethico-political orientation.

Another way of putting this is to say that while when she is 'doing ethics' she is also 'doing politics', nevertheless, Butler has no singular theory of politics that we might draw out from her ethical theory. Butler provides numerous tools to help us conceptualise, understand and intervene in politics and she offers us a number of theories (always plural) of the political. These two chapters of the book have elucidated a few of those concepts and have explored many of those theories of the political.[17] This strategy must be understood as clearly distinct from an approach to Butler's political theory that would first elucidate her ethics and then build from it her account of politics. Were that the approach taken here, then this chapter, ostensibly 'on ethics', would be followed by another, putatively 'on politics'. However, as we have just said, one cannot treat Butler's political theory in the singular, and one cannot produce a separate chapter that would sum up her politics (e.g. by listing out core principles, key abstract concepts or general approaches). For this reason, Part III of the book is not therefore a linear culmination to it. Instead, Chapters 6 and 7 cash out on the preceding sections in a very specific and circumscribed way, by investigating the politics of heteronormativity.

Part III
The politics of heteronormativity

6 Kinship trouble

In short, feminism must call for a revolution in kinship.

(Rubin 1975: 199)

This chapter is the first of two devoted to exploring 'the politics of heteronormativity'. Heteronormativity has quite recently emerged as a fully shaped and well-theorised concept in fields from gender studies, to literature, to film theory, and, while still little referenced in political science, this concept proves central to sexual politics and the politics of sexuality.[1] 'Heteronormativity' denotes the normative power of heterosexuality in both society and politics. Following the literal invention of 'heterosexuality' – a term introduced in the 19th century, and only after the coining of homosexuality – social norms, political practices and legal structures all developed to produce a practical truth that at the time was merely presumed (Katz 1995). This 'truth' is the idea that heterosexuality is the 'normal' or 'natural' way through which human physical and social experience must be lived. Heteronormativity constructs not only the natural domain of heterosexual practices and relations, but also the attendant realm of denigrated or despised sexualities, relationship forms and identities – particularly homosexuality and other putative threats to 'the family' (Foucault 1978; Evans 1993; Butler 1993; Fausto-Sterling 2000). Thus heteronormativity could be taken as a political concept that draws attention to those deviant, abjected or marginalised individuals who are somehow stigmatised or discriminated against by the dominant sexual norm. However, to read heteronormativity in this way would be to reduce it to a problem soluble by liberal tolerance. It would, on this reading, add little if anything to a rich tradition and a vibrant literature in political thought that calls on us to include the excluded, to defend the rights of the marginalised, to uphold the human dignity of those rendered abject.[2]

In this chapter we use Butler's work to mobilise the concept of heteronormativity in the service of a distinct set of political and theoretical ends. We make a focused intervention into the politics of kinship and 'the family' using Butler's writings on *Antigone* as our lever. Butler's troubling of kinship structures links up significantly with her earlier work on sex/gender, just as it makes a powerful contribution to previous work done by others on the concept of heteronormativity. Furthermore, by using heteronormativity and unintelligibility to read Butler's rethinking of kinship (through the figure of Antigone), we provide a useful exemplar of what we have chosen to name her 'troubling politics'. At the same time, we begin the process of articulating Butler's political theories of norms and normalisation, which we argue in Chapter 7 marks her most profound disruption of the status quo in the field of politics, i.e. it proves to be her most radical and important work in political theory.

In turning to the question of kinship in *Antigone*, Butler rethinks the political by challenging the so-called foundations of kinship as proposed by certain psychoanalytic arguments. Butler moves beyond universalising accounts in order to make possible a more open and culturally variable understanding of kinship. We argue here that Butler's 'troubling' of kinship structures takes up the challenge proposed 30 years ago by Gayle Rubin in her classic essay 'The Traffic in Women'. Rubin made the powerful claim that the roots of gender hierarchy lie in the structures of kinship and for this reason only a revolution in kinship would do for those who seek to eliminate that hierarchy: 'the oppression of women is deep; equal pay, equal work, and all the female politicians in the world will not extirpate the roots of sexism' (Rubin 1975: 198). As we have previously shown in other contexts in this book, Butler consistently refuses to allow the preservation of a 'natural' realm that somehow stands outside politics or precedes it. The 'pre-political' or 'non-political' always serves precisely political ends. This chapter focuses on Butler's politicisation of kinship structures in her reading of the figure of Antigone. Here she takes the critique of heteronormativity much further than it has gone before, by analysing the incest taboo as a power that both maintains heteronormativity and produces a particular configuration of the family. She does both through her introduction and refinement of the concept of (un)intelligibility – a term that eschews the framework offered by liberal tolerance and demands a more rigorous treatment of the politics of subjectivity – and by drawing attention to the 'incest-born' person.

The unintelligibility of the incest-born suggests a thoroughgoing reconsideration of the liberal concept of tolerance (contra Edelman 2004: 103; cf. Brown 2006). The concept of unintelligibility, as we develop it here, reveals the political blindspots of tolerance. We argue that unintelligibility gestures toward that sphere of existence of the non- or in-human; precisely because liberalism tries to fix and distribute all identities, particularly marginalised identities, it cannot grasp this 'other'. The unintelligible cannot be tolerated, for they have not been granted access to the category of the human. By analysing the incest taboo as a force that maintains heteronormativity through the production of a particular configuration of the family, Butler makes an important contribution to the theory of heteronormativity, she provides us with a powerful critique of the contemporary politics of 'the family' and, most importantly for our purposes here, she makes a crucial contribution to theorising the politics of norms.

Troubling kinship with Antigone

Antigone, of course, has generated extensive commentary since the time of Aristotle, and the figure of Antigone has become a classic of modern political theory (Tyrrell and Bennett 1998; Burns 2002; Tralau 2005; cf. Steiner 1984). While no theorist can afford to be cavalier in reading things into and out of any given textual object of engagement, it is not our purpose here to locate Butler's work within that history of commentary, or to criticise her construal of the characters and situations. Butler is no classicist; she says as much herself, and we take her at her word (Butler 2000a: 2; see Elden 2005: para. 2). *Antigone's Claim*, then, is not really about the classical tragedy. Butler's book centres instead on the structures of kinship and their imbrication with political power. Critics of Butler who take her to be reading *Antigone* inauthentically are therefore probably right, so far as their argument goes, but their challenges to Butler also miss her broader point concerning heteronormativity and intelligibility in relation to kinship, and therefore underestimate the most important implications of her work (see Markell 2003; Seery 2006; Elden 2005).

Like Rubin before her, Butler challenges putatively universal structures of kinship through her direct confrontation with the incest taboo. This 'law', as we all know, decrees as a matter of logical consistency and linguistic intelligibility that son and husband, father and grandfather, brother and father, for example, cannot be the same person. The incest taboo therefore dictates a fixed and constrained family structure, in which every member can be distinctly sorted into non-overlapping categories. And yet, as we will discuss in our penultimate section of the chapter, both historical and modern kinship structures have proved highly variable. Indeed, the taboo against incest has meant strikingly different things at different times and places: often prohibiting but sometimes allowing or indeed requiring opposite-sex marital relations between particular people *identified as family members* through the kinship structure. This is a crucial point established by Rubin but often overlooked in later analyses: the *function* of the incest taboo is not to prohibit incest. Rubin puts it this way: 'since the existence of the incest taboo is universal, but the content of their prohibitions variable, they cannot be explained as having the aim of preventing the occurrence of genetically close matings' (Rubin 1975: 173).

This variability in kinship structures is in significant tension with the supposed universality of the incest taboo. It thereby provides the context from which we extract and articulate Butler's critique of heteronormativity. This tension is one reason why Butler is interested in Antigone *not* simply as a proto-feminist rebel who stands against the political rule of men, nor perforce as a metaphorical challenge to the heterosexuality through which female gender subordination is constructed. Butler's Antigone, like many Antigones before, performs an anti-authoritarian intervention by repeating her acts of defiance and adhering to her own interpretation of her duties and rights. But Butler goes further: she links this reading to a critique of the limits of 'representation and representability' *in language itself*, given Antigone's incestuous (non-)position in the heteronormative kinship structure. Put simply, Antigone, like any incest-born person, confounds the language of kinship. Butler thus moves the focus on Antigone from her dramatic role as a woman (who acts) to a view of her as an *incest-born person* and therefore as both a figure of abjection and a representation of the unrepresentable – the unintelligible (Butler 2000a: 1–2).

Incest proves, obviously, to be an inescapable feature of the tale of Oedipus, from which this play presents an episode. The novelty of Butler's reading lies in her emphasis on an astonishingly neglected facet: Antigone is both the child of an incestuous relationship and also a sister quite possibly in love with her brother. Commentators have been centrally concerned with Antigone's public actions *as a woman*, but this has blinded them and their readers to *all* the incest at the heart of the story (see Seery 2006 for a contrary view). Antigone and her three siblings – and indeed her entire family as it devolves from the tragedy of Oedipus – represent a figural challenge to intelligible kinship. They *are* (even if in fictional terms) that which cannot be, the *unintelligible*. While commentators may mention the incest, and link it to the general and inevitable 'family' tragedy, in Butler's view they have missed the significance of the incest taboo in its power to order the language of kinship into a heterosexual matrix of logical exclusions.

That is, relationships within the heteronormative structure of kinship only make sense within stated terms of consanguinity, which *proscribe* sexual activity between 'close' relations (as variously defined) and thus also proscribe (via a presumed necessary link with reproduction) the possibility of any offspring. Such offspring would be living embodiments of linguistic disorder. They are, therefore, an uncategorisable impossibility. In a mundane sense, the incest taboo thus *prescribes* exogamous marriage outside the immediate 'blood-related' family (according to varying rules of consanguinity) in order to create the orderly and intelligible family as a set of necessary and consistent kinship relations and practices. With that order and intelligibility come the patterns of responsibility and care, permitted rules of inheritance and prescribed rules of intestacy, and innumerable other informal and state-sponsored categorisations of right, privilege and obligation (Stevens 1999; Butler 2000a: 71–2; Josephson 2005).

Within this order, as Butler shows, there are no categories for the incest-born. Or worse, there are too many categories, because they fit into more than one. In other words, like language itself, the incest-born always prove to be in excess of the categories of kinship (cf. Butler 1997a). In the case of Antigone, Butler states this logical and linguistic fact succinctly: 'Antigone's father is her brother, since they both share a mother in Jocasta, and her brothers are her nephews, sons of her brother-father Oedipus' (Butler 2000a: 57). 'Antigone', Butler says, 'is one for whom symbolic positions have become incoherent, confounding as she does brother and father, emerging as she does not as a mother but ... in the place of the mother' (Butler 2000a: 22). Butler then puts this very *confounding* to work, by explicating the relationship between kinship structures (which presume the incest taboo as a logical truth that mirrors 'nature') and heteronormativity (which is defined and enforced both through legally sanctioned institutions and through the lived norms of daily practices).

We give this phenomenon of confounding the name that Butler casually suggests: 'kinship trouble'. We define it as a theoretico-political practice of challenging current structures of kinship so as to open a space of intelligibility for both the incest-born and for those 'others' who are also subject to the defining and denigrating power of heteronormativity. In trying to make kinship trouble, our argument here takes a path distinct from, but complementary to, other recent work on Butler's political theory. Many of Butler's critics have been cynical or merely dismissive about her writings (Nussbaum 1999; cf. Benhabib 1995a, 1995b). For this reason, we engage instead with those who argue that Butler's work has political significance yet has been underdeveloped as a contribution to political theory (Lloyd 1999, 2005b; Stone 2005; cf. Salih 2002).

The unintelligible

The language of 'intelligibility' and explicit references to the category of 'the unintelligible' only emerge in Butler's later writings – particularly in *Precarious Life* and *Undoing Gender* (Butler *et al.* 2000; Butler 2000b, 2004a, 2004b). Here we offer an exegesis of this concept in the context of Butler's confounding of kinship structures, but it seems significant to note at the outset that the idea of unintelligibility can be traced back to a number of earlier ideas and arguments in Butler's work. It resonates in important ways with numerous previous concepts: 'interpellation' as Butler develops it from Louis Althusser, in *Psychic Life of Power* (Butler 1997b); the 'constitutive outside', which Butler reworks, drawing from Jacques Derrida in *Bodies that Matter* (Butler 1993); and 'abjection' as Butler reconfigures it from Julia Kristeva both in *Bodies* and in *Gender Trouble* (Butler 1999 [1990]). Ultimately, the genealogy of Butler's thinking of unintelligibility must be traced back, in general, to her crucial engagement with the Hegelian philosophy of reflection and, in particular, to the Hegelian theory of recognition. This is not the space to engage with Butler's interpretation of Hegel, but to put the point succinctly we can say that Butler reads 'recognition' in Hegel not as a status that one pre-given subject would bestow on another (Butler 1987a; see Hutchings 2003). Instead, 'recognition' names a reflective process in which *one comes to be only through being recognised*. This means that neither subjectivity nor human existence can be taken for granted in advance;

the process of recognition (not contained or controlled by any single subject) makes human being possible.

With this in mind, we turn now to elaborate Butler's conception of unintelligibility. We argue that one of the strengths of *Antigone's Claim* is Butler's evocation of Antigone not only as a metaphor for (un)intelligibility but also as a character we already feel we know, i.e. as a potential real person with a real dilemma. This makes *Antigone's Claim* a crucial site for grasping Butler's work on intelligibility, since we have, on the one hand, a greater chance of *relating* to the concept (through a story that most readers already know) and, on the other, a greater risk of *reducing* that concept to something else entirely (namely, the tolerance of an already-existent subject).

The stakes of this reading can be clarified by making a few distinctions. First, the unintelligible is not the marginalised or the abjected. Intelligibility is not the same as recognition thought in the sense of Charles Taylor's 'politics of recognition', since in Taylor's multicultural politics recognition requires a prior visibility that is ruled off-limits for the unintelligible (Taylor 1992). That is why the discourse of intelligibility is not the same as a discourse of oppression, and why the political response to the problem of unintelligibility cannot be the same as a response to oppression or discrimination. Butler writes:

> To be oppressed means that you already exist as a subject of some kind, you are there as a visible and oppressed other for the master subject. . . . *To be oppressed you must first become intelligible.* To find that you are fundamentally unintelligible (indeed, that the laws of culture and language find you to be an impossibility) is to find that you have not yet achieved access to the human, to find yourself speaking only and always *as if you were* human, but with the sense that you are not.
>
> (Butler 2004b: 30; first emphasis added, second emphasis in original)

To be oppressed you must *first become intelligible.* This is why the 'unintelligible' are not merely the oppressed, the victimised or the marginalised. The 'unintelligible' are those 'others' who are made invisible by the norm. To be rendered unintelligible, says Butler, is to be barred 'access to the human'. Thus, by definition, the 'unintelligible' cannot exist as 'human'. But this is no mere definitional stipulation. To say that the unintelligible cannot exist as human is to suggest that the category of the human is not a given, but rather an achievement or production. And to assert that one only exists if one is intelligible is also to contend that human existence cannot be presumed, since our very existence depends upon norms that precede, produce and constrain us. As we discuss further below, for Butler a 'livable life' may be impossible without intelligibility.

This means that the power of intelligibility, i.e. the normalisation of visible subjects, operates with a stealthy silence. That is, normalisation does not just categorise human subjects; it produces the conditions of possibility for the 'human' in the first place. Therefore, the power of normalisation can not only marginalise or oppress; it can render one unintelligible. This makes unintelligibility an unruly and paradoxical concept. If to be rendered unintelligible is to be made invisible, unrecognisable as human, then we will only 'see' the unintelligible after they have become intelligible. Every time we try to offer an example of the unintelligible (e.g. in the form of the incest-born, the transgendered, or all gays and lesbians in relation to heteronormativity)[3] we have already, by way of the example itself, rendered them intelligible. Nonetheless, this paradoxical logic does not prove that there is no unintelligible; it merely demonstrates that we have no immediate access to the unintelligible until 'we' have attempted to make 'them' visible.

For precisely this reason, Butler's argument does not centre itself on 'the abject' as a category of identity, already there and awaiting help or emancipation (and identified under labels such as 'victimised' or 'oppressed' or 'discriminated against'). And Butler's is not simply an impassioned plea to help the helpless. Instead, Butler designs her argument and structures her account of norms so as to reveal the very existence of 'the unintelligible' (always for lack of a better term) *as unintelligible*; this revelation occurs by exposing the workings of intelligibility as a normative force. Unintelligibility prevents one from even appearing within the political realm as a human being, a being with desires, wants or needs.

The concept has clear resonances with Jacques Rancière's description of politics as only occurring after those who are not supposed to 'count' within the political order appear and demand to be counted. Rancière also stresses a point that proves crucial to understanding Butler's notion of the unintelligible. For Rancière, 'parties do not exist prior to the declaration of wrong' (Rancière 1999: 39). This means, in Butler's language, that 'the unintelligible' can only be brought to light as a category of human subjects *after* they have been rendered intelligible – usually through their own struggle for recognition, but perhaps also through analysis that exposes or challenges those norms that would produce the unintelligible in the first place. 'The people' or 'the workers' cannot be taken for granted as a category of human beings that make political claims; 'the people' comes into existence *by way of* those claims. Butler's unintelligibility is like Rancière's 'declaring a wrong' in that it may make the unintelligible intelligible. Yet, once they have been *made* intelligible, we cannot presume that they always already *were* intelligible.

To be rendered 'unintelligible' in this way, to be forced, as Butler says in the quotation above, to speak only 'as if' you were human, is to render one's life unlivable. Butler introduces the notion of 'a livable life' on the very first page of *Undoing Gender*, when she argues that norms of gender can 'undermine the capacity' for a livable life. In this vein, Butler redescribes the task of the movements of 'The New Gender Politics' as follows: 'to distinguish... among the norms and conventions that permit people to breathe, to desire, to love, and to live, and those norms and conventions that restrict or eviscerate the conditions of life itself' (Butler 2004b: 8). To pull together these two strands of Butler's argument, we can say that the 'unintelligible' are those for whom the norm makes life unlivable.

Butler says that 'to find that you are unintelligible ... is to find that your language is hollow, that no recognition is forthcoming because the norms by which recognition takes place are not in your favor' (Butler 2004b: 30). With this set of arguments about unintelligibility Butler insists, counter-intuitively perhaps, that a 'livable life' cannot be presumed from the outset. Here we see a different way of asserting the point about unintelligibility, since the concept of unintelligibility counters our intuitive notion that 'everyone' counts as a human and is recognisable as such. Butler writes: 'if the answer to the question, is life possible, is yes, that is surely something significant. It cannot, however, be taken for granted as the answer' (Butler 2004b: 29). It might be the case that, for some, life is not livable.

It is tempting nonetheless to read *Antigone's Claim* as a passionate defence of the individual, a critical attack on the linguistic apparatuses that sustain the state-sponsored legislation and informal social rules that make some lives 'unlivable' by dictating abjection and victimhood (as exemplified in Antigone's fate). This makes the text into a moving political case for a more *inclusive* social and legal approach to human relationships, most particularly self-chosen ones of friendship, commitment and trust – including but not limited to sexual relationships polymorphously conceived.

No doubt Butler does mean to suggest much of that. But to read her argument in this manner would be to limit its political impact in profound ways, and it would be to overlook the depth and breadth of the power of heteronormativity. Inclusion cannot solve the problem of unintelligibility, since (again, by definition) the unintelligible cannot be included given that *they do not even exist* as human. Unintelligibility creates political problems that go well beyond the bounds of legislation or public policy. The concept of unintelligibility proves powerful because it reveals the constitutive difficulty of normative violence that we have already elucidated. Normative violence is a violence done not merely *to* subjects but *at* the level of subjectivity. If there is no subject position in which to appear, then one cannot inhabit the human.[4]

We develop Butler's concept of unintelligibility to make it clear that if one wishes to foster, not limit, livable lives, then only a significant restructuring of kinship will do. Rubin succinctly calls this a *revolution* in kinship, while Shane Phelan elaborates the point: 'the imbrication of kinship and citizenship, and the heterosexual formulation of kinship that defines gays and lesbians (as well as unmarried adults) as either outside kin networks or unable to form new ones ... suggests that kinship will have to be rethought. ... ' (Phelan 2001: 157). To use Butler's language, kinship must be confounded, must be profoundly troubled at its very core if we are to create conditions in which the unintelligible can emerge into the realm of intelligible humanity.

That is why Butler seeks the critical subversion of heteronormativity (see Chapter 7), a rupturing of the heterosexual matrix that creates new spaces for newly intelligible, livable lives. In turn, as Michael Warner suggested many years ago, this sort of kinship trouble also requires the reversal of almost all social theory *methodologically*, where the strategy until very recently has been to ground norms in nature, and thus to construct supposed truths or limits to which human society must conform, and according to which individuals must be disciplined (Foucault 1978; Warner 1993). Such a conclusion proves radical precisely because it refuses to shelter *any* realm from the force and conflict of politics. To *pre*-politicise kinship is to *de*-politicise those norms and practices that exclude the incest-born and the incestuously coupled, for example, from the realm of intelligibility.

This argument poses, in a different light, a well-known question in gender studies: if some form of behaviour is natural, why then does it need social and legislative protection (e.g. heterosexual marriage) – should not the natural survive quite well on its own? And if some form of behaviour is unnatural, why does it have to be demonised or prohibited (e.g. homosexual behaviour or same-sex marriage) – should not the unnatural suffer quite nicely on *its* own? (Connell 2002: 3–4). Further, how is the natural/unnatural coded in practice? And, above all, if that coding occurs through the mechanism of culture or politics, then is the natural really anything other than that which we code *as* natural (within the utterly contingent realm of the political)?

In making these queries, Butler refuses the psychoanalytic reading of incest. She captures that reading as follows: 'one might simply say in a psychoanalytic spirit that Antigone represents a *perversion* of the law and conclude that the law requires perversion', and thus the law is itself perverse (Butler 2000a: 67). That reading, argues Butler, merely pairs two static entities – the law and perversion – with one another, all to produce what she somewhat sarcastically calls a 'satisfying' result: 'that the law is *invested* in perversion' and is therefore other than it at first appears (Butler 2000a: 68). This 'satisfying' reading, however, does precisely nothing to make life possible. It makes no effort at all to render the unintelligible intelligible. Instead, it closes off that possibility by merely asserting that the law, which is still the law, is itself perverse. Mimicking Antigone's own resistance to the law, Butler challenges psychoanalysis: 'what happens when the perverse or the impossible emerges in the language of the law and makes its claim precisely there in the sphere of legitimate kinship that depends on its exclusion or pathologization?' (Butler 2000a: 68).

Structuralist and psychoanalytic accounts provide the target for Butler's critique, particularly because they so often render Antigone, and her desire for her brother, unintelligible. Butler consistently demands that we move away from accounts that would place kinship structures beyond question, that is, by situating them in a putatively universal realm. Instead, she asks *how, why* and *to what ends* such a universal is constructed; for Butler, the constitution of 'the universal' or of 'the human' is precisely a *political* issue (see, for example, Butler 2004b: 189–90). Once again, Butler makes a move that parallels Rubin: both ask us to look at the so-called 'foundations' of society in order to envision a radical approach to politics. Rubin says that the sex/gender system once organised *society* but now only organises *itself*, and she leverages this claim into a call to restructure the system of sex and gender (Rubin 1975: 199). Butler recognises that, today, heteronormativity, the incest taboo and universalist accounts of kinship all stand in the way of such restructuring, and for this reason Butler invites us to reconsider the politics of foundations.

Given this conception of politics as that which puts into place conceptions of the universal and the foundational, Butler wisely queries the putatively foundational 'division between the psychic or symbolic, on the one hand, and the social, on the other' (Butler 2000a: 71). The effect of her critique is to incorporate the psychic or symbolic within the social, and thus to see social variability and malleability as the means through which strategies of control and containment get their grip, and potentially the means through which this can be undone. Structures, even if said to be merely formal (or even vastly malleable), are still structures, Butler says; thus they domesticate 'in advance any radical reformulation of kinship' (Butler 2000a: 74). To effect serious change in kinship structures thus requires opening them up to cultural contestation.[5]

Incest and the family

While Butler is attentive to anecdotal accounts of new 'family' structures and sensitive to the dilemmas of neologisms and reinscription, she pays little attention to what the actual language of these new relationships might be, that is, the new terms of kinship that would produce non-heteronormative families/kinship structures and thus intelligibly human subjectivities. If Antigone had not been crushed by the state, which was keen to keep the heteronormative order both intact and in circulation, what could she have called herself and her loved ones? How could she name her desires and their objects? How might she designate the family of her own that she never had? How much language would have to be changed (or simply dismissed as archaic) to foreclose her extreme abjection and suicidal melancholia?

These are practical political questions. In turn, they render problematic a great deal of the institutional and legislative structures that support and maintain heteronormativity and the current structures of kinship. At present most countries have compulsory certification of birth including parental and sexual identification, and in many countries there are elaborated procedures for determining these facts of 'consanguinity'. The intelligibility of 'family' language supposedly arises from, but is in turn practically structuring of, these very 'facts' through which identities and relationships are mediated. These procedures function both to determine who can and cannot 'unite' to found a family and to institute a hierarchy in terms of next of kin for inheritance or other purposes once a family is founded. Some scholars question whether we need these state-sponsored recording of lineages at all (see Stevens 1999), and within the project of confounding kinship we might go on to ask other questions – questions about 'blood' relations, about the necessity of marriage, about the future of the incest taboo. As Rubin shows, these kinship rules may once have served external purposes but now seemed designed only to regulate kinship itself – and for reasons that are less than clear (Rubin 1975). Here we elaborate Butler's troubling of kinship by looking briefly at current political and scientific debates on precisely these issues.

In the current social-scientific and therapeutic literatures, and in many media and popular culture sources, incest is almost immediately contextualised as child abuse, or simply sexual abuse without regard to age – most particularly in father–daughter cases. This framing of incest renders the incest-born unintelligible: if incest is always and already an act of extreme abuse, then nothing human could arise from the act of incest. Indeed, the question of the incest-born is almost never raised, precisely because the category of the incest-born hardly exists; it is only intelligible as somehow less than human. If incest is nothing more than an event so inhuman (occurring only in a space 'outside the human') as to be unspeakable, then the act of incest must be prohibited and, if it should nonetheless occur, forgotten and erased. If society depends upon the prohibition of incest, a fundamental taboo against it, then the category of the human is based upon the impossibility of incest (or its erasure).

Antigone offers a provocative case of incest, then, since there the issues are mother–son and sister–brother and all parties are over the age of consent. With Antigone we do not have a potential case of child abuse. Moreover, sexual abuse as such is not in question, because the mother–son incest arises through mistaken identity, and the sister–brother incest arises as a feeling in only one party, if that. Neither case includes power or aggression. Thus any presumed identity between incest (as heterosexual activity between 'close' relations) and scenarios of sexual abuse is undermined; the horror and trauma that result from incest in the tragedy follow exclusively from the taboo itself.

Butler's critique of the heteronormativity of the kinship system and her call for attentiveness to the problem of (un)intelligibility both focus her critical sights on the incest taboo itself. 'The question', Butler asks, 'is whether the incest taboo has also been mobilised to *establish* certain forms of kinship as the only intelligible and livable ones' (Butler 2000a: 70).[6] Building indirectly from Rubin's claim that the incest taboo always serves a function *other* than the mere prohibition of 'close genetic matings', Butler suggests here that the taboo works in the services of heteronormativity. As

Rubin stated succinctly years before Butler would make the argument more famous in *Gender Trouble*: 'the incest taboo presupposes a prior, less articulate taboo on homosexuality' (Rubin 1975: 180).

The popular construction and understanding of incest contribute in their own way to production of the unintelligibility of the incest-born – that is, as a 'natural' and universal law – but it may therefore come as a surprise to many to learn that the concept of incest proves far more ambiguous, variable and controversial than might at first be assumed. The question of which relationships fall on which side of which boundary is culturally and legally variable, and occasionally even contradictory. For example, the marriage of widows to brothers-in-law is required in some religious systems and prohibited in others (Arens 1997; Bittles *et al.* 2001: 68–71). Not only is incest defined differently, and differently defied, in various cultures, but the supposed relation to 'blood' is sometimes even blatantly metaphorical, for example in cases of alleged incest involving family-members-by-adoption or even in-laws who are unrelated through normal kinship rules of 'blood'.[7]

Scientifically, a significant link between 'defects' in offspring and 'inbreeding' among successive generations of parents proves less than obvious. Instead, the purported 'links' prove to be fraught with cross-causalities, ambiguous comparisons and indeterminacy in individual cases (Bittles *et al.* 2001: 71–6). 'Defective' genes are not caused by 'inbreeding', although they can segregate in a limited gene pool. However, gene segregation already occurs, even in a large pool, and is today the occasion for voluntary genetic counselling, rather than proscription (or enforced sterilisation, which was often the case in the past). Indeed, in animal breeding the reverse prejudice is generally true: inbreeding is standardly understood to produce 'good' results and humans routinely organise compulsory inbreeding.

Bittles *et al.* come to this conclusion:

> in Western societies there is a strong belief that the progeny of close kin unions will exhibit elevated levels of physical and/or mental defect, the implication being that these adverse outcomes are caused by the expression of detrimental recessive genes which have accumulated in the kindred and/or community because of inbreeding. ... The evidence produced to support this contention often has been vague and largely anecdotal in nature, with little or no proof that the claimed pattern(s) of ill health stemmed specifically from the expression of specific recessive genes. An opposite and ultimately beneficial genetic perspective on consanguinity also has been advanced, suggesting that in communities in which close-kin unions were traditionally preferential there would have been a gradual but significant elimination of detrimental recessive genes from the gene pool.
>
> (Bittles *et al.* 2001: 71)

Inbreeding (endogamy) and outbreeding (exogamy) are in themselves *eugenic* arguments applied both to individuals and to 'the species'. Intriguingly, these arguments work both ways, and each is discredited in reputable practice – if not entirely in popular consciousness. Some individual characteristics can be linked to limited gene pools, but these can be evaluated positively for any number of reasons (e.g. dark skin in hotter climes, or blonde hair and blue eyes as a sign of beauty) or rather negatively (e.g. albinism, pygmyism), at least to the point of figuring in the advice offered by counsellors. A mixed gene pool is said to promote genetic variation and selective adaptation and therefore to be good for 'the species', but at the same time 'the species' is supposed to be defended against 'inferior stock' to preserve the 'fittest' genes from dilution. Over aeons of time, and in constantly changing circumstances, natural selection works with such a variety of reproductive strategies and produces such speculative and indeterminate outcomes that inbreeding/outbreeding has no causal purchase in the general theory, notwithstanding 'Darwinian' attempts to naturalise one particular model in 'progressive' accounts of human social groups (Agar 2004; Bittles 2001; Fausto-Sterling 2000).[8]

Although they are a fictional family, it is notable that Antigone and her three siblings have no obvious 'defects'. Of course, some contemporary royal families are notably 'inbred', and mistaken and deliberately consensual unions between siblings and half-siblings do, in fact, occur. It should be less than shocking to note, then, the existence of political groups advocating reform or abolition of incest laws.[9] In short, incest is a discursive artefact with an 'excess', and in Western culture it has been used as a cultural taboo through strategies of naturalisation which have no necessary functional or other validity in individual, social or biological terms (Bittles *et al.* 2001).

This brief survey of the recent scientific literature on incest elaborates on the point already articulated by Rubin: the incest taboo serves other purposes. It also helps to support a point made, or at least consistently raised, by Butler: incest may not always be the violation we take it to be. Indeed, in *Undoing Gender* Butler frequently uses the phrase 'when incest is a violation' in order to suggest two points simultaneously. First, sometimes incest is *not* a violation. We cannot assume the functional universality of the taboo; we may need to inquire, instead, into the role that the taboo plays in supporting heteronormativity. This means comprehending the incest taboo as a mechanism for producing unintelligibility. But, second, the phrase also suggests to us that sometimes incest *is* a violation and no critique of the political effects of the incest taboo can overlook this fact. Butler's argument thereby raises the question of how we decide when incest is and is not a violation.

Indeed, Butler frames this question directly: 'how do we account for the more or less general persistence of the incest taboo and its traumatic consequences as part of the differentiation process that paves the way for adult sexuality *without demeaning the claims made about incestuous practices that clearly are traumatic in nonnecessary and unacceptable ways?'* (Butler 2004b: 154, emphasis added). Butler will not give a specific answer to this question; nor will she provide a metric designed to measure and determine each and every case that comes up. However, Butler does provide a way to *approach* crucial questions such as this one, and such an approach depends precisely on refusing to decide the issue in advance. Butler returns to the so-called foundations of culture in the form of the incest taboo in order to demonstrate that such 'foundations' always prove to be political constructions. We must decide the question of violation in incest through the work of politics: through a rigorous and careful assessment of what counts as 'universal' and why, through a genuine engagement with questions concerning who counts as human, and through an understanding of the future as always unpredictable and contingent. This is one more reason why Butler's theoretico-political project exceeds the framework of liberalism.

Towards a livable life

Butler states her goal directly, and perhaps more succinctly and clearly than some readers might at first imagine. That goal is to make a livable life *possible*. And, she passionately asserts, 'possibility is not a luxury; *it is as crucial as bread'* (Butler 2004b: 29, emphasis added). To make a livable life possible means to challenge normative violence and the heteronormative structures of kinship in such a way as to render the previously unintelligible intelligible. In other words, Butler's project centres on an effort to open up spaces for the 'human' to exist, possibly to thrive. Many readers might see the concept of the 'livable life' as too vague to be of much use, too singular to offer political hope. Butler sees things differently:

> one might wonder what use 'opening up [gender] possibilities' finally is, but no one who has understood what it is to live in the social world as what is 'impossible', illegible, unrealizable, unreal and illegitimate is likely to pose that question.
>
> (Butler 1999: viii)

The question of (un)intelligibility cannot be dismissed as politically meaningless and it cannot be rejected as philosophically abstract. It takes concrete shape in relation to kinship structures and heteronormative practices – political, legal, constitutional and international. In other words, for some, unintelligibility is the most meaningful issue of all.

Examples could include both transgendered people who have no intelligible place in a system of binary sex and gender (even if that system affords equal rights to lesbians and gays) or those whose sexual practices will remain criminalised and only be further stigmatised by the legalisation of gay marriage. The politics of 'the livable life' demands a struggle against the norms that produce unintelligibility (thereby rendering lives unlivable). This politics need not eschew the legal arena but it will apply caution when entering. Thus certain kinship structures find themselves re-scripted within same-sex partnerships and marriage, such that the terms 'husband' and 'wife' make no sense, and where 'mother' and 'father' may apply in various ways to any number of parenting adults. These practices can alter norms, can make space for livable lives and can do so even without sanctioned legislation by the state. In addition, these discursive shifts can also challenge heteronormativity and rework kinship *through* political and legal processes (Wilson 1995; Petchesky 2001; Josephson 2005). One can cite analogous historical examples as well: the alleged moral and scientific grounds for anti-miscegenation laws have notably succumbed to contrary views in recent history. The politics of gender-equalisation, same-sex marriage, human reproductive and sexual rights, and an anti-eugenic backlash all have the potential to 'trouble' heteronormative kinship at its very foundations in the incest taboo (Goodenough 2004; Carver 2007).

However, within a politics of the livable life the focus must always remain on challenging the norms that make some lives unlivable, and this entails a necessary vigilance concerning legal remedies. Demanding rights from the state is not always the answer when doing so may also tend to reify certain heterosexual norms. And rights, once attained, *can* be lost and *must* be defended. Butler's politics, that is, sees the future as untimely: past victories are not guarantees of what is to come, and what is to come remains unpredictable. Butler contends that we must remain *open* to this future, and her politics therefore demands a continuous reassessment of our conceptions of universality, of norms, even of what constitutes politics itself.

To provide examples such as those above is not to reduce the argument to an individualised level: Butler's theorising of intelligibility applies broadly to sexed and gendered subject positions, not just to single individuals (Butler 1987b, 1989a). This is why Butler's political project will not boil down to a claim for lesbian and gay rights. Butler certainly does not stand 'against' lesbian and gay rights, but she conceives of politics both more broadly and more radically. Butler seeks to open spaces in which we might critically question, and sometimes challenge, the norms (and practices of disciplinary normalisation) that render some lives intelligible and some lives unintelligible. Thus in recent texts Butler maintains continual concern for precisely those who are rendered unintelligible by the very framework of 'lesbian and gay rights'. In certain cases and contexts the claim for identity-based rights can reinforce norms that render other lives unlivable; marriage provides but one obvious example.

We contend that it would be a mistake to take the critique of heteronormativity as merely the politics of tiny minorities, having little effect on the vast majority. And that is why, as we have maintained throughout, it would be seriously misleading to read Butler's politics as one of mere inclusion or simple multicultural recognition. Our effort here has been to elaborate the politics of heteronormativity through Butler's troubling of kinship. Butler's novel reading of Antigone/*Antigone*, in calling attention to the unintelligibility within the 'human' of the incest-born person, subverts the structures of kinship typically taken for granted and implicitly universalised. In our reading of Butler's work, we argue that she does much more than point out the 'constructed' character of sex and gender. She does a great deal more than call for an 'end to oppression' of the marginalised. In making kinship trouble Butler opens up the politics of heteronormativity beyond a narrow, liberal framework of inclusion/exclusion and policies of toleration. By demonstrating how the incest taboo both produces and sustains heteronormativity, Butler's makes a robust contribution to what Rubin named as the goal of feminism: to effect a revolution in kinship. This specific intervention into the politics of heteronormativity can thus serve as a guide as we now turn to explore both the critical theory of heteronormativity and the politics of subversion that Butler offers in response.

7 Subversion

This chapter focuses on the politics of heteronormativity, but it shifts from the analysis of specific manifestations of and particular engagements with heteronormativity to a political theory of the concept. This shift demands genealogical work on the concept of heteronormativity – as it can be reconstructed out of Butler's notion of the 'heterosexual matrix' – and it requires a critical retrieval of the theory of subversion. 'Subversion' appears repeatedly in Butler's earlier writings, and it plays a central role in her articulation of politics. Put another way, Butler invokes the language of subversion in her early works at precisely those moments when the stakes of her reading turn political. Her implicit, and frequently misunderstood, 'theory of subversion' takes sharper shape, we will argue, when read with and through the concept of heteronormativity. To explicate a politics of subversion at work in Butler's writing requires a concomitant redescription of subversion's critical target: namely, the power of heterosexuality when it operates as a norm. Following the lead of queer theory, we name this power heteronormativity, and in this chapter we seek to distinguish it rigorously from homophobia. While Butler draws the concept of subversion out of the writings of others, and while she neither coins nor even makes use of the term heteronormativity, we argue nevertheless that the subversions of heteronormativity both effected and advocated in Butler's work constitute precisely that which should not – indeed, cannot – be ignored by political theory.

This final chapter can be read in a number of different ways, all designed to help fill in Butler's political theory as a politics of troubling and a troubling of politics. Read together with Chapter 4, the concepts of normative violence and subversion can be considered central contributions that Butler makes to contemporary political theory. Read together with Chapter 6, we see emerge from Butler's work a full and powerful political theory of heteronormativity, which we argue here proves essential to politics writ large. Understood in light of arguments from Chapter 5, we see that Butler's political ontology and her ethical conceptions remain inextricably bound up with her political interventions and her theories of gender and sexuality.

This chapter does not close the book by *concluding* it, a process that would seek to establish 'the political theory of Judith Butler'. Rather, it closes the book by filling in the picture of Butler as a thinker *of* politics and 'the political'. That picture, like Butler's conception of the political, like her vision for radical democracy, will and must remain open-ended – awaiting a future-to-come that no theory can predict or forestall. With that vision of the political in sight, we turn now to articulating the 'troubling politics' in Butler's subversions of heteronormativity.

Subversive acts, subversive readings

Subversion is not a secret resource in Butler's oeuvre, hiding away to be discovered in some little-noticed or never published text. On the contrary, Butler places subversion in the subtitle of her most famous book; it seems clear that Butler's politics is, in one way or another, a 'subversive politics'; and we are not the first to highlight the term in reading her work. In the existing literature, one notes three distinct (though entangled) responses to the question of subversion in Butler's corpus.

First, some authors will take Butler's politics of subversion as a given frame for their investigation and then move on to focus on particular, specific questions concerning Butler's theory of politics. Thus one hears the language of subversion but sees little investigation of it. Alison Stone's recent work provides an excellent example of this approach to subversion: Stone structures her entire reading of Butler's work around the term subversion, but her questions are not what *is* subversion or what does subversion *target*. Rather, she asks about the *possibility* of 'subversive agency' and about the *desirability* of subverting 'gender norms' (Stone 2005: 5). Moreover, subversion frames Stone's discussion to such an extent that it allows her to discuss the famous contentious conversation between Benhabib, Butler and Fraser in terms of these questions about subversive agency and the subversion of gender norms, despite the fact that in those particular texts neither Butler nor Benhabib nor Fraser uses the word subversion much at all (Benhabib 1995a, 1995b; Butler 1995a, 1995b; Fraser 1995). We read Stone in this manner not to offer a criticism of her work; indeed, it is precisely the *focus* on questions of agency and the normative ground for politics that makes Stone's essay on Butler particularly relevant and helpful for placing Butler in the context of political theory. Our point is merely that while Stone certainly sees the significance of 'subversion' to Butler's (political) work, her task is not to explore the concept of subversion critically. Stone remains much more concerned with theories of performativity and resignification (on 'subversive resignification', see also Disch 1999; cf. Mills 2000). In like manner, Lloyd's important work on Butler takes account of subversion, recognising its significance to Butler's writings, but Lloyd's project concentrates instead on parody, agency and subjectivity (Lloyd 1999, 2005a, 2005b; see also Haraway 1991).

A second group of authors focus so closely on other issues that they simply pay little or no attention to the question of subversion. Instead, and again, agency often takes centre stage. McNay (2000) structures her critical account of Butler around the concept of resignification, within a text that treats questions of agency as primary. Other texts may not even have Butler as a central player, but will mention her in order to recall the critique of agency (Hawkesworth 1997; cf. Scott 1999b; see also Webster 2000) or to assert that Butler's arguments strip away the ground for either feminist action or normative judgement (Benhabib 1995a; cf. Hutchings 2003). Resignification and performativity (or 'performance') also draw their own share of critical concern (Disch 1999; Webster 2000).

Obviously, then, neither of these first two groups hold any explicit concern with the politics of subversion. In the third category we find Martha Nussbaum's famous review essay on Butler entitled 'The Professor of Parody' (Nussbaum 1999). Nussbaum responds to the question concerning subversion directly. Her answer? Nussbaum's polemic asserts that subversion is central to Butler's work, and goes on to insist that this is precisely why Butler should be *dismissed* as a political thinker. Nussbaum sees 'parodic subversion' as all Butler has to offer, and 'political quietism' as the only possible result of her project (Nussbaum 1999). We will not address Nussbaum's polemic in any detail, except to say that hers is not a careful explication of what Butler means by subversion; others have already made concise yet powerful responses to Nussbaum (see Lloyd 2005a: 147–8). Her work proves interesting for our account only because, as other writers place subversion in the background as a potentially positive context for thinking Butler's politics, so Nussbaum foregrounds subversion as if it could mean nothing more than the idle speculation of an out-of-touch academic.

Unlike the first two groups of thinkers, Nussbaum links subversion to Butler's wider political project. Our work here draws a similar link, yet reaches dramatically divergent conclusions. It will follow a somewhat parallel path to that traced by Penelope Deutscher, the one writer who emphasises the prominence of subversion in *Gender Trouble* and structures the opening of her reading around the concept (even though she abandons it in the end) (Deutscher 1997: 19–32). Our first task, then, will be to return to Butler's original accounts of subversion in order to retrieve it as a viable and productive political concept. Although it appears in the subtitle of *Gender Trouble*, the word subversion is not to be found in the index of *any* of Butler's first three books. Butler puts forward no theory of subversion; indeed, as we discuss below, she later eschews such a project. She provides little (if any) explicit conceptualisation of the term; nor does she define it. The most direct comments one finds from Butler on subversion come in a rarely cited interview she gave in autumn 1993. She asserts: 'you can't plan or calculate subversion. In fact, we would say that subversion is precisely an incalculable effect. That's what makes it subversive' (Butler 1994: 38).

Butler's statements here may well take the form of a definition, but 'subversion ... is an incalculable effect' hardly counts as one. The *OED* offers three entries for the verb subvert: (1) to demolish, raze or overturn; (2) to undermine, corrupt or pervert; and (3) to disturb, overthrow or destroy (*OED* 2002: 3,094). None of these is a weak verb: subversion clearly takes its place within a radical or revolutionary political vocabulary. However, we believe that Butler's critics may have implicitly (and sometimes explicitly) taken subversion only to mean the first and third definitions.[1] As Deutscher helpfully notes, '"subversion," after all, has the connotations of overthrowing, overturning, upsetting, effecting destruction', and yet this is not at all what Butler wishes to imply by subversion (Deutscher 1997: 26). Butler's broader theory roots itself closely on the second definition, and we will advocate a thinking of subversion as internal *erosion*. To make this case we first offer here a brief genealogical account of the concept of subversion in Butler's early writings, one designed to prove that subversion must be read more broadly than it has been before by those sympathetic to her project and more subtly than it has by those critical of that project.

Butler's first book, *Subjects of Desire*, includes an extra chapter added at the end and subtitled 'Hegel and Contemporary French Theory'. Subversion makes its first appearance towards the end of that extra chapter (at the conclusion of the book) in her discussion of Foucault. Indeed, the idea of a politics of subversion seems to emerge in Butler's work as an undertaking that she attributes to Foucault. At the end of *Subjects* Butler describes the project contained in Foucault's later writings as resting on a 'tactic of subversion', one that calls for 'the overthrowing of juridical models of power' (Butler 1987a: 222, 227; cf. Butler 1996). This is not the place to trace Butler's deep debt to Foucault or to engage in a close and critical reading of Butler's interpretation of his work. We would argue that Butler misreads Foucault, by attributing a politics of subversion (as radical overthrow) to him – a politics of subversion to which, in the end, Foucault himself does not subscribe.[2] Leaving that exegesis and argument aside, we turn to one central characteristic of that reading and one crucial conclusion.

First, as shown above, Butler broaches the possibility of a politics of subversion within the context of Foucault's work. Second, she does this so as to find his (presumed) account of subversion lacking (Butler 1987a: 228). These elements of Butler's reading of Foucault prove essential to our argument here, since they show that Butler uses tools provided by Foucault in order to build *her own* politics of subversion. Specifically, as will be discussed below, the central idea of subversion from within – what we might call genealogical subversion – derives from Butler's interpretation of Foucault. Thus her reading of Foucault proves significant, despite the fact that she is wrong to assess his work in terms of subversion. Rather, he consistently *rejects* the project that Butler *takes up* as her own.

Butler makes that project hers in the last section of *Gender Trouble*. Here again, subversion appears initially as someone else's endeavour – this time in Kristeva's celebration of the semiotic. Deutscher pinpoints Butler's critique as challenging 'the grounds of the adequacy of [Kristeva's] account of subversion' (Deutscher 1997: 23). On Kristeva's reading, the semiotic realm – constituted by the maternal body, poetic experience and lesbian existence – can *subvert* the paternal law. Butler notes: 'The semiotic is described by Kristeva as destroying or eroding the Symbolic' (Butler 1999: 101, 105). Butler takes on board a project of subversion by tacitly recognising its significance. She criticises Kristeva not because of the latter's politics of subversion but because that politics remains outside culture: '*cultural* subversion is not really Kristeva's concern, for subversion, when it appears, emerges from beneath the surface of culture only inevitably to return there' (Butler 1999: 112; cf. Deutscher 1997: 26). Here Butler offers her standard critique of Lacanian theory: nothing politically significant can come from a theory that displaces its radical element *outside* language, politics or history (see Chambers 2003a). Our concern lies not with this critique but with Butler's subtle appropriation of the project of subversion.

Butler's critical readings of Foucault, Kristeva and Wittig consistently demonstrate that subversion cannot serve as a radical practice or fund a radical politics if we conceptualise it as external to or beyond the system that it subverts. The above authors, along with Lacan and Žižek, are all called to task when they project the radical political moment 'outside' the system that it would disrupt (Butler 1993, 1997b). For example, Kristeva constructs the semiotic as 'before the law' and fully external to the symbolic realm. Žižek does the same with the Lacanian 'real', placing it beyond the realm of history, culture and politics in such a way that it serves as their very cause. While her literary texts prove subversive because they offer a 'subversive redeployment' of the values that belong within the regime of compulsory heterosexuality (Butler 1999: 160), Wittig's (1992) theoretical texts make the mistake of conceptualising subversion only outside the system (Butler 1999: 154). Butler repeatedly asserts, against these claims, that any 'prediscursive' is nothing more than a move from within a particular language game. There is no 'outside' of discourse other than as a (false) projection inside a particular set of discursive practices. For Butler, then, subversion must come from *within* culture, history and discourse if it is to be politically efficacious (e.g. Butler 1999: 185; cf. Butler 1993, 1995a, 1997a). We can never get outside the system that we wish to subvert, and to assert that we can is merely to undermine the possibility of subversion. For this reason, the agency involved in a subversive act or a subversive reading appears from inside the system that it attempts to overturn. Indeed, because it must remain internal in this way – yet still serve to overwhelm or transform the system to which it is internal – subversion undermines the very distinction between inner and outer (Butler 1999: 174; cf. Butler 2000a).

In the final chapter of *Gender Trouble* Butler's question comes into focus: *how to articulate a viable politics of subversion that remains inside of culture.* Subversion can only be possible within the terms of the law (Butler 1999:

119; cf. Deutscher 1997: 26, 31), which means that Butler, or we, will have to develop a more nuanced conception of subversion, one that eschews the definition of subversion as external overthrow or anarchic rejection of the law. To work within the law must be to subvert it differently, perhaps in a way that returns us to the Latin etymology of the word, *subvertere*, 'to turn from below'. Subversion must be a political project of erosion, one that works on norms from the inside, breaking them down not through external challenge but through an internal repetition that weakens them. A subversive politics thus becomes a subtle politics, one that requires patient, repeated, local action. We will return to this account below.

Despite Butler's own avoidance of codifying any sort of politics of subversion, of creating a metric that would distinguish the subversive from the non-subversive, the next three sections will reveal (in a way that shows its importance for the field of political theory) Butler's politics of subversion. We are not interested in the conditions of possibility for subversion, and we are not seeking to create the yardstick that Butler rightly dismisses. Our aim, instead, is to bring a politics of subversion into the foreground, to delineate that politics in the first place. The politics of subversion remains a politics of the incalculable, a non-programmatic and ungrounded politics of possibility, but the incalculable should not be conflated with the indescribable or the unthinkable (see Lloyd 2005a: 144). To grasp what is at stake in her politics of subversion demands a shift in the level of analysis; it requires a theory of heteronormativity. We make this move in the next section of the chapter by showing that, despite not using the term herself, Butler describes and attacks the workings of heteronormativity. Once heteronormativity has been brought into starker light as the target of Butler's own efforts at subversion, we can then fill out her politics of subversion – including its radical reworking of gender and thoroughgoing rejection of identity politics – in the final two sections.

From homophobia to heteronormativity

Subversion, then, is not only an 'incalculable effect' but also a critical theoretical and political practice of working on norms from within, of undermining those norms, eroding their efficacy, calling them into question either by merely calling them out (i.e. revealing their condition as norms) or by challenging their status, their grounding or their effects. As we discussed in the previous section, certain authors have explored Butler's politics of subversion indirectly, by investigating practices discussed by Butler that could potentially carry out a politics of subversion. Parody, performativity and resignification provide the three most common examples.[3] Deutscher takes subversion as central, but Deutscher turns away from subversion (and toward constitutive instability) at precisely the moment she suggests that Butler never tells us what subversion is (Deutscher 1997: 31–2). Here, we delve directly into the politics of subversion, specifying and clarifying our previous remarks about what subversion *is* by way of an argument about subversion's critical target.

Certain passages in *Gender Trouble* might lead one to believe that the text seeks a subversion of identity itself (e.g. Butler 1999: 163), and this reading gives rise to a series of criticisms (see, especially, Weir 1996). However, such a project, if interpreted narrowly, makes very little intuitive sense, and thus the criticisms of Butler on this front may rest on too literal a reading. Specific conceptions of gender might be subverted (Butler 1999: 179). The 'epistemological account of identity' that serves as the ground for a certain form of feminist politics can certainly be subverted (Butler 1999: 184). And if we go so far as to argue, as Butler does, that the sex/gender distinction is itself a product of the discourse of gender, then perhaps 'sexuality', or, as Foucault might say, 'sex itself', can be subverted (Butler 1999: 30–1; Foucault 1978: 152).[4] But how could one subvert identity itself? This last question proves very much rhetorical, since it names a project that is not Butler's. Butler herself makes no genuine effort to subvert identity or even gender (see below). Indeed, much of Butler's work goes to show that there is no such thing as 'identity itself'. Identities are produced through iterated practices; they are never self-identical. Butler offers us a genealogy of identity that destabilises it, renders it partial and contingent, and she theorises heterosexual identity as constituted by the disavowal of homosexual attachments (Butler 1997b: 146).[5] Butler's political project, however, despite both the subtitle of her book and the potential narrow (mis)reading of subversion by her critics, never seeks an 'overthrow' of 'identity itself'. While she does call for many of the other potential political outcomes that we have listed, Butler's fundamental object of attack in her early work is the normative structure that she names the 'heterosexual matrix'.

Central to Butler's account of the matrix is her conceptualisation of 'gender intelligibility' and her reading of 'regulatory practices'. Butler argues that '"persons" only become intelligible through becoming gendered' (Butler 1999: 22). In other words, the very idea of the self only makes sense if that self appears in gendered form. There can be no gender-neutral 'person', despite arguments to the contrary, since a person *without* gender would be unintelligible, would not make any sense to us. In other words, we could not understand such a non-gendered entity *as* a person. Butler appears to derive the concept of a 'regulatory practice' from her reading of Foucault. A regulatory practice is a *normative* practice: it can appear as an edict or law, but it usually functions much more subtly through societal expectation, peer pressure, propriety (i.e. as a norm). We pretend to believe that a set of internal essential features establishes personhood. Butler asks instead: 'to what extent do *regulatory practices* of gender formation and division constitute identity, the internal coherence of the subject' (Butler 1999: 23, emphasis in original). Butler wants to demonstrate that gender intelligibility has a great deal more to do with the power of norms, with the wide array of regulatory practices that police gender, than with any inherent features of a genderless self.

The heterosexual matrix is nothing more, though certainly nothing less, than an assemblage of norms that serves the particular end of producing subjects whose gender/sex/desire all *cohere* in certain ways. Butler writes: '"intelligible" genders are those which in some sense institute and maintain relations of coherence among sex, gender, sexual practice, and desire' (Butler 1999: 23). Butler introduces the term 'heterosexual matrix' at the very end of her first chapter in *Gender Trouble* (Butler 1999: 42–3), but her reference here, much earlier on, to a 'matrix of intelligibility' (Butler 1999: 24) in many ways gives a more lucid account of what is at stake for her in coining the phrase in the first place. The question of this matrix turns on 'subversive' possibilities that might be found within it: one articulates the matrix in order to subvert it. As a way of enhancing those possibilities for subversion, we want to give an account of the matrix *through the lens* of heteronormativity. This is not to suggest that one *replace* the heterosexual matrix with the concept of heteronormativity, but rather that one use the conceptual resources of the latter term in order to offer a more helpful, more vibrant, more politically productive reading of the matrix. We propose this reading not because of a theoretical deficiency in the 'heterosexual matrix', but because we do not believe the heterosexual matrix has been well understood by Butler's readers – and Butler later drops the term herself. Thus we are offering an extended interpretation *of* the heterosexual matrix and arguing for the centrality of the concept of heteronormativity *within* that reading, but we do not seek to substitute the latter for the former.

Heteronormativity is a regulatory practice of sex/gender/desire that thereby alters or sometimes sets the conditions of possibility and impossibility for gender intelligibility. Butler never uses the word heteronormativity in *Gender Trouble*, an unsurprising fact, given that the word was coined three years later by Michael Warner (1993; cf. Rich 1980). Despite – so far as anyone can tell – being the first to *use* the word (and it is still not in the *OED*), Warner did not really bother to *define* it, and no one has done much explicit conceptual work with it. Warner applies the term to suggest that society takes heterosexuality to be *normative* in terms of identity, practices and behaviour. This means that heterosexuality is the median point on the normal curve: not only that which is statistically dominant, but also that which is expected, demanded and always presupposed in society.

We use the term heteronormativity to articulate the political power that heterosexuality has when it functions as a norm. Heteronormativity is a regulatory practice in Butler's sense and *should therefore be rigorously distinguished from homophobia*. Butler herself often refers to homophobic discourses or responses (e.g. Butler 1999: xiv, 168; 2000a: 70; 2004b: 5; cf. Butler 1997b: ch. 5), but for our purposes the concept of homophobia proves theoretically reductive and politically limited. Homophobia connotes both an individual act (something done by a person who is 'homophobic') and a psychological disturbance (a problem located in someone's head). Used as a political concept, homophobia encourages an interpretation that would reduce the political effects of heteronormativity – effects that manifest broadly in the material world – to the explicit actions of a few homophobic individuals. If we take homophobia as the political problem, then we imply that the political solution depends upon changing individual attitudes.

Certain readers might claim that it is we who have construed 'homophobia' too narrowly; they might insist that homophobia can be thought more broadly than this, that it can be considered a social and political problem with social and political policy as its proper responses. We resist the temptation to think homophobia writ large for at least two reasons. First, to do so would be to run a different sort of reductionist risk – the risk of merely assailing 'homophobic society' without any mechanism to specify the particular political issues or concerns in play. More importantly, even when thought broadly the notion of homophobia has the tendency to flatten or erase some of the most significant critiques of sexuality (and the sex/gender system) that have been offered over the past two decades both by feminists and queer theorists. 'Homophobia' compresses the insights of feminist and queer critique within the constrained framework of interest-group liberalism. As Lloyd suggests, in a similarly critical vein, 'interest group pluralism has formed one of the dominant paradigms for thinking about' democratic politics (Lloyd 2005a: 153). And the hegemony of this model makes it difficult to discern the workings of alternative political and theoretical vocabularies. The worry, then, is that sexuality will not be thoroughly problematised but will instead be reduced to a mere problem of 'sexual orientation'. The 'solution' to this so-called problem then looks simple: reject, deny or throw off 'prejudice' against homosexuals, and refuse to discriminate against same. Indeed, the liberal state has the obvious solution here, even if it has not been fully implemented by any liberal states: simply make discrimination against homosexuals illegal.[6] This liberal fantasy contends that once straights stop being homophobic – that is, stop fearing gays and lesbians and stop discriminating against them – then equal treatment of gays and lesbians will follow. The 'right to marry' completes the telos of this anti-homophobic vision.

However, and as we will demonstrate below, heteronormativity cannot be translated into a problem of discrimination against autonomous individuals on the basis of their sexual orientation. 'Gay marriage' cannot 'solve' these problems; no wonder, then, that it is precisely those queer theorists most attuned to the workings of heteronormativity who have been willing to challenge the mainstream lesbian and gay movement's choice (particularly in the US) to make 'gay marriage' their central political goal (Warner 1999; Butler 2000b; see also Smith 2001). The concept of heteronormativity reveals institutional, cultural and legal norms that reify and entrench the normativity of heterosexuality. In other words, 'heteronormativity' tells us that heterosexual desire and identity are not merely assumed, they are expected. They are demanded. And they are rewarded and privileged. Thus heteronormativity must not be reduced to the idea of an assumption in the heads of individuals that says, 'my guess is that you're straight'. Heteronormativity is written into law, encoded in the very edifices of institutions (see below), built into an enormous variety of common practices – particularly since so much of society remains structured around dating/ romance.

In general, to reveal the norm may be to subvert it, since norms work best when they are never exposed. In other words, the optimal operation of the norm is an invisible operation. Once norms reach the point that they require significant shoring up, then they have already been significantly weakened. This means that reinforcing a norm can never bring it back to full strength, since the very act of reinforcement serves to expose the norm as weaker than it could be. To capture this particular meaning of subversion (and its political significance) requires maintaining a clear distinction between 'what the majority do/are', on the one hand, and normalisation, on the other. This distinction entails that one not take heteronormativity as merely pointing to a 'truth' about the world: namely, that a supermajority of people in it act/identify as heterosexual. The political concept heteronormativity offers not a bare description of fact (most people 'are heterosexual'). Rather, heteronormativity provides a political articulation of the normativity of heterosexuality. Taken out of context, this last claim might appear tautological; in context, however, it serves to stress the politics of norms that lie at the heart of Butler's project.

If we take the 'problem' to be heteronormativity in Butler's sense of a regulatory practice, then we simultaneously suggest strategies of reshaping and resisting normative structures and regulatory practices. Heteronormativity is both a theoretically richer and politically more salient concept; it makes it possible to *analyse* the political problems to which homophobia can only allude. Heteronormativity has been defined as a '*practice* of organising' beliefs around presumed heterosexual desire, as a set of '*rules* that force us to conform to hegemonic heterosexual standards' and as a *system* of binary gender (Dennis 2003; Felluga 2004; Weiss 2001). We prefer to emphasise the importance of *norms*, which proves so central to the concept, and therefore adopt the following theoretical articulation of the term:

> Heteronormativity means, quite simply, that heterosexuality is the norm, in culture, in society, in politics. Heteronormativity points out the expectation of heterosexuality as it is written into our world. It does not, of course, mean that everyone is straight. More significantly, heteronormativity is not part of a conspiracy theory that would suggest that everyone must become straight or be made so. The importance of the concept is that it centers on the operation of the norm. Heteronormativity

emphasizes the extent to which everyone, straight or queer, will be judged, measured, probed and evaluated from the perspective of the heterosexual norm. It means that *everyone and everything is judged from the perspective of straight.*

(Chambers 2003b: 26)

Heteronormativity carries regulatory practices within it, practices that produce and constrain gender intelligibility. This means that it structures the social, political and cultural worlds not just through its impact on ideas and beliefs, but also practically as well, in the way that it operates through institutions, laws and daily life. For such practices, we can think of marriage, of course. But we can also think of adoption, immigration and taxes. We can consider club memberships and car insurance. We can ponder blind dates, bathrooms and Valentine's Day. And none of this is to mention *weddings*. Any list of laws, customs and practices like this points to the fact that heteronormativity accrues privilege to those behaviours, practices and relationships that more closely approximate the norm, while stigmatising, marginalising or rendering invisible – *making unintelligible* – those behaviours, relationships and practices that deviate from it. Heteronormativity might be taken, then, as a concept that parallels that of *whiteness*: both call attention to seemingly invisible problems of sedimented and ingrained privilege that need to be *subverted* (see Roediger 1999; Olson 2004).

The shift from homophobia to heteronormativity also offers a powerful new frame for reconsidering some of the political concerns that have proved most worrisome to Butler's readers. As Stone (2005) and Lloyd (2005a) both stress, the question of political agency and the issue of normative judgement both arise repeatedly as areas of concern for Butler's interlocutors in political theory, even for those most sympathetic to her project. Framing the problem to which Butler responds in terms of heteronormativity (and not homophobia) draws attention to the ways in which Butler rejects a model of agency or normative judgement built on a conception of sovereignty. Borrowing the language of Patchen Markell to elucidate this issue, we can say that heteronormativity names a manner of 'patterning and arranging the world that allow[s] some people and groups to enjoy a semblance of sovereign agency at other's expense' (Markell 2003: 5). To challenge heteronormativity, then, requires a rejection of that very model of sovereign agency, an insistence that no individual is sovereign given our fundamental dependence on (being-with) others (Butler 2004a). Agency must thus be decentred and distanced from the sovereign model, which does not mean to do away with agency entirely (see Coole 2005). At the same time, normativity must not be reduced to a notion of deliberation, judgement or choice made by a supposedly sovereign agent. And this is why, as the following section demonstrates, the subversion of heteronormativity cannot be carried out by the single act of an autonomous agent. It is also why the critique of heteronormativity involves a subversion of the 'patterning and arranging' of the world that heteronormativity creates, but such a critique does not logically derive from a 'normative judgement' lodged against heteronormativity (as if the latter were simply an act of 'discrimination' or 'oppression' that could merely be condemned).

Heteronormativity and sex/gender: the matrix

Butler shows that the heterosexual matrix never remains static. The matrix can only be sustained through constant *repetition*: the matrix 'stands' only through the 'motion' of the regulatory practices that produce it. Subversion becomes possible precisely because temporal repetition is required in order to sustain regulatory practices.

> The 'unity' of gender is the effect of a regulatory practice that seeks to render gender identity uniform through a compulsory heterosexuality [that regulatory practice is heteronormativity]. The force of this practice is, through an exclusionary apparatus of production, to restrict the meanings of 'heterosexuality', 'homosexuality', and 'bisexuality'. ... That the power regimes of heterosexuality ... seek to augment themselves through a constant repetition of their logic ... does not imply that repetition itself ought to be stopped – as if it could be. If repetition is bound to persist as the mechanism of the cultural reproduction of identities, then the crucial question emerges: What kind of repetition might call into question the *regulatory practice* of identity itself?
>
> (Butler 1999: 42, emphasis added)

The emphasis added here proves essential. What must be subverted is not 'identity itself' but the 'regulatory practice'. And, as we have seen, the assemblage of regulatory practices, which produce intelligible genders within a heterosexual matrix that insists upon the coherence of sex/gender/ desire, is another name for heteronormativity. The target of Butler's politics of subversion must be that assemblage, the matrix itself, heteronormativity. To subvert the heterosexual matrix is to repeat the regulatory practices that maintain the matrix, but to do so in a way that alters its terms. Since its terms are precisely gender, sex and sexuality – and particularly the way they work together to produce particular gender identities – the subversion of heteronormativity will have radically significant consequences for our *understanding* of identity and our *practices* of identity politics (see Scott 1992, 1999a). The subversion of heteronormativity will not, however, do away with identity altogether. Making this point requires a close reading of *Gender Trouble* where it articulates a politics of subversion, i.e. the final twenty-five pages of the book.

Butler begins the section on 'performative subversions' by *describing* heteronormativity while using the *language* of homophobia. In a section that theorises the 'construction of the body', Butler cites Simon Watney's

(1988) work on the figure of the person with AIDS as a 'polluting figure'. In that context she castigates 'the media's ... homophobic response' and 'the sensationalist graphics of homophobic signifying systems' (Butler 1999: 168). Despite these claims, Butler's argument does not work against individual acts of violence against gays (that is, it is not really about homophobia, at least in a narrow sense); nor does it seek therapeutic understanding that would eliminate the fear of gays and lesbians. Instead, Butler offers an account of both heteronormativity and the acts that potentially subvert it:

> the construction of stable bodily contours relies upon fixed sites of corporeal permeability and impermeability. Those sexual practices in both homosexual and heterosexual contexts that open surfaces and orifices to erotic signification or close down others effectively reinscribe the boundaries of the body along new cultural lines. Anal sex among men is an example.
>
> (Butler 1999: 169)

But, as Butler's general description suggests, sadomasochistic sex among men and women is another example. The heterosexual matrix not only produces a certain linking between sex/gender/desire, but also, and concomitantly, generates a certain construction of the body as impermeable – or as penetrable or erotic in only certain predefined ways. In one narrow sense, then, sexual practices that deviate from these norms offer one site of *potential* resistance, a site explored in some depth by Foucault in his interviews with the gay press (see Foucault 1989; cf. Halperin 1995). We emphasise 'potential' here, since it cannot be forgotten that to deviate from a norm is not necessarily to subvert it; indeed, norms depend for their survival on a certain percentage of deviant cases.

That is one reason to insist upon the complexity of subversion, why subversion can never be the simple throwing off of identity and why the politics of subversion must centre on norms. We can begin to work toward this conclusion by starting with Butler's reading of Foucault's famous lines 'the soul is the prison of the body'. Foucault argues in *Discipline and Punish* that with transformations in modern penal practices and through the rise of the disciplines the 'soul' of 'man' comes to be signified externally, to be written *on* his body rather than preserved inside it. Butler reads that argument as follows:

> the soul is precisely what the body lacks; hence, the body presents itself as a signifying lack. That lack which *is* the body signifies the soul as that which cannot show. In this sense, then, the soul is a surface signification that contests and displaces the inner/outer distinction itself.
>
> (Butler 1999, 172; see Chambers 2003a).

Butler wants to apply the same logic to the production of gender: 'the redescription of intrapsychic processes in terms of the surface politics of the body implies a corollary redescription of gender as [a] disciplinary production' (Butler 1999: 172). Her account here, however, comes up slightly short, since it must be not merely a redescription of *gender*, but a thorough redescription and displacement of the sex/gender distinction. If sex has been taken by second-wave feminism as the inner essence of an outwardly manifested gender, then Butler's goal is not to subvert gender (that outward appearance) but to subvert the sex/gender distinction itself and thereby to move well beyond the inner/outer distinction. Butler tries to make Foucault's account of the 'soul' analogous to her account of 'gender', but the analogy proves faulty. The soul is *thought* to be internal, but Foucault shows that it is an external signification *of* the internal. Gender, on the other hand, is *thought to be external*. Thus it is an external signification of an internal essence, sex. Of course, this shows us that if sex is itself a project *of* gender, then in stylising gender we simultaneously perform sex. Sex, which is thought be prior to gender, turns out to be its product. Sex is the prison of gender, and it is sex itself that is written on the body. The analogy to Foucault's 'soul' must be 'sex itself', that which is thought to be internal but turns out to be written on the body (in the case of sex, it is written *with* gender).

This displacement, this undermining of the inner/outer (sex/gender) distinction, cannot be reduced to a subversion of gender, or even of sex. Butler refers to the surface politics of gender as a 'stylisation of gender', and she asks after its conditions of possibility. Her answer: the 'disciplinary production of gender effects a false stabilisation of gender in the interests of the heterosexual construction and regulation of sexuality within the reproductive domain' (Butler 1999: 172). In other words, the heterosexual matrix constitutes the chain of equivalence that is sex/gender/desire. Heteronormativity gives us gender as the outward expression of an internal essence, sex. The presumption of heterosexuality, of opposite-sex desire, links the two together.

The heterosexual matrix produces gender, both in the form of manifestations of masculinity and femininity and in the consolidation of the same in the shape of men and women. This production is thought to rely upon male and female sex as the foundation of gender. The third term of the matrix is opposite-sex desire, that which holds the matrix together. Heteronormativity is the force that maintains the matrix, since it is within this heteronormative core that sex becomes gender (or vice versa). Putting these three terms in motion, we typically presume that the male desire for a female manifests masculinity and consolidates the gender identity of 'man'. This circuit of desire is also the construction of masculine gender and the consolidation of the gender identity of man. However, the regulatory practice that insists that masculinity reside in a desire for women – or that to 'be a man' is to 'want a woman' – can itself re-entrench the very 'maleness' at the core of masculinity. In other words, just as maleness can produce a man (from sex to gender), so 'being a man' can produce maleness (the projection of gender back onto sex, the construction of 'sex' through norms of gender).

The matrix consolidates the strict identification of sex with gender; we normally assume that this line of identification runs in one direction, from sex to gender. Thus we presume that males become men and females become women somehow 'naturally', that is, all on their own. The notion of the matrix seeks to expose that which normally remains hidden. In other words, it reveals heteronormativity. The core presumption of opposite-sex desire, a presumption produced by heteronormativity, *that* is what makes it possible for sex to 'naturally' become gender. We only ever see – to the extent that we see anything other than the products of the matrix, that is, masculinity and femininity, 'men' and 'women' – the outside edges of the matrix, males who are (have become) men and females who are (have become) women. But while the matrix suggests an interior essence of femaleness that produces the external gender of woman, we see that the solidification of identity as woman can be just as much a projection of femaleness *from* the location of woman.

However schematic, this attempt to unpack the matrix proves worth the effort if it can throw into sharper relief the relationship between heteronormativity and sex/gender. Using the conceptual language of heteronormativity derived in the preceding section, our description of the matrix shows that both gender and sex *gain their very coherence* through heteronormativity. As categories of both thought and identity, sex and gender become intelligible within the terms of heteronormativity. And this is precisely why lesbian or gay identity is consistently rendered *unintelligible* by heteronormativity. A woman who desires a woman is an impossibility. Either the desiring person 'is not really a woman' or the object of desire 'is not really a woman'. Hence we see how thoroughly heteronormative is the notion of homosexuality as 'inversion'. Inversion theory tells us that a male homosexual is a 'woman trapped in a man's body', that is, 'he' *is really* a woman, hence his desire for a man. By showing clearly that Freud's theory of original bisexuality actually functions by way of a presumption of opposite-sex desire, Butler reveals (in the language we have been using) the heteronormativity at the heart of Freud's otherwise (and sometimes still) radical work on sexuality (Butler 1999). In her massive effort to theorise 'lesbian desire' as genuinely the desire *of* a woman *for* a woman, Teresa de Lauretis seeks her own subversion of heteronormativity, and does so precisely by working *inside* the terms of psychoanalysis (de Lauretis 1994).

To take another tack that explores the significance of the matrix, this working out of heteronormativity's relation to sex/gender (within the matrix) starkly illuminates a number of everyday practices. It does so in a way that connects heteronormativity directly to gender. For example, the typical strategies of harassment and abuse targeted against lesbians and gays focus not on 'sexual orientation' as a category of sexual identity, but precisely on gender. As is well known, epithets such as 'dyke' and 'fairy' attack perceived gender 'deviations' not abstract ideas of 'sexual orientation'. The heteronormative orderings of professional sport serve not to prevent same-sex sexual activity (indeed, gender-segregated teams would seem to provide opportunities for such activity, perhaps even to encourage it), but to preserve men/male and women/female as separate categories of sex and gender identity (Disch and Kane 1996).

And weddings prove to be the quintessential heteronormative practices not merely, and not even primarily, because marriage is reserved in most countries for heterosexual couples. Weddings play out and illustrate in practice the heterosexual matrix; they map it better than any diagram could possibly hope to do. A male who desires a female dresses up like a man – after spending the night before with a large group of other *men* engaged in thoroughly masculine activities. A female desires this male in such a way as to make her a woman, and she spends her own night out exclusively with women, engaged in stereotypically feminine activities. She becomes a woman, in the sense of both moving through the matrix and maturing, when her father places her on a pedestal next to her desiring groom (a word derived from the Middle English simply for 'boy' or 'man'). All of this must occur in front of dozens, if not hundreds, of friends and family who have travelled hundreds and thousands of miles to witness this presentation of the matrix: the literal movement down the aisle through the circuits of desire to stand before and above others as 'man' and 'woman', or, better, as 'husband' and 'wife' – or, even better, 'man' and 'wife'. Thus, to *see* the heterosexual matrix, just go to a wedding.

In any event, we insist that the politics of heteronormativity is the politics of the everyday. This means that while subversions of heteronormativity can be sought both in high-minded theory writings (say, Butler) and in collective political action (say, ACT-UP), they can also be found in daily life. Every time an individual, an institution, a text, a movie, a group practices, theorises, thinks or presents sex/gender in such a way as to erode the norm of heterosexuality from within, there is the *possibility* of subversion.

Subversions of heteronormativity

Butler turns to drag, to the practices of gender parody, as a strategy and site of this *potential* subversion. Drag is an *example* of gender performativity, not its paradigm, and this example appears within a theory of gender performativity, not performance. As Butler clarifies, performance 'presumes a subject', while performativity 'contests the very notion of a subject' (Butler 1994: 33). This is why, despite the excited early readings of *Gender Trouble* as a text that made 'anything possible' with respect to gender, Butler's theory of performativity rejects the notion of a pre-given subject who would then *perform*. For this reason, as Lloyd's work shows lucidly, Butler denies directly the idea that 'subjects can instrumentally perform genders in ways of their own choosing' (Lloyd 2005a: 137; cf. Lloyd 1999).[7]

After this analysis of the matrix, Butler's discussions of drag grow clearer, since drag concerns heteronormativity (and therefore sex/gender); it does not apply to gender per se. If we read drag as a political or cultural practice that tries to subvert gender, then we will always find ourselves trapped in the endless debate over whether drag successfully subverts or merely apes gender norms. Butler avoids these debates; she is not naïve about the possibilities for subversion. Thus, she writes: 'there is no necessary relation between drag and subversion' (Butler 1993: 125). Subversion does not happen automatically and its effects cannot be predicted in advance. Thus the subversive possibility of drag does not lie in the mere empirical chance that numerous individuals will 'do' drag, and thereby (by default, as it were) 'subvert gender'. As we have repeatedly made clear, Butler has taken her leave of that model of agency.

This is the case because drag cannot subvert 'gender itself', for drag, or any other practice of subversion, must target the coherence of sex/gender/desire and undermine the very internal/external distinction of sex/gender. A description of drag as subverting heteronormativity is not a radical rereading of Butler. She says as much herself: '*drag fully subverts the distinction between inner and outer*' (Butler 1999: 174, emphasis added; cf. Butler 2000a). It does not target gender in isolation, since it shows us that gender cannot be isolated in this way but must always be produced as a part of heteronormativity. Thus, as Butler puts it in *Gender Trouble:* drag subverts 'the law of heterosexual coherence' (Butler 1999: 175). She explains this point more fully in *Bodies that Matter* when she describes drag as a possible location for a 'certain ambivalence' about regimes of gender: 'to claim that all gender is like drag, or is drag, is to suggest that "imitation" is at the heart of the *heterosexual* project' (Butler 1993: 125). Drag cannot be turned into some sort of direct-action tool of queer activism. Yet drag holds subversive potential precisely to the extent that it exposes the internal structure of heteronormativity.

This makes it obvious that the subversion of gender would constitute neither a meaningful theoretical project nor a coherent political one. If we set out to subvert gender *while working within the terms of heteronormativity*, we can only ever fail. Thought on its own, in isolation from the matrix, no singular expression or practice of gender can be subversive. This is why Butler herself says that gender ambiguity proves as likely to shore up heteronormativity as it does to challenge it (Butler 1999: xiv). Heteronormativity has the power to capture attempts at gender subversion by reconciling them to the heterosexual norm. Indeed, the power of heteronormativity with respect to practices of gender is precisely that it makes it possible to reinterpret even the most dramatic deviations from gender norms (say, drag) as mere marginalisations of sexuality that attest to the power of the heterosexual norm. No practices of subversion can prove efficacious unless the target (intended or otherwise) of such subversion is heteronormativity itself. Gender can never be toppled or overthrown *within* the terms of heteronormativity. This argument proves utterly consistent with Butler's own point, against MacKinnon (1987) (see Butler 1999: xii), that if we work within the tautology that 'gender produces gender', then there is no way to escape it. The sex/gender system only coheres within and through heteronormativity. In other words, *without the heterosexual matrix we could not sustain gender identity* in its current form. Gender gets transformed (though not necessarily subverted) all on its own if political and cultural practices serve to undermine the heterosexual matrix.

Perhaps for some readers both the discussion of drag and the prior articulation of the matrix through heteronormativity will still beg the question of which strategies are subversive and which are not. They will be concerned not with the 'possibility' of subversion offered by the example of drag, but with specific strategies designed to actualise subversion. They will want to know not just *how* subversion works and *what* it targets, but what it *is* and how we can *produce* it. The first response to this line of inquiry must surely be Butler's own: 'judgments on what distinguishes the subversive from the unsubversive ... cannot be made out of context ... [and] ... cannot be made in ways that endure through time' (Butler 1999: xxi). Lloyd states the point succinctly: 'there is neither a single nor a guaranteed way of contesting heteronormativity' (Lloyd 2005a: 148). And we place a strong emphasis on Lloyd's second point: a politics of subversion must insist upon a future that is without guarantees, a future-to-come that cannot be predicted but which may well bring its own reinterpretation of the past (see Markell 2003; Chambers 2003a.) This requires a conception of democracy as always open-ended and always incomplete, and it entails a critical conception of ethics (see Dean 2008).

None of this is to imply that we cannot say what subversion might look like in practice; nor is it to suggest that we should not seek out subversions within practices already ongoing. Indeed, in the previous section we tried to suggest some sites within the everyday in which one could possibly find subversion. In the same context that she defines subversion as an 'incalculable effect', Butler goes on to describe the subversive activities of ACT-UP, arguing that their staging of 'die-ins' on New York streets challenged norms and forced witnesses to question their presumptions in significantly subversive ways (Butler 1994: 38). Even here, however, in a case that she clearly wants to call subversive, Butler consistently refuses to offer a set of standards by which one could judge it so. Indeed, Butler suggests that an act may prove more subversive because of its very *illegibility*, through its capacity to thwart our standard practices of reading (Butler 1994: 38). In other words, we cannot start with a metric that would judge an act subversive (or not), since subversion as a practice may alter our metric. That very transformation of our reading practices would be what makes it subversive.

We can fold this issue of legibility into our thinking of heteronormativity in the following manner: heteronormativity makes sexuality legible (Chambers 2005). It does so by allowing us, first of all, to assume that everyone is straight. And when that presumption fails, then heteronormativity demands that those who are not straight either pretend to be so (that is, allow 'us' to continue to presume they are straight) or declare their deviance from the norm clearly and explicitly (that is, come out). To subvert heteronormativity would therefore be to render sexuality less legible, to undermine the practices of reading sexuality produced by heteronormativity.

Moreover, the subversion of heteronormativity both accomplishes and is accomplished by something much simpler: namely, challenging, calling into question and/or undermining *the presumption of heterosexuality*. Thought in its broadest sense, heteronormativity affects daily life, shapes social norms and impacts on public policy by building the tacit assumption of heterosexuality into those practices, norms and policies. Subversions of heteronormativity cannot, again, be calculated in advance, nor can their gains be secured once they emerge. Nevertheless, subversions of heteronormativity can and will emerge whenever the presumption of heterosexuality is frustrated. Heteronormativity will be subverted – the norm will be gradually weakened, undermined, *eroded* from within – whenever the presumption of heterosexuality no longer holds. Further, and as should be clear from the earlier articulation of the concept of heteronormativity, contributions to the politics of subverting heteronormativity are also made whenever that presumption must be made explicit, when it must be defended rather than assumed.

Subverting heteronormativity, then, can occur in many ways. First, it can emerge in projects that deconstruct heterosexuality, that demonstrate its discursive effects and its internal contradictions (Halley 1993). It can appear in reconceptualisations of sex/gender/desire that interrupt the matrix, challenge the heteronormative presumptions of earlier theorists or reconceive the workings of desire (Butler 1999; Sedgwick 1990; de Lauretis 1994; etc.). Broadly speaking, the project in queer theory and the work produced within it since the early 1990s has contributed to a theory of sexuality (in its relation to gender and desire) that consistently thwarts the workings of heteronormativity (see also Carver 1996a, 2004).

But subverting heteronormativity is far from being a project reserved for theory. Heterosexuality can be practically deconstructed as well, and the presumption of heterosexuality can be frustrated in myriad ways in daily life. This reminds us of a college sketch presented in the residence halls by LGBT (lesbian, gay, bisexual and transgender) members: in it, three friends were discussing an upcoming dance, with two trying to set up the third. It quickly becomes apparent that the first two friends 'naturally presume' that their other friend is gay. They cannot understand why he grows so awkward and uncomfortable about their plans to set him up with 'the perfect guy'. Finally, the third friend embarrassingly mumbles/whispers that he is straight. The other two fail to hide their astonishment, but then quickly cover with comments such as, 'Oh, that's cool ... really, I have a cousin who is straight!' This is a practical deconstruction of heterosexuality, achieved by providing a brief, comic glimpse into a world in which the presumption of heterosexuality does not hold.

Other changed practices contribute to the subversion of heteronormativity on a daily basis. Within not only lesbian and gay communities but also a large number of academic communities, language use is changing in a way that rids discourse of its heteronormative presumption. 'Partner' is a gender-neutral term, but its significance lies not with gender equality but with the production of a gender ambiguity that foils the opposite-sex spouse presumption built into heteronormativity. Communities and institutions that have made the language of 'partner' common have thus taken one small step away from the continued presumption of heterosexuality. Bathrooms/lavatories offer another excellent example. The standard set-up of public facilities contains two separate lavatories, with doors side by side, each reserved exclusively for one sex, with icons on the door to indicate the singularity of each sex and the binary separation between them. This configuration *instantiates* the heterosexual matrix – from binary sex to binary gender, with segregation essential because of the presumption of heterosexual desire. Most people never ponder 'the bathroom problem' as it has come to be known in the literature (see Halberstam 1998). But those who deviate from the 'normal' find it a particularly painful and powerful 'problem'. One simple response to the 'bathroom problem' can be quite powerful as a reversal, as many bars and restaurants have discovered: simply remove the signs from the door and one makes a small but important subversion of heteronormativity.

Finally, heteronormativity can also be subverted at the level of public policy. The trend in recent years, particularly in the US, has been to make heteronormativity more explicit by *writing it into the law*, where it previously was not mentioned (and for potentially subversive countertrends, see Carver 2007). The Federal Defense of Marriage Act (DOMA) and the dozens of state DOMAs all serve to codify the presumption of heteronormativity by announcing it plainly. In one sense, this is a dramatic setback in the struggle for equal civil rights for lesbian and gay citizens – a fact that should not be downplayed. Nevertheless, in the politics of norms the very effort required to defend heteronormativity outwardly suggests a certain weakening of the norm. And legislators across the US have made it clear that they see themselves as responding to an imminent threat. This threat is certainly not, as those legislators would have it, against the 'sacred institution of marriage', but it may well be a threat to heteronormativity, to the easy presumption of heterosexuality. Perhaps the legalisation of gay marriage will prove subversive on this front, if and when it happens. Perhaps it will not (Warner 1999). However, and in any event, from within the theory of subversion that we have articulated here, the most subversive move of all would come, on the level of national public policy, in simply *eliminating state-sanctioned marriage altogether.*

A politics of subversion must insist, with Butler, that subversion always be thought as *internal* to culture, to history and to politics. Therefore subversion must, in general, target a norm or system of norms. This means, in particular, that Butler's radical politics of gender and her transformative queer politics all emerge more clearly when one reads her work as a subversion of heteronormativity. In other words, this reframing of Butler's project serves to short-circuit some of the debates concerning the status of 'the political' in Butler's work, since it brings the politics of subversion to the surface in Butler's writings.

Moreover, the impact of this reading should not be reduced to a plea for 'taking Butler seriously' *as* a political theorist, since it demonstrates the important contribution that Butler makes *to* political theory. Theorising heteronormativity in Butler carries out two tasks simultaneously: (1) it draws out the problem of normativity, in general, for both politics and political theory; and (2) it exposes Butler's writings as forming a sophisticated and powerful response to this problem. One can easily see two problematic tendencies in political theory that Butler's work counters. She challenges the propensity to talk about norms only as if they are things that individuals or legislatures self-consciously construct and then choose (or not) to embody. And she resists the proclivity to dismiss as conservative or quietist those theorists who take the power of normativity seriously and who confront its consequences for a sovereign model of agency (witness Nussbaum's reading of Butler). Butler contributes to political theory through her painstaking unfolding of subversion – a political response to norms that both political theory and politics need. And this is why political theory cannot afford to ignore either the theory of heteronormativity or the politics of its subversion.

8 Reflections

Nobody knows the trouble I've seen ...

(Traditional)

Butler has troubled the waters and caused a lot of trouble. As readers of this book will have seen, though, there is often a mismatch between what exactly she proposed to trouble and the troubled critiques that have emerged. Our presentation of Butler's thought in this book has been, of course, selective and angled in certain ways, as must necessarily be the case. While in no way uncritical in our examination of her work,[1] we write consistently in opposition to many of her critics. We have striven to make Butler's trouble productive in terms of political theory and possibly – down the line – in certain areas of political practice. On the whole, the commentary on Butler is guarded and grudging; why celebrate someone for making trouble? And indeed, on the whole, the trouble is not much appreciated; at best she is often damned with faint praise.

Unsurprisingly, feminist reaction has been the least appreciative, for reasons that were briefly if (eventually) famously announced in *Gender Trouble* and have been outlined at length in the foregoing chapters. For better or worse, however, Butler has self-identified as a feminist and engaged in recognisably feminist debates, and in any case self-identifies as a woman. In that way she's always going to be 'within' rather than 'without', and cannot be easily dismissed or ignored. In a thought-experiment – rather like Wittgenstein's 'picture of Goethe writing the Ninth Symphony' – we could imagine that *Gender Trouble* had been written by a man, and it seems likely that feminists would not have found quite so much trouble in it (Wittgenstein 1958: 183e). Butler deals much less with thinkers and issues particularly associated with the lesbian/gay/bi/transgender/transsexual movements, so in a sense they had less to complain about. But then they also had much less reason to be interested in the book or to find it troubling – though some have, of course. However, as our reflections emerge here, it is liberals who should be *really* troubled by Butler, but they have on the whole found it easy to view her work as primarily addressed to feminists and therefore about 'feminist' issues – as if such issues were unrelated to liberalism as such – or as a distant landmark in some 'emerging field' of queer theory that is not yet on the radar.

Without a doubt, commentators have every right to air their criticisms and concerns, but we are suggesting that the trouble about Butler is not quite what people think it is. Critics commonly worry that Butler has 'taken something away': for example 'politics' or 'agency', or even the body itself. Or they fear she has 'has not provided something': for example 'secure and convincing arguments' or 'well-worked-out tactics'. Clearly Butler's orientation to philosophy and politics is not the usual one; however, it is hardly unprecedented. Marx, Wittgenstein and any number of post-structuralists have taken stands that are oblique with respect to conventional philosophising and political action, and Butler's positions prove oblique in similar ways to these. She and her critics therefore often talk past one another. Butler does philosophy through textual engagement, she makes profoundly anti-foundational and language-centred assumptions, and she remains necessarily terse to the point of dismissiveness concerning the theoretical frameworks that make so much of conventional philosophy and politics possible (that is, intelligible on their own terms). On the one hand Butler finds herself with not much else to say, other than to outline her alternatives, which she does at prodigious length; on the other hand, if she engaged more thoroughly with conventional positions in conventional terms, then the critical difference that drives her work would disappear. Again, other writers have been in this position before Butler.

There are two overall points we have sought to make in this book. First, we draw out how and why Butler's work diverges so significantly from that of conventional thinking in philosophical and political terms. Second, we make the case that when taken on her own terms, and particularly when considered in specific areas of philosophical and political engagement, Butler's thought proves more engaging and more *politically* productive than many of the available alternatives. And it does so not necessarily despite but perhaps because of its alleged 'difficulty' and apparent radicalism. While Butler's critics are certainly entitled to their distinct views, we identify marginalising strategies within their arguments. Butler herself may have no interest in being more 'central' in any way defined by us or anyone else, but we hope our readers can respond positively to this suggestion, and in a sense this is what 'productive' has meant in our volume.

As we have construed it, Butler's overall philosophical project is one of denaturalisation. However, this proves to be a very robust, subtle and particular sort of denaturalising project, since, for Butler, revealing something as 'non-natural' can never be the end of a philosophical or political project. Butler wants not just to 'denaturalise' an object of discourse, but rather to analyse and articulate the manner and extent to which any discourse protects or secures the very 'prediscursive' realm that it produces. This project of denaturalising through challenging the prediscursive arises out of a concern for a politics that resists constraint. In other words, Butler points toward a politics that promotes a rigorous questioning of, and resistance to, all those arguments, laws and policies that introduce, pursue and multiply, intensify and normalise *constraint*. In some respects this looks like a mere restatement of mainstream liberalism, albeit in its rebellious phase, when political philosophies of legitimate government were 'grounded' in ontologies and epistemologies of 'individual' reason and 'natural' rights. The theoretical critiques, and critiques of liberal practice, that have ensued over 300 years or so are of course too numerous and voluminous to review here. But suffice it to say that Butler's politics has some – however distant – connection with liberalism, albeit the non-perfectionist and rigorously individualist wing. Certainly there seems little connection with any anarchist perfectionism, non-consequentialism or 'community' mindedness, however anarchistically libertarian she may be made to sound. However, if this is so, what is the problem?

The problem that Butler poses very starkly and quite directly affects conventional politics and philosophy, not just liberalism. And by no means can it be confined to 'identity politics' or any other supposedly narrow movement that would be cordoned off from mainstream views of the political. The problem is two-fold. Butler's denaturalising strategy really does kick away the 'groundedness' conventionally presumed to lie within any philosophical and political system. These systems seek out such grounds in concepts of 'human nature' or any number of other 'natures'. Examples include 'woman's nature', 'Nature' with a capital N, physical or moral 'naturalism', etc. Perhaps at more sophisticated levels this naturalism comes in the shape of 'bedrock' scientific facts (supposedly underpinning some 'truths' about human life and the world) or, at a rarefied level, in a 'realism' asserting that such 'truths' must necessarily be assumed, as otherwise coherent and justifiable thought will cease, or in any case lack credibility. Unsurprisingly this strategy consistently generates charges of 'relativism' or worse against Butler. And her own political riposte – that things simply are what we make them – can never satisfy the *desire* for something pre- or non-discursive through which to 'found' or 'ground' or 'secure' a system, argument or justification. This is a desire, in other words, to generate political power, and Butler's project to resist and challenge this move to the prediscursive thereby grapples with political power at the most fundamental level. This philosophical stand-off has been rumbling along for quite some time, and clearly neither side convinces the other of very much. Butler's explanation that 'the body' is a 'materialisation' in language merely adds fuel to the fire (Butler 1993).

More interestingly, Butler's particular politics of denaturalisation has identified how profoundly gendered and sexed liberal concepts are. Obviously many political philosophies and systems rest on overt naturalisms, but at least in some guises, and through certain textual citations, liberalism often appears to have a concept of 'the person' prior to, and accessible after, the sexing/gendering of persons as men and women. Politics is then a complex dialectic between these two positions: an abstract concept of 'the person', and sexed/gendered concepts of men and women. Conventional liberalisms are even quieter on the subject of sexuality than on sex and gender, and Butler's attack on heteronormativity, and the naturalisms defining and supporting its disciplinary institutions of constraint, is cutting-edge and prescient. Reproductive technologies and the attendant legalisms of prohibition and constraint that surround them have simply made Butler's point for her, if only those still attached to conventional naturalisms would care to notice. The point, drawn originally and repeatedly from Foucault, is that sex (as bodily sex) is as much a human creation as gender (conventionally understood as culturally and individually malleable behaviour) as is sexuality (given the demise of Darwinian and eugenic arguments 'rooting' this in 'biology'). Indeed, one might add reproduction to the list, disaggregated as it now is both in principle and in many areas of practice from either sexual feelings or sexual acts, and often involving more than two people anyway.

Despite all this, Butler certainly does not claim to solve the problem of the 'abstract' individual who could be either male or female (or anything else), masculine or feminine (or anything else), gay or straight (or anything else). Her deconstructive approach is to *create a problem*. Why? What does this do? Butler is making a problem for many areas of constraint where people are already *comfortable*, and not in rebellion. Indeed it would not be too strong to say they are emotionally invested. In effect, Butler offers a so-called hermeneutics of suspicion directed towards claims that establish constraint and justify power. She targets claims that emerge from centres of authority, but her project also works against the tyranny of social constraints and any pressures to conformity. And this is not because social constraint is wrong in all cases, or because conformity in itself is damaging or destructive, but because constraints should be justified through discourses of freedom and individuality rather than discourses of nature and fact. Nature and fact are conventionally taken to be knowable 'things' through which humans *learn* how to conform to norms and to which they *should* conform. Failure to do so brings on normative violence and the pain of unintelligibility.

For Butler these 'things' – nature and fact – are knowable *discourses*, and knowable *only as discourses*. Revealing them as such opens them back up to critical questioning. As it is, nature and fact are already the subjects of *answers* in discursive form that many politicians and philosophers are only too ready to offer. Butler clearly conceives of her democratisation of suspicion as liberating, and obviously considers its obverse, the authoritarianisation of certainty, as enslaving. Any political theorist will tell you that people are well known to rush headlong for their chains; Butler says the same (Rousseau 1997 [1762]; Butler 1997b). However, her project would make no sense if she had no hope for the open-ended character of human discourse and the individuality with which it is coincident. Most conventional philosophical and political discourses of theory and practice take place in a genre of security, that is, the discourses are constructed around and towards securitising language, on the assumption that this is the only way to make sense, be convincing and justify power-relations. Butler refuses this. Our claim is that this refusal is productive, and therefore anything but anti-political.

Butler offers her readers a clearly politicised philosophy but not a political philosophy or a 'theory of politics' through which some further structures are built from the ground up. It is hard, then, to see quite where Butler has gone so badly 'wrong' as to provoke such outrage, particularly about 'agency' and 'the subject'. Probably the issues go back to her attack, not on the embodied self (where she confessed to being a bad materialist) but on the self or subject as such: 'there is no doer behind the deed'. Butler identifies theories and doctrines of the self – along with agency as a property of that self – with the ultimate redoubt of naturalising discourses. These are the discourses that purport to explain what the self is and is not, what it can and cannot do; they tell us how the self works. The dark place for this is not so much the self-assured and disembodied 'Cartesian *cogito*' as the psychoanalytic self – ridden with anxieties, utterly embodied and a site of inevitable failure and irresolution.

Butler spends considerable time drawing psychoanalysis into her critique of naturalising discourses. In doing so, she disavows neither the *feelings* (even the subconscious) nor the embodied *desire* that the psychoanalytic enterprise has brought into the intellectual mainstream. She finds this the most disturbing area of all, more so than any bland liberal 'individual', because it is so individualised and internalised as a narrative of constraint, 'scientific' authority and God-like knowledge of the human psyche. In a sense she is the Foucault of micro-power and embodied disciplinary 'knowledge' brought to bear on the contemporary construction of 'the self' and the contemporary project of 'self-construction', where terrifying political work gets done, not least in 'correctly' gendering citizen-subjects. Working as a philosopher, rather than as a historical or simply pragmatic critic, she denaturalises, and hence politicises, important sites of disciplinary power and democratising resistance.

What, then, has she got to show for this, and to show us? What does this democratising resistance look like? The Butlerian answer is that it looks like what you make it look like, obviously depending on structures of power and constraint, discourses of agency that you find and deploy, and goals that you and any associates choose to pursue. Butler's critical reading cuts away at any claims to and by authority; it does not follow, however, that there is never anything left, merely that the thinking must be done by oneself, and with no fantasies of certainty and control. Butler's critics say that this 'leaves everything as it is', which indeed it might, but that then is up to us (Wittgenstein 1958: 124e). Butler's perspective on politics is undeniably one of resistance rather than authority, or even responsible office-holding. A theory of legitimacy is apparently missing, but then Butler dismissed social contract theories, as a naturalising 'before' ready to be mobilised *against* discourses of resistance. Butler is hardly alone in this regard, and she never purported to pursue political theory as such; instead, she consistently and rigorously pursues a politicised and politicising approach to philosophy and related intellectual disciplines. One could just as well complain that there is no Butlerian 'economics' or even much sustained attempt to 'add' class to gender, sexuality and race (and then give it a hearty stir). Like any good philosopher she has her eye on some things at the expense of others, and unlike most she has not made claims to comprehensiveness or systematicity. This position can be defended, but in our view her critics could show more awareness of its coherence, more concern for its forebears and more appreciation for its intellectual and political legitimacy.

Butler's work has challenged conventional thinking about politics and philosophy precisely by going 'all the way down' the linguistic road and bringing this experience to a number of 'real-world' issues of undeniable import. And – given that what have become her signature concepts (trouble, performativity and drag) are now entering the mainstream – political philosophy has acquired just a tiny bit of sparkle.

Notes

1 Power/sex/gender

1 In Chapter 7 we criticise Butler's reading of Foucault and power. We suggest that Butler's reading of Foucault on juridical power tends to collapse the distinction that Foucault always maintains (at least, analytically) between juridical power and disciplinary power. Thus, in her account here, Butler sometimes seems to misread Foucault by attributing to 'juridical systems' many of the elements of force that Foucault says belong to disciplinary power. While we will challenge this account later on, particularly as an interpretation of Foucault, we focus here on showing how much productive political work Butler does with this account.

2 Butler's reading of Beauvoir is not uncontroversial; see Coole (2008). However, Butler's point about the Cartesian *cogito* and agency reflects common presuppositions and usage.

3 The body

1 The title of this chapter could easily be read rather morbidly. We hope so. Butler's critics often focus on 'the body' as the brute fact that Butler is reputed to ignore, dismiss or overlook. When they use this phrase they mean for it to call up the actual, lived, daily existence of (women's) lives. Thus it strikes us as quite interesting that 'body' also signifies *lack of life*. It is only a body when it is no longer lived. It is only truly a body when it finally, once and for all, lacks the capacity for logos, when the only subject position in discourse that a person can take up is that of 'the body'. Joss Whedon gives the title of 'The Body' to his most critically acclaimed episode of *Buffy the Vampire Slayer*, and he does so precisely to direct our attention not to life but to death. Butler's own concern with a livable life means that her attention to bodies must always be mediated through discourses of life, of subjectivity – of practised, lived existence. In other words, we wonder if, in their stubborn insistence that Butler pay attention to 'the body', her critics may give the lie to the fact that they want Butler to deal not with real people, with real politics (as they imply), but merely with 'dead things' (the title of another *Buffy* episode).

2 This phrase, 'theory of gender', comes from Butler's readers (critics and supporters alike), not from Butler herself. Butler, we hope to show in the next section, consistently avoids theorising in the sense of producing a (singular) theory of some object, X. Furthermore, if Butler were to construct something along the lines of a 'theory of gender' it would always be a theory of sex/gender.

3 For a subtle and sophisticated exploration of the extent to which Butler does draw on existentialist thought, see Coole (2008).

4 On Butler's particular approach to Hegel – and particularly her understanding of the *Aufhebung* – also rests the evidence for whether Butler's reading of *Antigone* proves novel or not, and whether she does justice to Hegel within that reading. In Chapter 6 we follow through on the terms of this dispute in relation to John Seery's critique (see Seery 2006).

5 In our exegesis of her reading of Beauvoir and Foucault, in the next section, we will clearly delineate Butler's distance from Sartre. However, in the case of Descartes it should be stressed here that the entire project of doubting the existence of bodies is an *epistemological* project. We doubt whether bodies exist because we are trying to ground knowledge in certainty, trying to figure out what we can definitively know. This should be enough description of Descartes's undertaking to distinguish sharply it from Butler's: Butler has no interest in epistemological projects; hers is never an effort to ground knowledge or to produce a new theory of knowledge. Thus she has no inclination to doubt the senses; she does not presume that they cannot err (as an empiricist might want to do) but she does not assume they are unreliable (as a Cartesian would need to). It is wrong to attribute to Butler a scepticism about the body, since she is not engaged in the sort of epistemological project that depends upon doubting the existence of bodies. Here our reading diverges from that very recently offered by Zerilli (2005).

6 Although, as many recent commentators have stressed, this thesis says nothing about how easily change can come.

7 Butler does cite this passage in full within her earlier article on Beauvoir (Butler 1987b).

8 As will become clear as this line of logic develops, we contend that Foucault's argument does reinvigorate the sex/gender distinction but that Butler herself *misrepresents* the manner in which it does so.

9 This argument is elaborated in Chapter 7 (cf. Chambers 2003a).

10 Moreover, as should be clear from the argument that follows, this is not criticism of Butler's interpretation for its own sake. Butler's reading proves problematic precisely because it is not a productive misreading.

11 Contra Dreyfus and Rabinow (1982), Foucault's work cannot be confined to the frame of Heidegger's thought. Yet Foucault was certainly a close enough reader of Heidegger to comprehend fully one of his standard claims: to invert the terms of metaphysics means to remain trapped within those terms (Heidegger 1977; cf. Derrida 1982). Foucault thus offers *no* replacement for the foundational 'fictitious unity' of sex. On both of these points, see Chambers (2003a).

12 On this point it might prove productive to read the second of Jacques Rancière's '10 Theses on Politics', where he argues that the proper response to cause-and-effect logic lies not in its reversal, but in its rupture (Rancière 2001: thesis 2).

13 With this reading, we are making an indirect argument about the reception and interpretation of *La Volonté de savoir*. While the text was taken as important from the time of its publication, a great deal of attention was still given to those elements – bio-power, the critique of the repressive hypothesis – that Foucault himself downplayed. *Gender Trouble* draws from, and draws out, the more radical conclusion of Foucault's text: the discursive production of 'sex itself'. *Gender Trouble* begins to work out some of the implications for gender in Foucault's text, and this is one of the reasons why Butler's book has proved so important and enduring. *Gender Trouble* extends the implications of Foucault's conclusions for feminism in particular and for our understanding of sex/gender more generally. However, the stakes of that reading must be clarified; this we attempt to do here, and, we suggest below, Butler herself does throughout her career after *Gender Trouble*.

14 We champion Butler as one of the very best interpreters of constructivism. However, her misreading of Foucault on sex in the 1987 essay extends to the

constructivist conclusion she draws. Butler suggests that Foucault's tactic is to 'proliferate' binary oppositions until they have no meaning and 'to multiply' power relations until the juridical model no longer holds sway. Her dreadful conclusion is: 'when oppressors are themselves oppressed, and the oppressed develop alternative forms of power, *we are in the presence of postmodern relations of power*' (Butler 1987b: 138, emphasis added).

15 William Connolly's recent work on the literature of neuroscience powerfully illustrates that concern with material reality need not reduce one to the epistemology of realism or materialism; nor need it imply a critique of Butler's understanding of power, politics, gender or norms (see Connolly 2002).

16 'Sexed body' can be taken to mean, as we would probably intend it, merely that the body is not 'sexless', that any body carries a sexuality with it. However, in most countries today if one is not born into a body that appears clearly and properly 'sexed' in the sense of being distinctly male or female anatomically, then those societies *operate* (i.e. in general they 'act' and in particular they enforce surgery) so as to create the necessarily sexed body (see Fausto-Sterling 2000).

17 Embodiment, it should be noted, offers from the outset a rejection of those accounts that turn the body into nothing more than a neutral, material background. On this argument within feminist critiques of public man, see Carver (1996b: 679); and on this point in the writings of Nietzsche and Foucault, see Nietzsche (1921, 1967, 1974), Foucault (1984), Butler (1989b), Chambers (2003a).

18 As we stated at the beginning of this section, ours is not an effort to defend Butler against Coole's criticisms. Rather, we find the parallels in their arguments illustrative for theorising the body, just as Coole finds certain contrasts with Butler helpful for her account. However, one crucial difference between Butler and Coole needs to be highlighted. Coole moves from her argument on bodily intentionality to a discussion of the Nietzschean conception of 'interiority' and the agentic aspects of his account. She contrasts, again, with Butler, saying she 'reduce[s] interiority to a discursive effect' (Coole 2005: 133). Here we would make the potentially tragic attempt to agree with both Butler and with Coole. Coole is correct to show, with Nietzsche and Foucault, how interiority gets produced historically, and why it must be understood genealogically. Butler's point, however, also seems right: we have no access to the body except through language. This is therefore not the 'reduction' of interiority to a discursive effect; the two analyses (Nietzsche's, which Coole agrees with, and Butler's, which she rejects and uses as a comparison to highlight Nietzsche's 'phenomenological' account) operate at different levels. Nietzsche describes how interiority comes about historically. Butler finds herself dealing with a quite different set of accounts, those that *call on* interiority. Thus Butler does not seek to reduce interiority to a discursive effect, but to demonstrate *how* claims made on behalf of interiority, claims made to have access to interiority, are always precisely 'claims made'. We cannot get at the interior that history has produced except through language. Interiority is a historical effect, not a discursive one, but our relation to it is never unmediated – we can only ever get there through language.

19 Linda Zerilli formulates a similar point in this way:

> what persists once binary sex difference as an object of knowledge is destabilized ... is sexual difference as a question of meaning. It is a question we do not stop thinking about and a condition we do not eliminate once we know that binary sex difference is a contingent social and historical construct.
>
> (Zerilli 2005: 72)

Zerilli argues that Butler's critics have often misread her project as a purely sceptical project of *doubting*, an effort merely to question truth on epistemic grounds. She also suggests that Butler herself sometimes falls into the trap of arguing in epistemic terms. And, finally, Zerilli calls for theory to break out of the rut of debates over knowledge claims and instead to do the work of the productive imagination – to produce 'figures of possibility', to create 'new ways of seeing'. We strongly support Zerilli's contention that we must not merely doubt the truth of binary sex but also produce new ways of understanding and of living sex and gender; however, she herself may have underestimated the extent to which Butler repeatedly calls on figures of possibility in the form of the queer communities in which she has lived and for which she hopes to continue to 'make life possible' (Butler 1999: xvi–xvii).

20 This is also to suggest that Butler may well have an answer to her critics' concerns about the disappearance of sex, but particularly in *Gender Trouble* (the text of Butler's that will always get the most attention) she fails to articulate this answer. Yet we can see the beginnings of such a response, even in that book, by conceiving of the heterosexual matrix as a device that parses people based upon sex (and this means also that it parses them based upon their bodies). The heterosexual matrix provides a way of *seeing* people and then placing them into categories; *it tells us what to look for* (see Zerilli 2005). And that 'what' is sex/gender, where sex is bodily but marked through gender. Perhaps it is best put when put bluntly: how, on first glance, do most individuals *see* femininity? By seeing female body parts (e.g. breasts, hips, hair, facial features, etc.); or, better, by seeing outward signs – clothing, hair, jewellery, make-up – that are *taken* as symbols of what lies beneath. Resistance to the heterosexual matrix, resistance to heteronormativity, must be understood as a challenge to the *way* that we currently categorise bodies. This does not imply a doing away with bodies; it suggests a critique of *how* we see them. Thus, in a utopian, alternative universe not governed by the heterosexual matrix, we will still see people with bodies and with bodily differences, but genitalia will no longer be the guiding difference, the key mark for cutting between people.

21 An earlier draft of this chapter went so far as to claim 'she rejects *all* ontology'. In Stephen White's (2000) sense of 'strong ontology' that claim would hold, since nothing for Butler serves as ultimate ground; she rejects any attempt to shield a concept from the critical scrutiny that would explain its historical production, cultural proliferation or political contestation. Nonetheless, as Chapter 5 will go on to argue, Butler maintains close concern for questions of being, and her political theory is intimately bound up with what we will call her 'political ontology'.

4 Normative violence

1 As will become clear below, we plan to complicate, and to move beyond, this distinction Derrida makes between 'originary' and 'derivative' violence. But first a few clarifications are in order. It needs to be stressed that Derrida's sense of originary does not entail a denigration of that which is derivative. Physical violence, 'derivative' though it may be, still proves crucially important. Derrida produces a paradoxical temporality: that which appears after turns out to come before. Derrida names arche-writing an 'originary' violence precisely so as to call attention to its very existence, but this does not imply a denial of the existence of physical violence. Next, we would suggest the importance of keeping separate and distinct Derrida's two-fold distinction between derivative violence and the violence of arche-writing, on the one hand, and the later three-part classification of arche-violence/moral violence/empirical violence, on the other. Elizabeth

Wingrove, for example, has critically questioned the idea of locating political violence (both rape and war) at a 'tertiary level' (Wingrove 2000: 190). Wingrove is right to render problematic the political efficacy of this notion; however, we think she is wrong to attribute it to Derrida. The idea of three levels of violence (and the attendant notion of political violence as 'tertiary', Wingrove's word) comes *not* from Derrida, but, according to Derrida, from Lévi-Strauss. To elaborate: the Derrida quotation concerning arche-writing that we produce in the text above, appears in a section in which Derrida is generalising about *his* understanding of writing. The passages to which Wingrove poses her challenge to the notion of tertiary violence come from within the context of an exceedingly detailed reading of Lévi-Strauss's *Tristes Tropiques*. Derrida himself never proposes or defends this notion of 'tertiary violence' and he does not locate it in Rousseau (Wingrove's topic) but in Lévi-Strauss. Sincere thanks to Elizabeth Wingrove for helpful discussions on this point (E. Wingrove, Personal communications, and email to author SC, 2004).

2 Rodolphe Gasché (1986) names Derrida's quasi-concepts 'infrastructures'. Arche-writing, as an infrastructure, can be considered both the condition of possibility for the speech/writing distinction (that which makes it possible) and also the condition of its impossibility (that which marks its limits). 'Infrastructures' are neither words nor concepts, though they look like both (hence 'quasi-concepts'). They are attempts to carry out the work of deconstruction by revealing that the highest, most originary or final concepts of metaphysics may not be either highest, final or originary.

3 Having now unravelled the paradox of 'normative violence', it seems worth noting that for thinkers less inclined to think juridically (more inclined to read Foucault) normative violence might be more likely to seem redundant than to come across as a contradiction in terms. 'Normative violence' would prove to be a redundancy to the extent that all norms inherently contain and, in their own way, wield a certain violence. That is to say, norms are not just common practices, not merely typical or expected behaviour; norms contain both the median point on the normal curve and the tails at the edges of the curve. Thus a norm is not a norm without the marginal, the deviant, the outliers that sustain it. Practices and behaviours that 'deviate from the norm' are precisely practices and behaviours that make the norm possible, in that they establish the distance between 'the normal' and the abject. In a sense, then, one is never really 'outside' the norm. Or, as Butler puts it: 'being outside the norm is in some sense still being defined in relation to it' (Butler 2004b: 42). Thus one only finds oneself in tension with the norm, in conflict with it. The power relations within norms, relations that affect individuals no matter where they fall on the normal curve (i.e. the power of normalisation), wield a certain violence. Norms then are always already 'violent' in this way, and normative violence becomes a redundancy. We do not reject this sort of analysis, but this is not a redundancy to be overcome or eschewed; it is to be embraced. Butler, implicitly, and we, explicitly, do just that, by putting normative violence to work as a political concept. 'Normative violence' sounds redundant to just the extent that it draws attention to the inherent violence of norms, and this is an area, we argue, that *demands* more attention, both *in* politics and *from* political theorists. Most political scientists would see nothing redundant about the concept, and this is why, in the text, we approach normative violence through its apparent paradox of self-contradiction (not through its redundancy).

4 And, finally, to 'undo gender' – as suggested in the title of Butler's recent book – is not to do away with the concept and category entirely. The project of undoing gender maintains the goal of reducing the chances of doing gender wrong; it thereby increases the prospects for a livable life (Butler 2004b).

5 At first glance, 'child abuse' might seem to provide a counter-example to our logic here. That is, society clearly shuns physical harm done to children in much the same way (perhaps more so) as it reject torture, yet we name this harm 'abuse' even in this extremely serious case. But this is only a surface appearance. Indeed, 'child abuse' works *within* the logic we articulate here. A child is 'abused' and not 'tortured' precisely because a child is not yet an adult, not fully human. A child is abused because he or she is always already presumed to be in the care of a fully adult human. To use the same word we apply to children in order to describe the treatment of prisoners is thereby to suggest that they are not fully rational, mature, adult humans. It is to dehumanise them, to render them less than fully intelligible as human. Children are intelligible as human, but precisely as immature, non-adult humans. To take adults as children is, then, to misrecognise them.

5 Political ontology

1 Deep thanks to Rob Watkins for urging us to underline this crucial point and for helping with some of the language used to do so.
2 On this final point, witness Nietzsche, a 'philosopher' repeatedly accused of amoralism or immoralism. Despite this, it seems impossible to deny that few thinkers, if any, held a greater *concern* for morality than Nietzsche.
3 Much could also be made of the texts Butler chooses to study in this book, particularly those by Adorno and Levinas, in order to build the case for the unique or special character of this text. And, again, the dust-jacket descriptions, and even the blurbs by fellow authors, emphasise the 'stunningly original interpretations of Adorno and Levinas' as a new and profound contribution to moral philosophy. But, even here, one finds as much, perhaps more, that is familiar in this text. Levinas, it should be noted, plays a prominent role in Butler's thinking in *Precarious Life* (and he even shows up in a footnote all the way back in *Subjects of Desire*). Moreover, *Giving an Account* calls once again on the literature of psychoanalysis that has fascinated Butler since *Gender Trouble*. And, finally, this text, like most of Butler's work, spends more time on Foucault than any other thinker. This means, once more: it is not that one finds nothing new here, but that 'new' elements prove intimately related to the 'old' ones.
4 We owe a deep debt here to Charles Phillips for both the elaboration and formulation of this claim.
5 This serves as a powerful rejoinder to Habermas's account of 'performative contradiction', which he attempts to a wield as a tool of critique. Butler shows here how the charge of performative contradiction might not be damning at all; she shows why performative contradictions might be embraced rather than avoided (Habermas 1987; see Chambers 2003a).
6 One should emphasise that, since this impossibility is constitutive, 'giving an account of oneself' is not something one cannot or should not do. Its failure does not prohibit it, but always intrinsically possesses it. Thus, giving an account is not only impossible but also *necessary*.
7 White offers the standard critiques (an oblivious denial of the existence of bodily pain and suffering, an evacuation of the necessary grounds for political agency) and he cites the standard critics (Benhabib 1995a and Fraser 1995, but also Digeser 1995).
8 Butler's tendency to *sound* as if she repudiates all ontology certainly wanes as her writings develop over the years, and her explicit use of the language of ontology increases along the same timeline. White himself sees this clearly in his charitable and grounded reading of Butler's theory of mourning, as found in *Psychic Life of Power*. However, White is rather uncharitable (perhaps even unfair) in his highly selective quotations from Butler used to support the implication that she denies

ontology wholesale. White ignores a large number of places where Butler embraces ontology (even in her early work), and he quotes selectively from places where Butler is not making an argument against ontology, but showing specifically how feminist conceptions of gender sometimes *presuppose* an ontology. It is the assumption of a prior ontology that Butler wants vehemently to resist, not the actual work of ontology itself. Thus Butler does not really have what White calls 'a thoroughgoing critique of ontology' (White 1999: 156). In the beginning of his essay, White draws this conclusion from selective quotations from *Gender Trouble*, places where Butler speaks specifically about feminist coalition politics, not about a general theory of identity (Butler 1999: 16). Toward the end of his argument, White claims that for Butler 'identity ... *is best seen* as *nothing more than* a site of "insisting rifting"' (White 1999: 169, emphasis added). He goes on to hammer Butler rhetorically with this phrase 'insisting rifting', implying that it constitutes the watchword of her conception of identity. However, White draws the phrase from the concluding paragraph of a little-read 1990 essay, where Butler draws broad conclusions about the possibility for an 'ungrounded ground from which feminist discourse emerges' (Butler 2004c [1990]: 200). To our knowledge, she never uses the phrase again; she surely does not make 'insistent rifting' the mantra for her understanding of identity in the way that White's rhetoric tends to imply.

9 In his effort to alert philosophy to its historical 'forgetfulness of Being', Heidegger proposed and for a time insisted upon the ontic/ontological difference – 'the difference between *das Seinde* (that which is, beings) and *das Sein* (that by virtue of which beings are beings, Being)' (Chambers 2003a: 69). The ontic level refers to beings (plants, people); the ontological refers to their very existence as beings.

10 Indeed, Markell goes so far as to claim that the latter notion, state sovereignty, proves to be a particular instance of the former, sovereign agency.

11 For an effort to read Butler less charitably, to read her as in fact falling back upon a variant of 'methodological individualism', see Boucher (2006); cf. Edelman (2004).

12 We have made this point in an earlier context, but at the risk of repetition we would rework it in this one. The displacement of individual accountability indicates plainly that Butler's concept of 'relationality' cannot be taken as a characteristic of a particular subject (women, caregivers, etc.); relationality characterises subjectivity – it makes the subject possible just as it makes sovereign agency impossible.

13 We have highlighted Butler's quotation of Nietzsche, 'punishment is the making of a memory', because it illustrates the somewhat bizarre nature of Butler's reading. Butler suggests that Nietzsche positively declares this as a definition of punishment. Yet the quotation comes from section 13 of essay II, in which Nietzsche argues that punishment has no singular meaning, that it is in fact 'totally *indefinable*'. 'To give an idea of how uncertain, how supplemental, how accidental "the meaning" of punishment is' Nietzsche goes on to list all the things punishment has been taken *as*. By our count he lists 14 different descriptions of 'punishment as'; in the middle of this list one finds 'punishment as the making of a memory'. To pull this out of the middle of the list, change the 'as' to 'is' and present it as Nietzsche's definition of punishment strikes us as a difficult reading to defend (Nietzsche 1967).

14 Butler attempts to cull a narrow concept of responsibility from Nietzsche and force it into the constraining frame of 'moral philosophy'. For his part, Nietzsche discusses responsibility within a richly historical and highly political context. In section 38 of *Twilight of the Idols* Nietzsche famously suggests that 'liberal institutions cease to be liberal as soon as they are attained'. They are liberal only while they are being fought for, and thus it is war, the war for these institutions,

that produces freedom. In this context, Nietzsche proceeds to give one of his definitions of responsibility:

> For what is freedom? That one has the will to assume responsibility for oneself. That one maintains the distance which separates us. That one becomes more indifferent to difficulties, hardships, privation, even to life itself. That one is prepared to sacrifice human beings for one's cause, not excluding oneself.
>
> (Nietzsche 1954 [1888]: section 38, p. 542)

15 Nietzsche: 1967: essay II, sections 1 and 2. See Kaufmann's helpful explanatory footnotes here, particularly his references to Kantian morality.
16 And we would locate the efforts of someone like Tronto and her 'ethic of care' within the terms of a project that seeks to increase 'responsibility *for*' but that does not move to the ontological concern with 'responsibility *to*' (Tronto 1993: 132).
17 Here we would note that Butler's conception of ethics reveals a great deal about her understanding of politics even at those moments when the focus on ethics displaces politics. It is worth recalling that in the laboratory we often take the measure of a thing through displacement.

6 Kinship trouble

1 For the literature on heteronormativity, see the following brief genealogy: Rich 1980; hooks 1982; de Lauretis 1987; Sedgwick 1990; Wittig 1992; Halley 1993; Warner 1993, 1999; Halperin 1995; Watney 1996; Kaplan 1997; Chambers 2003b, 2005, 2006a; Dennis 2003. For a few key texts (especially recent texts) in sexual politics and the politics of sexualty, see Pateman 1988; Carver and Mottier 1998; Butler 1999; Phelan 2001; Blasius 2001; Babst 2002; Currah 2001; Shanley 2004; Josephson 2005; Segura *et al.* 2005.
2 For a few examples, see Rawls 1971; Mendus and Horton 1985; Mendus and Edwards 1987; Mendus 1988, 1989; Young 1990; Benhabib 2002; Young 2002.
3 Eve Kosofsky Sedgwick's path-breaking work on 'the closet' can clarify our point here that, *in relation to heteronormativity*, all gays and lesbians are rendered unintelligible (Sedgwick 1990). The closet is not a protected space that shields one's sexual identity; nor is it a relic of ignorance and deception that 'out' gays merely leave behind. Building on Sedgwick's work, David Halperin explains as follows: 'the closet is an impossibly contradictory place: you can't be in it, and you can't be out of it' (Halperin 1995: 34). You cannot be *in* the closet because others may always suspect you are gay. And heteronormativity makes it impossible to be *out* of the closet because many people will continue to assume you are straight (see Chambers 2003b). The closet is a liminal realm of unintelligibility because the closet is *uninhabitable*. Heteronormativity produces the closet and therefore creates, for gays and lesbians, this unavoidable liminal place.
4 We use the Foucauldian language of 'subject position' here only as a way of sharpening the point. We do not wish to imply that 'the human' can be reduced to or exhausted by a distributed set of subject positions. The human, as Butler would certainly emphasise, 'exceeds its boundary in the very effort to establish' both the category of the human and its boundary. And, of course, no subject fully inhabits the human, since 'life' relates the very category of the human to that of the non-human (Butler 2004b: 12). Our point is a simple one: *in order to inhabit the human*, one must have a space from which to speak *as human*. The Foucauldian term 'subject positions' conveys this notion nicely (and, of course,

Foucault himself would have strenuously resisted the reduction of his notion of 'subject position' to a structuralist version that takes subject positions to be rigidly allocated and productive of a closed social totality).

5 Butler herself provides examples of this 'opening up': she points to those cases in which the so-called 'perverse' *demand*, even in the face of their own abjection, to be accounted for. For example, Butler describes those 'blended families' in which a child can say 'mother' and more than one person might respond, or a family in which 'father' might represent both a phantasm and a real person in living memory. These arrangements are something of a commonplace (even if not fully accepted) in liberal societies, as are shared parenting arrangements in which genetic 'relatedness' is ignored or sometimes even obscured (Blasius 1994; Weston 1991; Weeks *et al.* 2001).

6 As already established above, the incest taboo licenses only heteronormative sex within identities that are already constituted by 'the family', that is, sexual relations only between 'unrelated' men and women, and therefore no sexual relations between 'related' men and women. And if the naturalised language of un/relatedness must be reworked in order to validate fully same-sex and other unconventional families and their offspring, as Butler seems to imply, then it would follow that in such a world incest will already have been resignified, because un/relatedness would no longer be construed on the basis of the incest taboo. It should also be noted that the language of un/relatedness or kinship already has a considerable penumbra of metaphorical extensions, for example half-, step-, adoptive relations and in-law relations, as a matter of tradition, and, more recently, egg-mothers (up to two per zygote), sperm fathers and womb-mothers. This may possibly extend in the future to the cloning of a human individual (who might in the first instance arise from a foetal rather than adult cell) – all of which leads to a rather extensive unravelling of the heteronormative 'sexed' model of reproduction (Harris and Holm 1998; Harris 2004).

7 For example, UK legislation forbidding in-law marriages was struck down by the European Court of Human Rights in September 2005 and is currently therefore under revision (Kennedy 2005).

8 Cases of egg and sperm donation between siblings for technologically assisted conception raise an interesting issue: 'incest' may take place entirely apart from bodies or sexual feelings (as opposed to non-sexual feelings of closeness and care) (Edwards 2004). Rather than inscribing a naturalised taboo and setting the stage for abjection, genetic and family counselors are generally advised to provide reassurance both to the incest-born in order to help them cope with stigma and to those in consanguineous marriages (typically first cousins, double first cousins and uncle–niece) (Bittles and Makov 1988).

9 See, for example, http://www.consang.net (accessed on 5 June 2005).

7 Subversion

1 Nussbaum's critique lends the first round of support to this claim. In addition, one can note that the criticisms launched against Butler's account of agency often ask about the *possibility* of subversive agency, but they go on to presume that the litmus test would have to be dramatic, drastic and immediate social change (e.g. Stone 2005). One also detects the presumption in critical readings of Butler that since her theoretical approach to sex and gender seems so philosophically radical her political position must be similarly 'radical' – and thus 'subversion' must allude to an anarchic, destructive, transformative politics. Butler's politics may prove much more modest than all this.

2 Butler's misreading hinges on her mistaking Foucault's rejection of juridical *models* of power for a call to subvert juridical power itself. Butler's reading flattens

Foucault's historical account by reading a Hegelian notion of history into Foucault's very much anti-Hegelian account.

3 On parody, see Lloyd 1999, 2005a; cf. Tyler 1991; Hawkes 1995. On performativity, see McNay 2000; Lloyd 2005b; Disch 1999; Webster 2000; Zivi 2006 On resignification, see Disch 1999; Lloyd 2005a.

4 As always, by sex we refer not to sexual activity, sexual behaviour, so-called 'sexual orientation', or intercourse, but to the project of 'sexing the body', to the assemblage of elements used to distinguish 'male' from 'female' (see Fausto-Sterling 2000).

5 Although we are much less concerned to shore up Butler's normative foundations, we are very sympathetic to Stone's effort to highlight the centrality of genealogy to Butler's work and to strengthen Butler's account with Nietzsche's (Stone 2005). We omit a discussion of Butler's engagement with psychoanalytic theory in order to focus on her conception of subversion and the theory of heteronormativity. In rejecting the idea that Butler seeks to subvert either identity or gender, we put to one side her melancholic theory of gender identification.

6 The UK took a large step toward such full implementation when it recently passed new anti-discrimination laws.

7 Many readers, we fear, have also read Butler's example wrongly, in that they have taken her to be describing *drag performances* on stage (and presumably for straight audiences). This shows the risk of reading Butler's writings out of a queer context. We would suggest that Butler's example of drag refers not to a politics of performance, but to a politics of the everyday. This means that she's calling forth the image not of a drag queen on stage, watched by a straight audience, but of a drag queen, for example, sitting on the subway along with everyone else. Butler might even be suggesting that you, her reader, be the one dressed in drag. See Chapter 1 for more on this point.

8 Reflections

1 See, in general, our consistently critical comments concerning Butler's tendency to overlook historical and institutional factors, and see in particular our critique of her reading of Nietzsche (and sometimes Foucault) in Chapter 5.

Bibliography

Agar, N. (2004) *Liberal Eugenics: In Defense of Human Enhancement*. Oxford: Blackwell.

Allen, C. and Howard, J., eds. (2000) *Provoking Feminisms*. Chicago and London: University of Chicago Press.

Arendt, H. (1958) *The Human Condition*. Chicago and London: University of Chicago Press.

Arens, W. (1997) 'Incest Taboos'. In *The Dictionary of Anthropology*, ed. T. Barfield, 257–9. Oxford: Blackwell.

Austin, J.L. (1962) *How to Do Things with Words* [William James Lectures, 1955], ed. J.O. Urmson. Oxford: Clarendon Press.

Babst, G.A. (2002) *Liberal Constitutionalism, Marriage, and Sexual Orientation: A Contemporary Case for Dis-establishment*. New York: Peter Lang.

Benhabib, S. (1995a) 'Feminism and Postmodernism: An Uneasy Alliance'. In *Feminist Contentions: A Philosophical Exchange*, 17–34. New York and London: Routledge.

Benhabib, S. (1995b) 'Subjectivity, Historiography, and Politics'. In *Feminist Contentions: A Philosophical Exchange*, 107–26. New York and London: Routledge.

Benhabib, S. (2002) *The Claims of Culture: Equality and Diversity in the Global Era*. Princeton: Princeton University Press.

Bittles, A.H. (2001) *A Background Summary of Consanguineous Marriage*. Perth, Australia: Centre for Human Genetics, Edith Cowan University.

Bittles, A.H. and Makov, U.E. (1988) 'Inbreeding in Human Populations: Assessment of the Costs'. In *Human Mating Patterns*, ed. C.G.N. Mascie-Taylor and A.J. Boyce, 153–67. Cambridge: Cambridge University Press.

Bittles, A.H., Savithri, H.S., Venkatesha Murthy, H.S., Baskaran, G., Wei Wang, Cahill, Janet and Appaji Rao, N. (2001) 'Human Inbreeding: A Familiar Story Full of Surprises'. In *Ethnicity and Health*, ed. H. Macbeth and P. Shetty, 68–78. London: Taylor & Francis.

Blasius, M. (1994) *Gay and Lesbian Politics: Sexuality and the Emergence of a New Ethic*. Philadelphia: Temple University Press.

Blasius, M., ed. (2001) *Sexual Identities, Queer Politics*. Philadelphia: Temple University Press.

Boucher, G. (2006) 'The Politics of Performativity: A Critique of Judith Butler'. *Parrhesia* 1: 112–41.

Brown, W. (1995) *States of Injury: Power and Freedom in Late Modernity*. Princeton: Princeton University Press.

Brown, W. (2006) *Regulating Aversion: Tolerance in the Age of Identity and Empire.* Princeton: Princeton University Press.

Burns, T. (2002) 'Sophocles' Antigone and the History of the Concept of Natural Law'. *Political Studies* 50: 545–57.

Butler, J. (1987a) *Subjects of Desire.* New York: Columbia University Press.

Butler, J. (1987b) 'Variations on Sex and Gender: Beauvoir, Wittig, Foucault'. In *Feminism as Critique*, ed. S. Benhabib and D. Cornell, 128–42. Minneapolis: University of Minnesota Press.

Butler, J. (1989a) 'Gendering the Body: Beauvoir's Philosophical Contribution'. In *Women, Knowledge, and Reality: Explorations in Feminist Philosophy*, ed. A. Garry and M. Pearsall, 253–62. Boston: Unwin Hyman.

Butler, J. (1989b) 'Foucault and the Paradox of Bodily Inscriptions'. *Journal of Philosophy* 86: 601–7.

Butler, J. (1989c) 'The Body Politics of Julia Kristeva'. *Hypatia* 3: 104–18.

Butler, J. (1993) *Bodies that Matter: On the Discursive Limits of 'Sex'.* New York: Routledge.

Butler, J. (1994) 'Gender as Performance: An Interview with Judith Butler'. *Radical Philosophy* 67: 32–9.

Butler, J. (1995a) 'Contingent Foundations: Feminism and the Question of "Postmodernism"'. In *Feminist Contentions: A Philosophical Exchange*, 35–58. New York and London: Routledge.

Butler, J. (1995b) 'For a Careful Reading'. In *Feminist Contentions: A Philosophical Exchange*, 127–43. New York and London: Routledge.

Butler, J. (1996) 'Foucaultian Inversions'. In *Feminist Interpretations of Michel Foucault*, ed. S.J. Hekman, 59–76. University Park, PA: The Pennsylvania State University Press.

Butler, J. (1997a) *Excitable Speech: A Politics of the Performative.* New York and London: Routledge.

Butler, J. (1997b) *The Psychic Life of Power: Theories in Subjection.* Stanford: Stanford University Press.

Butler, J. (1998) 'Merely Cultural'. *New Left Review,* 227: 33–44.

Butler, J. (1999 [1990]) *Gender Trouble: Feminism and the Subversion of Identity.* 2nd edn. London and New York: Routledge.

Butler, J. (2000a) *Antigone's Claim: Kinship Between Life and Death.* New York: Columbia University Press.

Butler, J. (2000b) 'Politics, Power and Ethics: A Discussion Between Judith Butler and William Connolly'. *Theory & Event* 4.2.

Butler, J. (2003) 'Peace is a Resistance to the Terrible Satisfactions of War, an Interview with Judith Butler'. *The Believer* (May).

Butler, J. (2004a) *Precarious Life: The Powers of Mourning and Violence.* New York and London: Verso.

Butler, J. (2004b) *Undoing Gender.* New York and London: Routledge.

Butler, J. (2004c) *The Judith Butler Reader*, ed. S. Salih. Oxford: Blackwell.

Butler, J. (2005) *Giving an Account of Oneself.* New York: Fordham University Press.

Butler, J., Laclau, E. and Žižek, S. (2000) *Contingency, Hegemony, Universality: Contemporary Dialogues on the Left.* London: Verso.

Carver, T. (1996a) *Gender Is Not a Synonym for Women.* Boulder, CO: Lynne Rienner.

Carver, T. (1996b) '"Public Man" and the Critique of Masculinities'. *Political Theory* 24: 673–86.

Carver, T. (2004) *Men in Political Theory.* Manchester and New York: Manchester University Press.

Carver, T. (2007) '"Trans" Trouble: Trans-sexuality and the End of Gender.' In *The Future of Gender*, ed. J. Browne, 115–35. Cambridge: Cambridge University Press.

Carver, T. and Mottier, V., eds (1998) *The Politics of Sexuality: Identity, Gender, Citizenship.* London: Routledge.

Cavarero, A. (2002) 'Politicizing Theory'. *Political Theory* 30.4: 506–32.

Chambers, S. (2003a) *Untimely Politics.* Edinburgh and New York: Edinburgh University Press and New York University Press.

Chambers, S. (2003b) 'Telepistemology of the Closet; Or, the Queer Politics of *Six Feet Under*'. *Journal of American Culture* 26: 24–41.

Chambers, S. (2005) 'Revisiting the Closet: Reading Sexuality in *Six Feet Under*'. In *Reading* Six Feet Under, ed. J. McCabe and K. Akass, 24–41. London: I.B. Taurus and Palgrave.

Chambers, S. (2006a) 'Cultural Politics and the Practice of Fugitive Theory'. *Contemporary Political Theory* 5.1: 9–32.

Chambers, S. (2006b) 'Desperately Straight: The Subversive Sexual Politics of Desperate Housewives'. In *Reading* Desperate Housewives, ed. K. Akass and J. McCabe, 71–85. London: I.B. Taurus.

Connell, R.W. (2002). *Gender.* Cambridge and Malden, MA: Polity Press and Blackwell.

Connolly, W. (1995) *The Ethos of Pluralization.* Minneapolis: University of Minnesota Press.

Connolly, W. (2002) *Neuropolitics: Thinking, Culture, Speed.* Minneapolis and London: University of Minnesota Press.

Connolly, W. (2005) *Pluralism.* Durham and London: Duke University Press.

Coole, D. (2005) 'Rethinking Agency: A Phenomenological Approach to Embodiment and Agentic Capacities'. *Political Studies* 53: 124–42.

Coole, D. (2008) 'Butler's Existentialism'. In *Judith Butler's Precarious Politics: Critical Encounters*, ed. T. Carver and S.A. Chambers. London and New York: Routledge.

Currah, P. (2001) 'Queer Theory, Lesbian and Gay Rights, and Transsexual Marriages'. In *Sexual Identities, Queer Politics*, ed. M. Blasius, 178–99. Princeton: Princeton University Press.

D'Emilio, J. (1992) *Out of the Closets: Voices of Gay Liberation.* New York and London: New York University Press.

de Lauretis, T. (1987) *Technologies of Gender.* Bloomington and Indianapolis: Indiana University Press.

de Lauretis, T. (1994) *The Practice of Love: Lesbian Sexuality and Perverse Desire.* Bloomington and Indianapolis: Indiana University Press.

Dean J. (2005) 'The Politics of Avoidance: The Limits of Weak Ontology'. *The Hedgehog Review: Critical Reflections on Contemporary Culture* 22.1: 55–65.

Dean, J. (2008) 'Change of Address: Butler's Ethics at Sovereignty's Deadlock'. In *Judith Butler's Precarious Politics: Critical Encounters*, ed. T. Carver and S.A. Chambers. London and New York: Routledge.

Dennis, J. (2003) 'Heteronormativity'. In *Men and Masculinities: A Social, Cultural, and Historical Encyclopedia*, ed. M. Kimmel, 207–9. New York: ABC-CLIO.

Derrida, J. (1974) *Of Grammatology*, trans. Gayatri Spivak. Baltimore and London: Johns Hopkins University Press.

Derrida, J. (1982) *Margins of Philosophy*, trans. A. Bass. Chicago: University of Chicago Press.

Descartes, R. (2004 [1637]) *Meditations on First Philosophy*, ed. J. Bennett, trans. J. Cottingham. Cambridge: Cambridge University Press.

Deutscher, P. (1997) *Yielding Gender: Feminism, Deconstruction and the History of Philosophy*. London: Routledge.

Digeser (1995) *Our Politics, Our Selves? Liberalism, Identity, and Harm*. Princeton: Princeton University Press.

Disch, L. (1999) 'Judith Butler and the Politics of the Performative'. *Political Theory* 27: 545–60.

Disch, L. (2008) '"French Theory" Goes to France: *Trouble dans le Genre* and "Materialist" Feminism – A Conversation Manqué'. In *Judith Butler's Precarious Politics: Critical Encounters*, ed. T. Carver and S.A. Chambers. London and New York: Routledge.

Disch, L. and Kane, M. (1996) 'When a Looker Is Really a Bitch: Lisa Olson, Sport, and the Heterosexual Matrix'. *Signs: Journal of Women in Culture and Society* 21: 278–308.

Dreyfus, H. and Rabinow P. (1982) *Michel Foucault: Beyond Structuralism and Hermeneutics*. Chicago: University of Chicago Press.

Edelman, L. (2004) *No Future: Queer Theory and the Death Drive*. Durham, NC, and London: Duke University Press.

Edwards, J. (2004) 'Incorporating Incest: Gamete, Body and Relation in Assisted Conception'. *Journal of the Royal Anthropological Institute* 10: 755–74.

Elden, S. (2005) 'The Place of the Polis: Political Blindness in Judith Butler's *Antigone's Claim*'. *Theory & Event* 8:1.

Elshtain, J. (1987) *Women and War*. New York: Basic Books.

Eribon, D. (1991) *Michel Foucault*, trans. B. Wing. Cambridge, MA: Harvard University Press.

Evans, D.T. (1993) *Sexual Citizenship: The Material Construction of Sexualities*. London: Routledge.

Fausto-Sterling, A. (2000) *Sexing the Body: Gender Politics and the Construction of Sexuality*. New York: Basic Books.

Felluga, Dino (2004) 'Guide to Literary and Critical Theory'; available at http://www.sla.purdue.edu/academic/engl/theory/genderandsex/terms/heteronormativity.html (accessed 26 February 2007).

Feuerbach, L. (1957 [1841]) *Essence of Christianity*, ed. E.G. Waring and F.W. Strothmann. New York: F. Ungar.

Foucault, M. (1972) *The Archaeology of Knowledge*, trans. M. Sheridan Smith. New York: Pantheon Books.

Foucault, M. (1977a) *Discipline and Punish*, trans. A. Sheridan. New York: Vintage Books.

Foucault, M. (1977b) 'What Is an Author?' In *Language, Counter-Memory, Practice*, ed. D. Bouchard, trans. D. Bouchard and S. Simon, 113–38. Ithaca and New York: Cornell University Press.

Foucault, M. (1978) *History of Sexuality*, vol. 1: *An Introduction*, trans. R. Hurley, New York: Vintage Books.

Foucault, M. (1981) 'The Order of Discourse'. In *Untying the Text: A Poststructuralist Reader*, trans. and ed. R. Young. London: Routledge.

Foucault, M. (1984) *History of Sexuality*, vol. 2: *The Use of Pleasure*, trans. Robert Hurley. New York: Vintage Books.

Foucault, M. (1989) *Foucault Live*, ed. S. Lotringer. New York: Semiotext(e).

Foucault, M. (1998) *Aesthetics, Method, and Epistemology: Essential Works of Foucault, 1954–1984*, vol. 2, ed. P. Rabinow. New York: The New Press.

Foucault, M. (2003) *Society Must Be Defended: Lectures at the Collège de France, 1975–76*, ed. M. Bertani and A. Fontana, trans. D. Macey. New York: Picador.

Fraser, N. (1995) 'False Antitheses'. In *Feminist Contentions: A Philosophical Exchange*, 59–74. New York and London: Routledge.

Gasché, R. (1986) *The Tain of the Mirror: Derrida and the Philosophy of Reflection*. Cambridge, MA: Harvard University Press.

Gilligan, C. (1982) *In a Different Voice: Psychological Theory and Women's Development*. Cambridge, MA: Harvard University Press.

Goodenough, P. (2004) 'Legalize Incest Suggestion Shocks Lawmakers'; available at http://www.cnsnews.com/ViewCulture.asp?Page = %5CCulture%5Carchive%5C200405%5CCUL20040521a.html (accessed 18 July 2007).

Habermas, J. (1987) *The Philosophical Discourses of Modernity*, trans. F.G. Lawrence. Cambridge, MA: The MIT Press.

Halberstam, J. (1998) *Female Masculinity*. Durham, NC: Duke University Press.

Halley, J. (1993) 'The Construction of Heterosexuality'. In *Fear of a Queer Planet*, ed. M. Warner, 82–102. Minneapolis: University of Minnesota Press.

Halperin, D. (1995) *Saint Foucault: Toward a Gay Hagiography*. Oxford: Oxford University Press.

Hampsher-Monk, I. (1992) *A History of Modern Political Thought: Major Political Thinkers from Hobbes to Marx*. Oxford: Blackwell.

Haraway, D. (1991) *Simians, Cyborgs, and Women: The Reinvention of Nature*. New York: Routledge.

Harris, J. (2004) *On Cloning*. London: Routledge.

Harris, J. and Holm, S., eds (1998) *The Future of Human Reproduction: Ethics, Choice and Regulation*. Oxford: Oxford University Press.

Hawkes, G. (1995) 'Dressing-Up: Cross-Dressing and Sexual Dissonance'. *Journal of Gender Studies* 4: 261–70.

Hawkesworth, M. (1997) 'Confounding Gender'. *Signs: Journal of Women in Culture and Society* 22: 649–85.

Hay, C. (2004) 'Taking Ideas Seriously in Explanatory Political Analysis'. *British Journal of Politics and International Relations* 6: 136–41.

Hegel, G. (1977 [1807]) *Phenomenology of Spirit*, trans. A. V. Miller. Oxford: Oxford University Press.

Heidegger M. (1977) 'Letter on Humanism', trans. F. Capuzzi. In *Basic Writings*, 213–65. New York: Harper and Row.

Heitmeyer, W. and Hagan, J. (2003) *International Handbook of Violence Research*. Boston and London: Kluwer Academic Publishers.

Home Office (UK) (2000) Report of the Interdepartmental Working Group on Transsexual People. London: Home Office.

hooks, b. (1982) *Ain't I a Woman: Black Women and Feminism*. London: Pluto.

Human Security Centre (2005) *Human Security Report 2005*. Vancouver, Canada: University of British Columbia.

Hutchings, K. (2003) *Hegel and Feminist Philosophy*. London: Polity.

Jackson, S. (1999) *Heterosexuality in Question*. London: Sage.

Jebb, R. (1900) *Sophocles, the Plays and Fragments: Part III: The Antigone*. Cambridge: Cambridge University Press.

Josephson, J. (2005) 'Citizenship, Same-Sex Marriage, and Feminist Critiques of Marriage'. *Perspectives on Politics* 3: 269–84.

Kaplan, M. (1997) *Sexual Justice: Democratic Citizenship and the Politics of Desire.* New York: Routledge.

Katz, J.N. (1995) *The Invention of Heterosexuality.* New York: Dutton.

Kaufman-Osborn, T. (2006) 'Gender Trouble at Abu Ghraib'. *Politics & Gender* 1: 597–619.

Keane, J. (2005) *Violence and Democracy.* Cambridge: Cambridge University Press.

Kennedy, M. (2005) 'Say I Do, Judges Rule after Overturning British Legal Bar on Marrying the In-law'. *Guardian*, 14 September.

Kolko, G. (2002) 'Another Century of War?' *CounterPunch*, 26 November.

Lenski, G. (2003) 'Eugenics'. In *Blackwell Dictionary of Modern Social Thought*, ed. W. Outhwaite, 217. Malden, MA: Blackwell.

Lloyd, M. (1999) 'Performativity, Parody, Politics'. *Theory, Culture and Society* 16: 195–213.

Lloyd, M. (2005a) *Beyond Identity Politics: Feminism, Power and Politics.* London: Sage.

Lloyd, M. (2005b) 'Butler, Antigone and the State'. *Contemporary Political Theory* 4.4: 451–68.

Lloyd, M. (2008) 'Towards a *Cultural* Politics of Vulnerability: Precarious Lives and Ungrievable Deaths'. In *Judith Butler's Precarious Politics: Critical Encounters*, ed. T. Carver and S.A. Chambers. London and New York: Routledge.

Locke, J. (1960 [1689]) *Two Treatises of Government.* Cambridge: Cambridge University Press.

MacKinnon, C. (1987) *Feminism Unmodified: Discourses on Life and Law.* Cambridge, MA: Harvard University Press.

McNay L. (2000) *Gender and Agency: Reconfiguring the Subject in Feminist and Social Theory.* Cambridge: Polity.

Markell, P. (2003) *Bound by Recognition.* Princeton: Princeton University Press.

Markell, P. (2006) 'Ontology, Recognition, and Politics: A Reply'. *Polity* 38.1: 28–39.

Marx, K. (1987 [1859]) 'Preface' to *A Contribution to the Critique of Political Economy.* In K. Marx and F. Engels, *Collected Works* 29, 261–5. London: Lawrence & Wishart.

Marx, K. (1996 [1867 and 1872]) *Capital*, vol. 1, in K. Marx and F. Engels, *Collected Works* 35. London: Lawrence & Wishart.

Mendus, S., ed. (1988) *Justifying Toleration: Conceptual and Historical Perspectives.* Cambridge: Cambridge University Press.

Mendus, S. (1989) *Toleration and the Limits of Liberalism.* Basingstoke: Macmillan.

Mendus, S. and Edwards, D., eds (1987) *On Toleration.* Oxford: Clarendon Press.

Mendus, S. and Horton, J., eds (1985) *Aspects of Toleration: Philosophical Studies.* London: Methuen.

Mills, C. (2000) 'Efficacy and Vulnerability: Judith Butler on Reiteration and Resistance'. *Australian Feminist Studies* 15: 265–79.

Minh-ha, T. (1991) *When the Moon Waxes Red: Representation, Gender and Cultural Politics.* New York: Routledge.

Nietzsche, F. (1921) *Werke, Band V: Die fröliche Wissenschaft.* Stuttgart: Alfred Kröner Verlag.

Nietzsche, F. (1954 [1888]) *Twilight of the Idols*, trans. W. Kaufmann. Princeton: Princeton University Press.

Nietzsche, F. (1967 [1887]) *The Genealogy of Morals*, trans. W. Kaufmann. New York: Vintage Books.

Nietzsche, F. (1974 [1887]) *The Gay Science: With a Prelude in Rhymes and an Appendix in Songs*, trans. W. Kaufmann. New York: Vintage Books.

Norton, A. (2004) *95 Theses on Politics, Culture, and Method*. New Haven, CT: Yale University Press.

Nussbaum, M. (1999) 'The Professor of Parody'. *The New Republic Online*, February; available at http://www.tnr.com/archive/0299/022299/nussbaum022299.htm (accessed 5 August 2004).

Olson, J. (2004) *The Abolition of White Democracy*. Minneapolis: University of Minnesota Press.

Pateman, C. (1988) *The Sexual Contract*. Cambridge: Polity.

Petchesky, R.P. (2001) 'Sexual Rights: Inventing a Concept, Mapping an International Practice'. In *Sexual Identities, Queer Politics*, ed. M. Blasius, 118–39. Princeton: Princeton University Press.

Phelan, S. (2001) *Sexual Strangers: Gays, Lesbians, and Dilemmas of Citizenship*. Philadelphia: Temple University Press.

Rancière, J. (1999) *Disagreement: Politics and Philosophy*, trans. J. Rose. Minneapolis: University of Minnesota Press.

Rancière, J. (2001) 'Ten Theses on Politics'. *Theory & Event* 5.3.

Rawls, J. (1971) *A Theory of Justice*. Cambridge, MA: The Belknap Press of Harvard University Press.

Rich, A. (1980) 'Compulsory Heterosexuality and Lesbian Existence'. *Signs: Journal of Women in Culture and Society* 5: 631–60.

Richardson, D., ed. (1996) *Theorising Heterosexuality: Telling It Straight*. Buckingham: Open University Press.

Roediger, D. (1999) *The Wages of Whiteness: Race and the Making of the American Working Class*. London: Verso.

Rottenberg, C. (2003) Passing: Race, Identification, and Desire'. *Criticism* 45.4: 435–52.

Rousseau, J. (1997) [1762] *The Social Contract and Other Later Political Writings*. Cambridge: Cambridge University Press.

Rubin, G. (1975) 'The Traffic in Women: Notes on the Political Economy of "Sex"'. In *Toward an Anthropology of Women*, ed. R.R. Reiter. New York and London: Monthly Review Press.

Salih, S. (2002) *Judith Butler: Essential Guides for Literary Studies*. New York and London: Routledge.

Sartre, J. (1947) *Being and Nothingness: An Essay in Phenomenological Ontology*, trans. H.E. Barnes. New York: Philosophical Library.

Sawicki, J. (1991) *Disciplining Foucault: Feminism, Power, and the Body*. New York and London: Routledge.

Scott, J. (1992) 'Multiculturalism and the Politics of Identity'. In *The Identity in Question*, ed. J. Rajchman, 3–12. London: Routledge.

Scott, J. (1999a) 'Some Reflections on Gender and Politics'. In *Revisioning Gender*, ed. M.M. Ferree, J. Lorber and B.B. Hess, 70–96. New York: Sage.

Scott, J. (1999b) 'Comment on Hawkesworth's "Confounding Gender"'. In *Provoking Feminisms*, ed. C. Allen, 189–94. Chicago: University of Chicago Press.

Sedgwick, E. (1990) *Epistemology of the Closet*. Berkeley and Los Angeles: University of California Press.

Seery, J. (1999) 'Castles in the Air: An Essay on Political Foundations'. *Political Theory* 27.4: 460–90.

Seery J. (2006) 'Acclaim for Antigone's Claim Reclaimed (or, Steiner, contra Butler)'. *Theory & Event* 9.1.

Segura, G.M., Lewis, G.B., Hillygus, D.S., Shields, T.G., Liu, F., Macedo, S., Gerstmann, E., Riggle, E.D.B., Thomas, J.D., Rostosky, S.S., Smith, M., Egan, P.J., Sherrill, K., Haider-Markel, D.P. and Joslyn, M.R. (2005) 'A Symposium on the Politics of Same-Sex Marriage'. *PS: Political Science and Politics* 38: 189–239.

Shanley, M. (2004) *Just Marriage*. Oxford: Oxford University Press.

Shorter OED (2002) *Shorter Oxford English Dictionary*. 5th edn, vol. 1. Oxford: Oxford University Press.

Smith, A.M. (2001) 'Missing Poststructuralism, Missing Foucault: Butler and Fraser on Capitalism and the Regulation of Sexuality'. *Social Text* 19: 103–25.

Sophocles (1967) *The Complete Plays of Sophocles*, trans. R. Claverhouse Jebb, ed. M. Hadas. Bantam: New York.

Squires, J. and Kemp, S., eds (1997) *Feminisms*. Oxford: Oxford University Press.

Steiner, G. (1984) *Antigones*. Oxford: Clarendon Press.

Stevens, J. (1999) *Reproducing the State*. Princeton: Princeton University Press.

Stone, A. 2005. 'Towards a Genealogical Feminism: A Reading of Judith Butler's Political Thought'. *Contemporary Political Theory* 4: 4–24.

Taylor, C. (1992) *Multiculturalism and the Politics of Recognition: An Essay*, ed. Amy Gutmann. Princeton: Princeton University Press.

Tralau, J. 2005. 'Tragedy as Political Theory: The Self-Destruction of Antigone's Laws'. *History of Political Thought* 26: 377–96.

Tremlett, G. (2004) 'Hate Mail Drove Us out of Britain. Now We've Found a Place in the Sun. Gay Dads Take Children to Live in Spain'; available at http://observer.guardian.co.uk/uk_news/story/0,1143435,00.html (accessed 11 July 2005).

Tronto, J. (1993) *Moral Boundaries: A Political Argument for an Ethic of Care*. New York and London: Routledge.

Tyler, C. (1991) 'Decking Out: Performing Identities'. In *Inside/Out: Lesbian Theories, Gay Theories*, ed. D. Fuss, 32–70. New York and London: Routledge.

Tyrrell, W.B. and Bennett, L. (1998) *Recapturing Sophocles' Antigone*. Lanham, MD: Rowman & Littlefield.

UK Parliament (2004) *Gender Recognition Act*; available at http://www.opsi.gov.uk/acts/acts2004/40007-a.htm#2 (accessed 5 June 2005).

Warner, M. (1993) *Fear of a Queer Planet*. Minneapolis: University of Minnesota Press.

Warner, M. (1999) *The Trouble with Normal: Sex, Politics, and the Ethics of Queer Life*. New York: Free Press.

Watkins, R. (2008) 'Vulnerability, Vengeance, and Community: Butler's Political Thought and Eastwood's Mystic River'. In *Judith Butler's Precarious Politics: Critical Encounters*, ed. T. Carver and S.A. Chambers. London and New York: Routledge.

Watney, S. (1988) *Policing Desire: AIDS, Pornography, and the Media*. Minneapolis: University of Minnesota Press.

Watney, S. (1996) *Policing Desire: AIDS, Pornography, and the Media*. 3rd edn. Minneapolis: University of Minnesota Press.

Webster, F. (2000) 'The Politics of Sex and Gender: Benhabib and Butler Debate Subjectivity'. *Hypatia* 15.1: 1–22.

Weeks, J., Donovan, C. and Heaphy, B. (2001) *Same-sex Intimacies: Families of Choice and other Life Experiments*. New York: Routledge.

Weir, A. (1996) *Sacrificial Logics: Feminist Theory and The Critique of Identity*. London: Routledge.

Weiss, J. (2001) 'The Gender Caste System: Identity, Privacy, and Heteronormativity'. *Law and Sexuality* 10: 123.

Weston, K. (1991) *Families We Choose: Lesbians, Gays, Kinship*. New York: Columbia University Press.

White, S. (1997) 'Weak Ontology and Liberal Political Reflection'. *Political Theory* 25.4: 502–23.

White, S. (1999) 'As the World Turns: Ontology and Politics in Judith Butler'. *Polity* 32.2: 155–77.

White, S. (2000) *Sustaining Affirmation: The Strengths of Weak Ontology and Political Theory*. Princeton: Princeton University Press.

White, S. (2005) 'Weak Ontology: Genealogy and Critical Issues'. *Hedgehog Review*, 22 June.

Whittle, S. (1996) 'Gender Fucking or Fucking Gender?' In *Blending Genders: Social Aspects of Cross-Dressing and Sex Changing*, ed. R. Ekins and D. King. 196–214. London: Routledge.

Wilson, A., ed. (1995) *A Simple Matter of Justice: Theorizing Lesbian and Gay Politics*. London: Cassell.

Wingrove, E. (2000) *Rousseau's Republican Romance*. Princeton: Princeton University Press.

Wittgenstein, L. (1958) *Philosophical Investigations*, trans. G.E.M. Anscombe. Oxford: Blackwell.

Wittig, M. (1973) *Le Corps lesbien*. Paris: Editions de Minuit.

Wittig, M. (1992) *The Straight Mind and Other Essays*. Boston: Beacon Press.

Wikipedia (2004) 'Heteronormativity'; available at http://en.wikipedia.org/wiki/Heteronormativity (accessed 22 February 2007).

Young, I. (1990) *Justice and the Politics of Difference*. Princeton: Princeton University Press.

Young, I. (2002) *Inclusion and Democracy*. Oxford: Oxford University Press.

Zerilli, L. (2005) *Feminism and the Abyss of Freedom*. Chicago: University of Chicago Press.

Zivi, K. (2006) 'Rights and the Politics of Performativity'. Paper presented at the 2006 meeting of the American Political Science Association, Philadelphia PA.

Index